Valentina Pinna-Pattison

TO THE HORIZON
AND BEYOND

Bookland Publishing Co.

Canada   2003

Illustratons: Natalia Vetrova
Cover design: Natalia Vetrova & Farkhad Muratkhodjaev

Printed in Victoria, Canada

National Library of Canada Cataloguing in Publication

Filina-Pattison, Valentina, 1940-
      To the horizon and beyond / Valentina Filina-Pattison.
ISBN 1-4120-0036-X
      1. Soviet Union—History—Revolution, 1917-1921—Personal narratives, Russian.   2. Soviet Union—History—20th century.   3. Soviet Union—Social conditions—20th century.
I. Title.
   DK510.38.F54 2003   947.084
         C2003-901361-8

TRAFFORD

This book was published *on-demand* **in cooperation with Trafford Publishing.** On-demand publishing is a unique process and service of making a book available for retail sale to the public taking advantage of on-demand manufacturing and Internet marketing. **On-demand publishing** includes promotions, retail sales, manufacturing, order fulfilment, accounting and collecting royalties on behalf of the author.

Suite 6E, 2333 Government St., Victoria, B.C. V8T 4P4, CANADA

Phone	250-383-6864	Toll-free	1-888-232-4444 (Canada & US)
Fax	250-383-6804	E-mail	sales@trafford.com
Web site	www.trafford.com	TRAFFORD PUBLISHING IS A DIVISION OF TRAFFORD
HOLDINGS LTD.			

Trafford Catalogue #03-0399   www.trafford.com/robots/03-0399.html

10   9   8   7   6   5   4   3   2

CONTENTS:

This book is dedicated to three important people in my life: my husband Jan Holly, my daughter Larissa and my grandson Gleb who have been patiently supporting me on my endeavors to publish this work, which as Janko said was the reason he fell in love with me, having read my life story.

I would like to express my gratitude to my late husband John Pattison, who encouraged me to write a manuscript and who proofread it (him being British by birth), this was to become a book based on true life stories of me as well as of my family in Russia.

TO A READER

Take pen in hand, ye man, put into words a chronicle of your life.

As the words are written they become as a star in the endless night, a light which shines and guides, a good work and a noble act which may touch a soul and inspire it.

To transcend and rise above the every day struggles, pains, hurts and in so doing attain a strength of spirit. For within the spirit of a man there lies a potential for all the greatness and virtues which make a man a human being.1 hope these words, dear reader, written by me, can help you to better understand the events of my life, the times in which I lived and how they shaped my outlook of the life I will be sharing with you. The language of "To the Horizon and Beyond" is chosen English but because of my Russian mentality this is why a special set of images and associative phrases and rhymes at some moments are reflective of a confluence of two cultures of which I am a part and from whence I draw my style of writing.

The book you are about to read is not a biography in the strict sense of the word, but an essay which portrays the life of a family set in a period of time in Russia that encompasses the vast panorama of history and historical events: revolutions, wars, great up heavals which effected not only this family but as well as had a worldwide influence that is still felt to-day. In spite of all this we survived, lived day by day, worked, loved, raised our children and created...

These mists covered mountains
Are a home now for me,
The Russian soul on the rolling plains,
Calling thee forever be.

Someday we will return to
Our forests and streams,
And we'll no longer happen
To be as wandering pilgrims.

Through fields of enlightening,
I had walked and in so doing,
I've watched all your suffering,
Your defeats and triumphs.

And if they did hurt me,
Causing fear and alarm,
You did not desert me,
My dreams in the calm.

In my reveries I see the worlds
Of different kinds,
Where peace and tranquility
Of the higher realm abound.

Now the sun's gone beyond the hills,
And the moon's rising aloft.
Friend, let me bid you farewell,
And leave you with a thought.

But it is written in the starlight,
And every line on your palm,
We are fools to make war,
Trading good for harm.

The Author

PREFACE

"February,   the 14th,1997,
Valentine's Day,
St.Petersburg,
Russia.

DEAR MOM,

All the best and congratulations on the Day of Saint Valentine, the same name as you have. I wish you on your Name Day may there be the most pleasant suprises of love!

Some people have a way of bringing out the best in you by their caring and the interest that they take in all you do.

Some people make you comfortable right from the very start, for their smiles and love of life come from a warm and giving heart.

Some people are so special, that whenever they're around, it seems the world is filled with joys, just waiting to be.

A Saint Valentine's wish to tell you that you mean so much to me, for you have that extra something that I very rarely see - it's a warmth, an honest caring, that draws others close to you and makes you someone every day special the whole life through!

Love me and be loved by somebody special.

Your

LARISSA

P.S. God bless you, my dearest MOM, you're very far from home in America, in New York, among strange people surrounding you. If my grandma MARIA were alive, she would have blessed you as I'd done."

PART ONE

MARIA

"Oh, that bloody damned bastard has gone! He will never return. I loved him so much. I want to die. Life without him lost all meaning." Maria thought putting a great deal of pills in front of her, intending to commit suicide.

"'I am going to die", she said aloud.

She felt no relief, no despair, no fear. The moment of her end would not grant her even the dignity of seriousness. It was an anonymous moment; a few minutes ago, she had held a toothbrush in her hand, now she held medicine with the same casual indifference.

One must not die like this, she thought. One must feel a great joy or a healthy terror. One must salute one's own end. Let her feel a spasm of dread, and she'll swallow some pills. Then she felt nothing.

"Who are you?" she asked herself.

After a while she answered, "Maria Yakovlevna Bakunova, an average simple woman, born in 1907, from the Pochep village of the Orel region. An ordinary cashier from the railway station.

Who was he? A graduate of the Bryansk Forest-Technical Institute, a mechanical engineer, a handsome man with higher education and perspectives for the future. I am nothing compared to him. I did not graduate from either high schools or academies. My parents did not allow me to attend school.

They used to say, "You can read and write. That's enough for girls. Go to work. Do the weaving of ropes. It's more important."

But him. It's another deal. He wanted to study and he was a brilliant student. I used to be proud of him as if I were his mother. Really - we were the same age. Of no great importance it was that I had to work days and nights helping him to learn subjects and earning money for living, he was attending classes in the early

9

morning, preparing for lectures in the daytime and late evenings. There he met a new girl-friend, who was a student. It was of no importance for him that I was pregnant and about to bear a baby. He is in love with a new woman, the same education as himself, an equal pair for him," so she thought.

A bitter offence struck her sharply, tears rolled on her cheeks. Maria did not know how long she cried as if she were unconscious. She was alone now. The curtains were open. There was only one window in a tiny, one bedroom and living room flat, above the sixth floor of a great residential hotel-like house, in the city of Bryansk about of six hundred kilometers from the city of Moscow.

Dust-blue suede curtains to be pulled across the walls enclose the room when she wished; there was nothing to cover the ceiling. Lying in bed with her Boris she could see the stars over her head through the window, or flashes of lightning, or watch the rain smashing into furious, glittering sunbursts in mid-air above her, against the unseen protection. She liked to extinguish the lights and pull the curtains open, when she lay in bed with him.

She was fantastically sexy. Her imagination worked with great forces. In front of her eyes there arose different images of their intimate relations: he lay on her body motionless, after half an hour sexual love, whispering the only words to her: "Oh, Maria, Maria, Maria!" in delight. It was sounded as if a prayer was being uttered. Everything had melted at that moment. There remained exclusively the desire, the love, nothing more. Or, she lay on him, cuddling and kissing his young, strong body. Without words, tingling his sex, his balls, space between legs and above, looking for every time new and new sexual spots.

From those remembrances she felt her head dizzying. She looked at herself at the mirror. Out of it peeped at her a face, not belonging to modern civilization, but to ancient Russia; the face of an eternal beauty. Her hair, pitch-black and straight, was pleated into a long thick plait. Her skin was pulled tight over the high sharp bones of her face; her mouth was long and thick, her eyes, under slanting eyebrows were pale blue and photographed like two sardonic white ovals. An artist had asked her once to sit for a "painting of a Russian collective farm worker", she had laughed, refusing, and the artist had watched sadly, because the laughter made the face perfect for his purpose. Her small short-raised nose, as called among the regular people 'kartoshka'-type, gave to her face an unusual expression of defenselessness and simplicity. She had a face which cannot offend or insult, opposite, it can protect and realize. As an addition to everything, her complexion was so fresh, even after a flood of tears, that natural essence of a living being, being suppressed; the moment could not destroy her. It was because of her pregnancy, her natural pride of maturity, the female celebration of carrying a baby inside. All of a sudden she felt somebody pushing in her tummy. One time, another, then once more. She leaped on her feet, leaning against the wall, feeling the cold paint through the thin, dark cotton of her night gown. A tiny living creature asked insistently to come into the world. She shrugged and lowered the arms; she stood tapping a fingertip against the top of her stomach. People always speak of a black death or a red death, she thought; yours, Maria, will be a grey death. Why hasn't anyone ever said that this is the ultimate horror? Not screams, pleas, or convulsions. Not the indifference of a clean emptiness, disinfected by the fire of same great disaster. But this - a mean, smutty little horror, impotent even to frighten, you can't do it like that, she told herself, smiling coldly; you forgot about another person in you, Shame on you! To hell, that bastard Boris! Let's bear the lovely child, yours the only connection to the ugly, contradictive, mad world around you.

In a while the birth convulsions repeated, Maria knocked on the neighbor's door, she was called Emma, begging her to help with the birth. She responded immediately starting to spread the pills on the table, Maria's exciting voice exclaimed, "Doctor, please, Emma!"

The ambulance came soon. That happened on the fifth day of March in nineteen thirty five. Maria was twenty eight; it was her primary birth-baby, named after a friend, which helped her in a very difficult moments of her life. Beyond the window the spring burst into blossom, the country entered the next five-year plan of the economical development, in all the corners of the town streets, in every flat or a village house there were pronounced the boast-ings, proud words of the certain successes, records of the industry and agriculture. From every radio-set the political propagandists held speeches about the congress of the Soviet Comnunist Party - "Congress of the Winners". Everywhere, everyone was infused with a contagious enthusiasm for the country's agricultural and economic expansion. Each young person wanted to be a national hero, like Stakhanov, pilots Chkalov, Gaidukov. The examples in labor existed in all branches of life. Maria was a cashier and followed the Aladin's method of selling the railroad tickets. It meant that she had to work days and nights and sell as many tickets as possible, and at last she was awarded with the three Labor medals of the Third degree.

Maria, do you hear big vague words "Universal Harmony"- "Eternal Spirit" -"Divine Purpose" -"Nirvana" - "Paradise" -"Racial Supremacy" -"The Dictatorship of the Proletariat"?

Internal corruption, Maria. If you listen to any prophet speaking of sacrifice, run faster than from a plague. Because where there's sacrifice, there's someone collecting sacrificial offerings.

Where there's service, there's someone being served. The man who speaks to you of sacrifice, speaks of slaves and masters. And intends to be the master. And there was the only master in Russia, "the father of all nations and peoples", Joseph Stalin.

All newspapers, all mass media at those times spoke of what a great personality Comrade Stalin possessed, how long Comrade Stalin's working day had lasted, how clever Comrade Stalin was thinking only about the troubles and cares of the ordinary people. Everybody was obliged to work hard and that was considered to be the greatest happiness in the world. It was disgraceful to speak aloud about the personal, private life. The main principal in a person's life was to sacrifice in the name of the good of the Communist society. The propagandists promised that in the future everybody would live better. "AII of us must live for a better future," they used to say.

Maria, as everyone in this society believed, hoped and expected the better future and wondered when it would begin.

Soon she was to meet a young man who captured her heart. He was not only handsome, a quality she admired. But he was also gentle and kind, and she got married to him. He was twenty eight, she - thirty three, the age when the sexual health was something of an enigma for them.

Really, it is taken for granted when we have it and sorely missed when we don't. Sexual health is assumed to be automatic that we pay little attention to how it can be maintained.

The name of Maria's new husband was Nickolay Alexeyevich Filin, a brilliant partner, the new sexual response cycle. For her, the first excitation phase was relatively slow, the muscles grow increasingly tense, the vagina began to lubricate, normally, about ten to thirty seconds after stimulation began; its interior started to dilate, and the clitoris and nipples began to swell with dammed-up blood. Phase two, the plateau, was a continuation of this shivering buildup of tension - heart rate and respiration increased, the skin started to flush, and the outer third of the vagina began to swell dramatically.

All this came to a fantastic climax at orgasm, when all that muscular tension and engorged blood were suddenly, ecstatically released.

"What is an orgasm anyway?" thought Maria to herself.

"So which is it, the body or the mind?"

"For me," she answered, "it is as if it were a journey into an alternative state of consciousness, complete with an almost psychedelic warping of her sense of time and space. The French call it 'le petit mort'(the little death) - a lovely allusion to that ineffable sense of having been transported to another, perhaps higher realm and state of mind."

Who knows how often she had been submerging into the heavens with her Nickolay, body leaned back against her. It was a body of long straight lines and angles, each curve broken into planes.

He stood rigid, his hands hanging at his sides, palms out. He felt his shoulder blades drawn tight together, the curve of his neck, and the weight of the blood in his hands. He felt the wind behind him, in the hollow of his spine. The wind waved his hair against the sky seen through the open window. His hair was neither blond nor brown but exact colour of ripe walnut rind. He smiled at the things which had happened to him and Maria this morning and at

13

the things that now lay ahead.

"Darling, are you so attractive and amazing to have another man on the site before I've come?" asked he.

"Sweetie, are you jealous? You'd rather think of the future work what are you going to do? What can you do?" asked she honestly.

"Oh, no, I'm not jealous but all the men are very selfish. They want to possess one beloved woman and not to share this feeling with anybody. I love you, my sweetheart. You're the only treasure in my life. All the rest is senseless. Even my job!" Nick said passionately.

"I love you, too, my dearest. All the past is out of reckoning. My daughter remained like a souvenir from my hard-loving fortune. Now everything sounds better", answered Maria.

Oh, Maria, Maria, Maria!

Who knows your future? Nobody. Even the God. It was the time in Russia when the Communist Party Government celebrated its victory. But Maria now recollected her childhood, survived after the First World War; her parents took her to the Orthodox Church. Her mother, as everyone there, was a peasant woman, with a kerchief over her head. Those simple women could mingle with princesses in furs and jewels. People of every class and age stood for hours holding candles, their minds and souls absorbed in the overwhelming display taking place around them. From every corner of the church golden icons glittered in the glowing light. From the iconostasis a high screen before the altar, the miters and crosses of gold-robed bishops, blazed diamonds and emeralds and rubies. Priests with long beards trailing down their chests walked among the people, swinging smoking pots of incense. The service was not so much a chant as a linked succession of hymns, drawing unbelievable power from the surging notes of the deepest basses. Dazzled by sights and smells, washed clean by the soaring notes of the music, the congregation came forward at the end of the service to kiss the soft hand of the bishop and have him paint a cross in holy oil upon their foreheads.

The Church offered the extremes of emotion, from gloom to ecstasy. It taught that suffering was good, that drabness and pain were inevitable. "As God wills", the Russian told himself, and, with the aid of the Church, sought to find the humility and strength to bear his earthly burden.

The hardest burden then was the First World War with Germany starting in August 2, 1914, when Tsar Nicholas issued a formal proclamation of hostilities at the Winter Palace in St.Petersburg, the Russian capital.

It was a blazing-hot midsummer day, as Maria remembered. The Pope slowly made his way through the crush of people, dropping to their knees and frantically tried to kiss his hand. All village people seemed to jam themselves beneath the glittering chandeliers. On the altar stood the miraculous icon, the Vladimir Mother of God. Perhaps it was a copy of St.Petersburg one. Everybody knew of that icon, brought to Moscow in 1395, it was said to have turned back Tamerlane, one of the khans of Tatar -Mongol's invasion with the help of that icon.

Everybody knew also that before the icon in 1812 the grizzled General Kutuzov had prayed as he was leaving to take command of Tsar Alexander the First's armies in the war against Napoleon.

At that time, at the beginning of a new war, Nicholas the Second invoked the icon's blessing.

Each woman or a man knew the words of the oath taken by Alexander the First in 1812, now repeated by his relative "I solemnly swear that I will never make peace so long as a single enemy remains on Russian soil".

In those early days, patriotism was closely tied to a deep-rooted fear of the Germans. "For Faith, Tsar and Country!" and "For the defense of Holy Russia!" were the calls that stirred the barracks, factories and villages.

Maria's old grandpa said then, "If we are unlucky enough not to destroy the Germans, they'll come here. They'll reign over the whole of Russia and then they'll harness you and me - yes, you as well as me - to their plows, damned sons of a bitch, fuck you!" added the old peasant woman sadly.

The Duma, then the government, sat only one day, August 8, passing the military budget without a dissenting vote.

"War was declared and all at once, not a trace was left of the revolutionary movement", declared Kerensky, the prime-minister:

"Even the Bolshevik members of the Duma were forced to admit - though somewhat sullenly - that it was the duty of the proletariat to cooperate in the defense".

Maria did not understand anything, everything was confused in her small pretty head.

In 1917 the Revolution had come. Everywhere is the blood, shooting and violence. Many political trends were on the arena: "the Reds", "the Whites", "the Bolsheviks", "the Mensheviks", "the Essers" etc. - for her it was the same as if to jump into the fire or out of the frying pan.

The propagandists screamed aloud with all their strong throats, who was the loudest, that was the winner.

Lenin, a brilliant dialectician, managed to get Russia, after living comfortably in exile, having taken no part in the overthrow of tsarism, having been transported back to Russia under the protection of the most autocratic and imperialistic regime remaining from Europe.

Most important, he demanded an end to the war and urged the troops at the front to begin fraternizing with the enemy. Lenin was the winner, and what happened further - nobody knew, Maria less of all.

It was in the past, but now her thoughts were coming back to her tore mentor. The Church was cut from the state according to one of Lenin's decrees, one of the main ideologists here. In fact, it meant that all religions were expelled, cathedrals were dynamited and exploded, nobody was allowed to attend churches to pray, including pronouncing the name of God.

The only God was the Communist Party and the General Secretary of its Central Committee - Stalin, the most prominent Lenin's succeeder and the father of the ideology of collectivism. The ideology of collectivism - to act together. To think -together. To feel - together; to unite, to agree, to obey. To obey, to serve, to sacrifice. Divide and conquer - first. But then - unite and rule. We've discovered that one at last.

Remember the Roman Emperor who said he wished humanity had a single neck so he could cut it? People have laughed at him for centuries. But we'll have the last laugh. We've accomplished what he couldn't accomplish. We've taught them to unite. This makes one neck ready for one leash. We found the magic word, COLLECTIVISM. Look at Europe, Maria. Can't you see the nonsense and recognize the gist of the problem? One country is dedicated to the proposition that man has no rights, that collective is all. The individual held as evil, the mass -as God. No motive and no virtue permitted - except that of service to the proletariat. That's one version.

Here's another. A country dedicated to the proposition that man has no rights, that the State is all. The individual held as evil, the race - as God. No motive and no virtue permitted - except that of service to the State. Give up your soul to a council - or give it up to a leader. But give it up, give it up, give it up. In Russia there were two versions: the proletariat state was united as one whole, and above all it was PROLETARIAT as a God. The Propaganda stressed this ideal very well. "Religion is opium for the people", "The Communist Party is the brains, the honor and the consciousness of the people", "Lenin is now alive more than other living beings in the world", "Lenin is our force, our banner, and our weapon" - such and many similar slogans are still hung on the walls of buildings in communist regions and areas. The propaganda thoughts were forced into the heads of the people for a special purpose: to make people think in one and the same way. The single technique was to offer the propaganda poison as food and poison as antidote. Go fancy on the trimmings, but hung on to the main objective. Give the fools a choice, let them have their fun - but don't forget the only purpose you have to accomplish. Kill the individual. Kill man's soul. The rest will follow automatically, Maria. In the big and small plants in cities and towns, at enterprises and at every collective farm in villages there were committees and representatives of the Communist Party of the Soviet Union, the lectures' groups and volunteers leading the principal guidelines of the only ruling Party.

Everywhere had been trumpeted triumphantly about the advantages of the socialist system over the capitalism, how dreadfully went the slogan "the damned stagnating capitalists", how huge the achievements of socialists and communists in labour.

17

Maria tried to understand the social policy in her country but of main concern was her husband Nick. All the time he dreamt of his new job. He wanted to be a draftsman. By that moment Nick managed to acknowledge something useful about architecture. He read the special column in the newspaper in this respect: some technicalities of the Five Orders, the post and lintel, the flying buttress or reinforced concrete.

Nick had received his job. He had come to the drafting room every morning, had done his task, and had heard no word of comment. He was fond of the lines, pencil movements, all sorts of views on sheets of paper: elevation view, front-back-top-bottom views of a building settled in future with tenants. He liked dreaming about studios, flats and apartments.

He himself lived in Maria's studio shared with neighbors. Difficult to fancy that eight-ten studios enclosed each one bedroom and a sitting room in itself were provided with only one toilet and one bathroom for all tenants. It meant, in fact, that every morning Nick should wake up at the dawn to come to the toilet first because later it would be crowded, many tenants had wanted to use it. The same picture seemed to repeat itself about the bathroom and the toilet. In some houses both things were simply absent. The architects had been drawing but the seniors - cancelled the buildings which were cheap. So Nick's biggest dream was to design and build up the cheaper dwellings for simple people as well as for himself. A flat with a separate bathroom, where he could with his wife - Russian beauty Maria take a bath or a shower in a soft gentle soapy tub.

Maria would enter the drafting room and stand behind Nick for a long-long time, looking over his shoulder. It was as if his eyes concentrated deliberately on trying to throw the steady hand off its course on the paper. The two other draftsmen botched their work from the mere thought of such an apparition standing behind them. Nick did not seem to notice it. He went on, his hand unhurried, he took his time discarding a blunted pencil and picking out another. "Uh -huh," Maria would sigh suddenly. Nick would turn head then, politely attentive.

"What is it, darling?" he would ask, Maria would turn away

18

without a word, her narrowed eyes underscoring contemptuously the fact that she considered an answer unnecessary, and would leave the drafting room. Nick would go on with his drawing. He was usually disliked, from the first sight of his face, anywhere he went. His face was handsome, deep blue eyes and a straight nose, his character was closed like the door of a safety vault; things locked in safety vaults are valuable; people did not care to feel that save Maria. She adored him without understanding any sign or line, or turn in his drawing. The fascinating, undiscovered world for her, whose education had been stopped long ago by her father's words, "The girls do not need being educated very bloody damned long. Go to work - it is your task", said gloomy Daddy's order.

On the seventeenth day of March of nineteen forty she had born the second baby-girl, Valentina by name. Nick was glad as a child, smiled often and used to stand long periods of time before Val's cot: he enjoyed every new tooth appearing in the baby's mouth, every new sound distinguished in the silence, every new movement of the baby's body or head. He began to compose the rhymes in honour of the little child Val, daughter and Maria united his heart in one whole sum, so called - great love for life. Life itself was senseless without his family. He was not "bolsheviks" communist "parvenu" to build up a new society, his nature of common sense demanded the single thing: to love in order to live, and to live in order to love.

Simple stuff, however, was not allowed here to anticipate, to speak aloud and so deeply became hidden in Nick's soul that nobody can guess but Maria.

Oh, Maria, Maria, Maria!

She was delightful in bed. For her as for most women, being touched and stroked all over was an essential prelude to sexual arousal, perhaps because it took them longer to become aroused than men. Erogenous zones were found out practically because all sexual brochures were underground, except sexual diseases. No kidding! Maria was one of the women who could reach orgasm merely by the kissing or foundling of her earlobes, she could actually climax through the stroking of her eyebrows!

Maria -Nick have never forgotten that physical love which did not only mean intercourse - there was always kissing, hugging, caressing, stroking, massaging and a thousand of other variations on the ecstasy of touch.

That was specific, when kids went asleep, they created a wonder of love. He invented more and more new unthinkable positions of sex but Maria preferred comfort best of all. All the same for her, either day or night, on top on him or, beside, the main thing was she loved his body, that moment of interconnecting when the dull hard - working life stopped existing and her spirit raised high in the sky, and in the ears sounded Nick's voice "I love you, Maria!" Love and life were synonymous, poured into one word "joy".

Suddenly the joy had been stopped - early on Sunday morning, June 22, 1941, the German flood poured across the Soviet frontier, in three great parallel surges between the Baltic Sea and the Carpathian Mountains.

The Germans had thrown 151 divisions - just over three million men - into the battle, accompanied by an armored fist of tanks, guns and airplanes.

Stalin despite the warning given to him by British prime-minister Churchill and his own spies, seemed to have taken completely by surprise. In Berlin in the Wilhelmstrasse the Soviet ambassador was told that Germany had entered Russia in response to "border violations".

In fact, the invasion was the culmination of months of planning by the German general staff, acting on Hitler's orders. Operation "Bar Barossa" was designed to destroy the Soviet Union and Bolshevism. Hitler was certain of success. He had told General Alfred Jodl: "We have only to kick in the door and the whole rotten structure will come crashing down". In a proclamation broadcast that morning Hitler boasted that the German army's movements were "the greatest the world has ever seen".

June, 27, 1941. USSR. Members of Communist Party and of the Komsomol (League of Communist Youth) were mobilized as "political soldiers".

June, 28, 1941.USSR. Finnish troops pushed towards Murmansk.

20

June, 29, 1941.USSR. The new Committee of defense, headed by Stalin, took complete control of the country.

June, 30, 1941.USSR. The western front commander, General Dmitri Pavlov, and his leading officers were executed for incompetence on Stalin's orders.

Moscow, June, 29, 1941. Stalin, recovering from the shock of being attacked by his former ally, had put himself at the head of a Committee of Defense, in which the whole power of the state would be concentrated to fight the Nazis. The Red Army, too, was recovering from its initial unpreparedness and its well-armored, fast T-34 tank had given the Germans a nasty surprise.

What had really surprised the Germans, however, was the resistance being put up by the ordinary Russian soldiers fighting in defense of their homeland.

Moscow, July, 3, 1941. USSR. Stalin broke his silence on that day and calling the people "brothers" and "sisters" rather than "comrades", called on them to fight a total war against the invading Germans not only in the modern sense but also in the grim "old Russian" way.

In a speech broadcast throughout the Soviet Union, he called on the people to lay the land waste before the invader. Everything possible must be removed, he said, and that which cannot be moved must be destroyed.

It was a speech designed to stir the people's ancient love of Russia: "We must not leave a single pound of grain or a single gallon of petrol to the enemy". He called on the people whose ancestors had helped to defeat Napoleon by "scorching the earth" to follow their example and deny Hitler's invaders food and shelter. Crops and villages are to be burnt, livestock killed, dams destroyed. Partisan bands are to be formed "with the launching of guerilla warfare everywhere, with blowing up bridges and roads, with wrecking telephone and telegraph communications and with setting forests, depots and trains on fire. It is necessary to create in invaded areas unbearable conditions for the enemy".

Fuel was of special importance in this scorched - earth policy, for the German supply lines were becoming over - stretched and the thirsty tanks and aircraft had to rely to a large extent on captured fuel.

The burning of houses was not important at the moment, for the weather was hot and fine, but if the campaign extended into the bitter Russian winter then the lack of shelter could have hit the Germans as cruelly as it did Napoleon's men. Stalin had demanded a great deal from the people of the Soviet Union.

Some of them did not obey him - in some areas the invading Germans had been welcomed with bread and salt - but others had done anything for Holy Mother Russia, if not for communism.

The total mobilization of the men's population began. Everywhere there were hung the placards "Holy Mother Russia is calling", sounded the especially composed music - military Hymn: "Raise, the country, great and vast, to fight against the enemy to the death!"

The Filins' family was split. He went to his native village in Orel region; she stayed with the children at home expecting what would happen further.

Nick never told stories about his military years because of either hard recollections or of an unhappily sad life. Once, his mother, Nataly Iwanovna from Rostov-on-Don, talked about him, but rather shortly.

He appeared to be in her house where as usual the cellar had been used. Nataly Iwanovna did not remember then, she was over 90, who was the first to use that idea to hide in the underground cellar, from the Nazis. But it was accomplished; the great fear had conducted their souls: fear of being noticed and killed. And not because of his nationality, he was Russian. His crime was simply to be a pacifist, he hated the war.

Since the Germans entered the village a fortnight ago, he had known no peace. And now it is his turn to be stripped, humiliated, punched and kicked.

The rumours came to his ears that the Nazis had raped, tortured the Jewish, Russian, Byelorussian women in jail, killed people in the streets. The Nazis had exploited a local tradition of nationalism and anti-Semitism to suit their evil purposes. Photographs of Ukrainian nationalist prisoners slaughtered by the retreating Russians were posted up in the village and captioned

"Jewish killings". The Germans recruited a local militia. Just two days after the Germans arrived, local people were massacring Jews and Russians at the same time.

The conditions of the cellar were drastic, wall - wet, stuffy. Soon he felt the oxygen lacking. Mommy brought the food and drink at night-time. They conversed with gestures. Nobody wanted to break the silence. Everywhere ruled the fear. The fear of being murdered, hung, torched by the Nazis or by the Russians. Because there was the Stalin's order: don't let yourself be captured, these people were considered to be "the enemies of the Russian people". There remained only one right - to die for the Holy Motherland.

So, five long years had passed in fear. Even after the finishing of the World War the Second on the 9th of May, 1945, he still stayed in his refugee's place in fear not believing that the real peace had come. He went out of his safety spot grey-haired, a crippled man in his 34. All his thoughts were about Maria.

How is she?

On September 30, 1941, Maria with her two daughters, six and one, left the town of Bryansk in the steam-train for evacuation, directed to the depth of the Russian city of Chelabinsk in the Urals.

Compartments inside were overcrowded: military men were mixed with civilians, kids were crying, men were cursing with the fucking words; Maria's youngest couldn't help screaming all the time; the train doc said it was diarrhea, if she had wanted to have the child alive, she would have to get off and take her to medical assistance, to help her daughter recover. So she got off the train and made up her mind to visit a real pediatrician to consult her case. It was a wonderful woman, who gave her medicine and examined the pretty woman, too. For the first time Maria was told that she was pregnant and it was too late to abort the baby. Again there was a sleepless night; frankly speaking, it was not a proper time for childbirth - everybody ran away from the Germans.

September 30. 1941. Guderian's Second Panzer Army, back in the north, attacked towards Orel and Bryansk, von Kleist's First Panzer Army headed for Donetsk.

October,m, 8, 1941. Mud and rain had started severely to hinder the German progress on the Moscow front, where many battles raged in the Bryansk front and the Red Army's counter - offensive is grinding on against fierce German opposition. A critical battle is being fought for Rzhev, as the Russians thrust south towards Vyazma in an attempt to trap the German Army Group South. Similar battles are being fought further south as General Zhukov aims for Bryansk to sweep up behind Vyazma, and Marshal Timoshenko flights towards Izyum in attempt to recapture Kharkov.

The poor, exhausted people did not understand anything, except the words "our attack" or "our surrender". Having heard the familiar names of towns and villages they began crying. Tears poured and poured against their cheeks. After hearing them the children started crying. Sometimes, the crying transformed to hoarse sobs without pronouncing any word. It was not habitual to complain to somebody.

Everybody was in equal position: no husband, no relatives, no bread, no food, no shelter, and no transport.

About transport. On the tiring, unbearable way from the enemy, they were awarded with horse-carts, open in the air with the sledges on the wheels and covered with straw. Oh, what happiness happened to shine in the people's eyes! The feet were shoeless, suffering from pain, bleeding and blooded. And now the carts and additional horse power helped greatly - it grew more feasible to travel by cart, but still dangerous.

The damned bloody war was around them.

"Look! Look! Look at the sky! Nazis!" cried the general soldier. "All of you! Down! Down, on the ground, bloody fools!"

Maria fell down, covering with her body a tiny child, the other - next to her.

Luftwaffe pilot aces did their raid on the walking civilians and the railways, not far from them.

Nazi planes loaded with four - pound incendiary bombs were lighting the way for the squadrons with high - explosive bombs.

It was something impossible to describe in words: the sky was dark, smoky and stuffy. Somewhere it was burning, many were injured, others bootless and shirtless, still shouldering their poor belongings. Every man had his own horror story. For Maria, it was the sight of a four-year-old trying to spoon-feed her dead mother. She watched the people getting up. "They look like scarecrows", she noted, "But they look like soldiers, too."

Oh, Russian soldiers! Legends were composed to praise them. The Russian soldiers were fighting with their usual dogged courage. The Red Army had taken the offensive with a two-pronged attack on Kharkov, and tonight the Soviet High Command was claiming that the Red Army had broken the German line after one of the biggest tank battles of the war. It was a new period of liberation of Soviet lands from the Hitlerite rabble.

The Soviet troops began the decisive offensive against their vilest enemy, the German Nationalist Army, exterminating its manpower and war materials and hoisting the glorious Soviet banner over the liberated cities and villages. In one village the column of refugees had stopped after ten-days'-way on the carts. The village was full of Russian soldiers and officers.

Maria jumped off the cart very easily, helping her kids to follow her example, encouraging them with the words: "Darlings, be quick. Now it's the right time to have a rest, to eat something, to drink a drop of water. Maybe some kind people will help", she said.

"Come on, dear sweeties, come on. Don't be lazy."

A minute passed. But the girls did not move. Maria approached them closer, took Val off, then the turn came for Emma. The latter tried many times to release her left leg and could not. It hurt her immensely. The child burst into tears.

"What's happened? What's happened?"

The thought burnt into her mind, the girl did nit move because during the last bombardment a piece of bomb shrapnel had fallen into Emma's calf and for the ten last days' journey she was in an immobile position traveling in the cart with her calves pressed to her thighs. This was terrible with bad results. The calf had stuck to the thigh. She could not move her leg. She needed a doctor immediately.

Fortunately, there was a surgeon there. Without narcosis, any-

25

thing to dull the pain, Emma was given a surgery, the shrapnel was out, swelling had stopped, poisoning of her flesh and blood stopped. The little child spent all of her time on the cart's bed; the horse became her best friend, whom she could talk to for a long time, disclosing her intimate childish dreams and cares. She got crutches from her helpful friends after some time.

This was a horrible true picture of the war. Although her little leg was wounded but saved for the future. Sufferings will be chasing her unceasingly.

The next chapter of this book will be exclusively dedicated to Emma.

The narration keeps on.

January 18, 1942. USSR: Soviet paratroopers landed behind enemy lines south-west of Vyazma. Russian partisan detachments living and fighting behind the German lines have linked up with the 250-th Airborne Regiment and two battalions of the 201-st Airborne Brigade dropped south-west of Vyazma, which was now under heavy attack by the advancing Red Army.

The guerillas and the paratroopers were fighting side by side to cut the German communications with the front. With the partisans acting as guides, the white - shrouded paras were ghosting through the forest to launch swift hit -and -run raids on supply lines and headquarters. This combination of irregular and regular troops was a new tactic on the Russian front. Individual officers and experts had been dropped to the partisans before, but this was the first time that they had been used in a coordinated campaign by the Stavka, the Russian High Command.

With the German Defense line breaking up into defended localities, known as "Hedgehogs", there was room for such forces to maneuver, and even to hold large areas with established bases and landing strips for light aircrafts. On the same day when the Russian partisans began their active actions, Maria had born her third baby-boy. She named him Gennady in honour of the brilliant "golden-handy" surgeon gratefully. The worries had been increasing for her. Everyone in the village of the Voronez region was in need; everyone was in lack of money, in lack of food, in lack of light, in lack of clothes. Again the war gave her the bad signs;

again she was forced to think over her elementary life means. She managed to work at the nursery school as a manager - the simplest way of feeding her own three children and the strange ones when their mothers went to the fields to collect the harvest or to plant potatoes, corn, and grain and so on. Males were at the front line, females had done all the work on the farms without help of men, dividing it among themselves. Everybody worked hard. Sometimes food was not enough for them. Maria had to take care now of all the kids of the village, especially of newborn, such as Gennady. For them she organized a small milking farm, where not just cow milk, but also goat milk was used.

In the lonely, long evenings she read the cards for the women, psychologically predicting their future lives, reading their palms. Even she learned to pray in whispers when she remained alone and nobody could notice her, because religion was forbidden in Russia and somebody could report on her, Maria took out of her secret pockets an iron cross, kissed it and began her prayer:

"Hail Mary, full of Grace,
The Lord is with Thee,
Blessed art Thou amongst women,
And blessed is the fruit of Thy womb, Jesus,
Holy Mary, mother of God,
Pray for us, sinners, now
And at the hour of our death. Amen".

Maria had seen a vision that someone had chosen to use Russia as the instrument of punishment for the whole world if the people did not, by their obedience, prayers and sacrifices, obtain the conversion of Russia to the faith.

If God's requests were granted Russia would spread her errors throughout the world rising up wars and persecutions against the Church, the good would be martyred, the Holy Father would have much to suffer, various nations would be annihilated.

The whole surviving part of the world would be enslaved by the atheistic tyrants of Russia. However the present Russia was enslaved itself by Nazi soldiers and suffered from them much.

September, 17, 1943.USSR. The Red Army recaptured Smolensk, Bryansk, Gomel, and other small Russian cities. The liberation resulted in General Popov's Bryansk front actions.

Describing the action which liberated the city after several days of heavy fighting, Moscow said that Popov's men broke into the northern suburbs and drove the Germans back street by street until the cities were cleared.

Berlin Radio said that bad weather prevented the Luftwaffe from intervening in the battle and that "the German formations were faced with the extremely difficult task of holding their positions against the numerically superior enemy. That was why the Army was now so successful."

More men, more tanks , more guns, more aircraft - that was the secret of the Red Army's astonishing turnabout success against the most professional army in the world just when it seemed that "the Soviet Army was about to collapse".

The inexhaustible supplies of men and materials emerging from the depths of Russia had ground down the Germans.The Red Army now fielded 6,5 million men against 4,3 million Germans.

The Russians had 5600 tanks against the Germans 2600. They had 90 000 guns against 54 000 and 8800 aircraft against 3000. But it was a matter of quality as well as quantity. Russian tanks and aircraft now matched the once superior German equipment.

The Russians had also learnt how to fight a modern war. New commanders had emerged to use new tactics. But most important of all had been the fortitude and patriotism of the Russian soldier, the Russian man or woman.

Maria returned home.

Bryansk, the key railway town in the battles, had suffered grievous damage. Many of its fine buildings had been destroyed. Things were still lying in the streets, bits of things and bits of people. A horse's head was lying in the gutter. There was a pram hood all twisted and bent and there was a little baby's hand still in its wooly sleeve. Outside the former post-office building there was a crumpled bus, still with rows of dead people sitting inside, all covered in dust. Where Maria's house had been, there was nothing left. Just an enormous crater has been covered by clouds of dust. No buildings, just piles of rubble and bricks and underneath it all, people, screaming.

In the occupied suburbs the retreating Germans looted and set fire to everything on their way, and left the bodies of partisans hanging from the trees.

Even the plants, the weather had solidarity with the people, moaning about the perished. The sky was dark - cloudy, the dogs-and-cats-rain started, the wind blew, the earth as if a human being groaned, sighing heavily and intensely. As the sound of gunfire faded from the town for the first time for nearly two years, the people, gaunt and tired, emerged from their shelters to celebrate in the unusual safety of the streets.

They withstood all that the Germans threw at them and had not died of starvation, had to work to live through.

Maria had come up to the General soldier asking for help. She was given a permission to stay at a long barrack-type two-storied building, in a room shared with another twenty-thirty people. No water, no toilet, no electricity. Only the roof is over their heads.

How happy Maria was! She did not know then that in Washington forty-four nations on that day signed into being the first United Nations' organization - the Relief and Rehabilitation Administration (UNRRA) promising to bring immediate relief to the population of liberated countries. It was hard to grasp the magnitude of the needs of the people. They have been robbed of their foodstuffs and raw materials, and even of their agricultural and industrial machinery.

It will be for the UNRRA first to assure a fair distribution of available supplies among all of the liberated people, and second - to avoid death by starvation or exposure among those people. The forces of the United Nations will march forward and the people of the united nations will march with them.

Maria did not know yet about "Lend-lease" lifetime; she heard these strange to her ear words "United Nations", "Lend-lease" and did not understand them. She knew the only thing - the war was over, but problems of peace now began, very grave and disquieting, the severe shortage of food and prolonged rationing.

Once she was given an American stewed beef tin, then some

more overseas' products, and those strange words became closer to her, more familiar. Her friends and she united in one brave women's team, used to go to the fields to dig the fast frozen potatoes out of the ground, to bake the bread or pancakes, "toshnotiki" by name. They were disgustful, sweetish by taste.

Dinner of the post-war time consisted, often of all, the weeds' soup and toshnotikies. It was not surprising that little kids did not start walking for a long time until three years, they sat on the bum without moving, legs bent. The rickets disease had been progressing. That was the image of the post-war child, whose Maria's Gennady was of.

The kids were aware of the parents' business and jobs: they were told what to do and what not to do. Among the children there used also to be a community with the only aim to survive. That was why the seniors helped the juniors. The unwritten law of a children's society was never broken; respectfulness and seriousness were the most distinguished traits of their characters of those years.

The eldest eight-years-old Emma was a commander, so called "marshal-in-fields", Val and Gen, her subordinates. She taught them how to fix up the toys from the rugs, scraps of paper and of all sorts of fiddlesticks.In between she had to clean up the room, wash the floor and the dirty children's clothes and Mom's boots, warm up the prepared food on the kerosene stove, feed up the youngsters and a great deal of the errands to be run.

In 1946 there was a government's decree of the first-turn reconstruction of one hundred small Russian towns, including Bryansk. Maria by the way was in search of a job. For too little payment she worked as a builder helping to reconstruct her native town. At the same time she bought a Nanny-goat with the idea that milk was the most necessary food product for her children.

Again luck visited her: Maria was given a vegetable garden and the seeds for the first planting. It was nice! It was her dream to come true, although the place was ten kilometers from the plot. Potatoes seemed to be very popular for cultivation among the Bryansk people, who helped each other to plant and to harvest them.

Frankly speaking, post-war people were very generous, kind, and attentive to each other. Perhaps they had nothing to share except the sorrows and grief, grief for the death of murdered relatives. There was no family in Russia who did not suffer from the war: someone was killed, someone - hung, someone - died of starvation.

"Kids, have you eaten this porridge up to the end or, are you pretending to deceive me?" interrogated Maria, addressing her dearest ones because all of them were sweet to her as she bore them all equally, in her birth pains, and as if take your five fingers, and cut one, equally painful for the whole hand, the children are not divided for a real mother, her love for kids is one which was given to her by God and blessed by the Father.

Suddenly a knock on the door. Maria was hurrying to it, holding the empty plates from the supper in her hand.
The kids heard the dishes breaking into pieces, on the threshold stood her beloved husband Nick, safe and sound.

She pressed him heartily and sobbing whispered: "Alive, alive, alive. God has heard me. I prayed every night, I begged the God for you to be alive, and Christ had heard my words. I am the happiest woman in the world", she cried, dancing and circling around the room.

Some while after, she questioned him: "By the way, where have you been for the whole year? The war had finished in forty five, but now the forty sixth is in the yard, have you lived with another woman, my sweetie?"

"Oh, no, my darling. I love you so much, I need no woman but you. And I have missed my children, too", answered Nick, embracing the little ones and caressing them and kissing them. The whole family was reunited for further hardships to overcome and fight the consequences of that "totally unnecessary war"; it was so called by Liddell Hart in his "History of the Second World War".

Many events had happened in Russia in those years.

March, 5, 1953. Joseph Stalin died, aged 73, after expanding Russia by 182,480 square miles and Soviet influence by 763,340 square miles after the war, and drew the "Iron Curtain" round the USSR and its satellites. Continuing his ruthless rule at home, he began the Cold War against non-communist countries. His foreign policy was unknown to the little people. Home policy was directed by the Marxism-Leninism guidelines in rising the Soviet economy.

Maria remembered Stalin's order, for five-minutes' being late for work, someone can be dismissed. No excuses will be considered except when illness strikes.

Her work was far from home, buses were overcrowded constantly, which could make her late. Her position as a cashier on the railway station did not allow her being late not for a minute because there were long lines of people for tickets to travel in different directions throughout the country. The terrible fact was being late. She immediately grasped that according to the Stalin's order she would be punished, fired, or even sent to prison.

The decision came up to her in no second - to go to the hospital and take a document about visiting the doctor. The fear settled in her soul, as well as in everybody else's. You must not do this, but do that; ought to go there, but not here; give your souls to the Communist state.

If one learns how to rule one single man's soul, one can have control the rest of mankind. It's the soul, Maria, your soul. Not whips or swords or fire or guns. That's why the Caesars, the Attila, the Napoleon were fools and did not last. The soul, Maria, is that which can't be ruled. It must be broken. Drive a wedge in, keep your fingers on it - and the man or the woman is yours. One won't need a whip - he or she'll bring it to you and ask to be whipped. Set him in reverse -and his own mechanism will do your work for yours. Use him or her against himself or herself.

There are many ways. Here's one. Make a person feel small. Make him feel guilty. Kill his creative inspiration and his integrity. That's difficult. The worst among you gropes for ideals in his own twisted way. Kill integrity by internal corruption. Use it against itself. Direct toward a goal destructive of all integrity. Preach - selflessness. Tell man that he must live for others. Tell men that altruism is the ideal. The people must live for future, for better communist society. Nobody has ever achieved it and not a single one ever will.

His every living instinct screams against it. But don't you see what you accomplish?

Man realizes that he's incapable of as the noblest virtue - and gives him of sin, of his own basic unworthiness.

In that respect, Maria used to say sincerely, "World is bardak and people bloody".

Since the supreme ideal is beyond his or her grasp, she or he gives up eventually all ideals, all aspiration, all sense of their personal value. They feel themselves obliged to preach what they can't practise. Their souls give up their self-respect. You've got them, they'll obey. They'll be glad to obey - because they can't trust themselves, they feel uncertain, frightened, they feel unclean.

When the Soviet people grumbled, they roundly cursed, but never Stalin. He was far away in a Kremlin Tower, a place nearer to heaven than earth, and He did no wrong. He was the Father of all the nations, and He did not know what suffering they had to endure. "It is very high up to God! It is very far to the Tsar!" said the Russian proverb. If only we could get to the Tsar and tell him, our troubles would be at an end - so runs the plot of a hundred Russian fairy tales.

For the Russian people, Stalin was like the Tsar and the Father-God but one face, sitting in the heart of Moscow, in Kremlin, the somber medieval citadel of Russian power with its massive red walls jutting from the bank of the Moscow River.

Not a single building but an entire walled city, it seemed to a romantic Frenchman no less than a mirror of Russia itself, "This is curious conglomeration of palaces, towers, churches, monasteries, chapels, barracks, arsenals and bastions. This incoherent jumble of sacred and secular buildings; this complex of functions a fortress, sanctuary, seraglio, harem, necropolis, and prison; this blend of advanced civilization and archaic barbarism; this violent conflict of crudest materialism and most loft spirituality; are they not the whole history of Russia, the whole epic of the Russian nation, the whole inward drama of the Russian soul?"

Maria's soul had cried with bitter, endless tears when Stalin died.

She did not realize then why her neighbor cobbler once suddenly disappeared. It was very convinient to have his shoe repairing shop next to her house. Now it was closed. Nobody knew what had happened to the poor unlucky cobbler and his family. Rumours told that he said something out of turn aloud. Nobody was allowed to tell anecdotes which were so popular among the Russian people, about Vasilij Chapaev, the famous national hero and his favorite female friend Anka, about the Armenian Radio or the Northern local Nanai people, so primitive in their developing. Everybody was scared of saying odd things.

One could not leave the village, passports had not been given to the people. What was life for a person without a passport. Every species of animals and every fruit tree had to be paid the taxes for, for the state's benefit. Hard times were in the country, they talked over the tax burden if they failed with the agricultural deals, and they would not be permitted to visit a town. They felt like slaves in their Holy Stalinland.

The life in cities and towns was not easy, either as the wages were small, no one could make ends meet and salaries were so low in every family.

After seventeen-years-work, twice awarded with Medals for successful Labour for her native Motherland, Maria quit the work. She bought a cow, named Subbotka, putting her in a barn near her modest studio home downtown, and began breeding the only pet. The eternal law of gravity on the earth had stirred the blood in her veins, love for animals, for mother-nature overfilled her. She used to get up at dawn. The sun rose against powerful, dark weather rolling in from the west, clouds formed, then broke, and for a moment the huge forest of southeastern Bryansk glowing with yellow-red warmth, it was a glorious awaking to the morning. The sky was a deep blue, the sun rose and became huge and shining and the dew drops on the grass blades sparkled like masses of diamonds till the sun soaked them up.

Maria drove Subbotka onto the grass field, milked her, cleaned and brushed her, fed her in the stable, and kept saving the hay for winter-time. It took Maria a lot of time to keep everything in order, particularly, mowing the grass, drying it with the following up of hay-stacking, and transporting it home.

Her beloved husband, although be was a village man, did not help her. Every time when the mowing season came, Nick had a habit of having a vacation, referring on his tiredness for the whole working year, and that he possessing the legal right for a rest at long last.

"Sweetie, are you going to escape again when I need you most of all?" she said angrily.

"No, darling. I am not escaping, the only possible date of my holiday is today. There is a schedule of holidays and today's my turn", replied he softly. And he continued insistently, "My plan is not to sit at home with you, but to visit my mother's and brother's place in Rostov-on-Don". He used to leave her alone with her cares and troubles and returned when everything had been done for winter preparations.

Nick was egoistic by nature.

He pleased his "ego" every Saturday or Sunday; " it got to be time to visit the sauna ('bannya' - in Russian). Nothing could change that routine: even the calf -birth or arrival of VIP (very important person) of the family. Nick was tidy, accurate and always fresh, bannya's procedures took a specific place in his life.

Actually who does not know the Russian bannya!

That who had once visited it, could never forget it: nothing could be compared with it. Turkish bunnyas with their special massagists leaping along one's body were very well described by a great Russian poet Alexander Pushkin. Throughout the whole world the Finnish saunas are widely known with their dry steam and obligatorily bathing in the swimming pool or somewhere else.

Oh, Russian banya, it is a great sweat! In direct and figurative sense of the word. The Wonder in Wonderland. Even Lewis Carroll could not figure it out!

Everything had been started in the early June when the birches were greening: there began the preparation of the birches, bushy bunches of young branches to be used in bannya procedures.

First, these ones should be dried in the shade, saved at certain room temperatures and not to allow them to be under or over-dried. Second, when you entered the bannya, you ought to fill a basin with hot water and put this bunch into it to soak it. Then your naked body and, particularly, your nostrils will get the smell of the young birch woods. When you are climbing on the top step of the stairs mounted here and beginning to accumulate all the smells of the bushes, you should be bit against your bared skin with the birch bunch.

Your sweating back will sound like a flock of birds highly flying in the sky; your soul seems to be separated from the body, following the flying spirit. And into the members of your body there will come such tenderness and pleasure that cannot be liked with any massage in the universe - even the phillipine girls' body massage although good cannot be compared to a bannya.

The more wet hot steam in Russian bannyas is the better. The nostrils are blowing, the heart is beating very fast - it is high time to go out and take a water-bath, rolling out in the frosty prickling snow.

One can after using them may wish to dance and sing, compose verses, do everything your poor little heart-and-soul desires.

Nick's soul badly wanted tea."Maria, the samovar is ready, isn't it?" he would ask as usual.

"Certainly, my heart. I have added fresh carbons into the chimney, and pumped nicely with my boot, igniting the fire, making a new portion of tea in the big kettle on the top. And now, would you be so kind as to come to the table and help yourself with the tea?" answered Maria. Nick looked at his wife with great respect. Together they were sitting down at the round table covered with the linen cloth embroidered with red-and-white cocks and for many winter-and-summer hours they bad been drinking Russian tea. Habitually it was Georgian, Armenian either Indian, Azerbaijan or Crimea~blends like British Lipton, PG tea leaves' tips. As addition to this fascinating procedure there was a hard sugar in big rocky cubes. He chopped a little piece of sugar from this raw limb with special shears.

Holding in the left hand this tiny sweet bit of sugar and a big cup of tea in the right hand, Nick could have drunk ten-fifteen cups of delicious tea at a time. Maria who was a bad tea drinker very soon fell behind.

She was a master of cattle-keeping, and her pet Subbotka answered her with mutual love. Often she spoke to her as if she were a human being, "Hello, honey, how are you?" sounded Maria's voice in the early morning.

"Does anything hurt you? Is everything okay? Show me your teeth, please.1s the straw layer enough for you, my Subbotka?" And the black-eyed, brown coloured cow replied to her with a long mooing, faithfully staring at her hostess and licking Maria's palms. After having milked her, Maria had to rush to her permanent clients who needed fresh milk and who paid her in advance. So she earned money to bring up her children and to educate them. That was not the easiest of tasks.

Those years were the challenging for education: everybody wanted to learn everything. The propaganda also had great influence on the people helping to summon the young brilliant brains. At the Universities and High and Secondary Schools, big competitions took place constantly.

Education was free, it is why among twenty-thirty applicants one could be most successful. In such an atmosphere the bribes to professors were a usual thing. Maria's eldest daughter studied at the Technical Secondary School, Val - at the University, the youngest - at the Technological Institute. All of them were students at the same time, fast transforming from teenagers into adults. Subbotka helped all the family wherever it was possible by her milk, she dressed them, she fed them and was a helpful, reliable friend, figuratively speaking. In the family's albums there were many photos of beautiful Subbotka. It was not so important that she gave not as lots of milk as others-only around twenty liters per day, and its fat - only 2,5%. Subbotka was a really valuable asset to the family.

In those days one government changed for another: Malenkov, Bulganin, Khrushchev, who ruled each in his own way. Khrushchev, however, issued the order, forbidding the town people to keep the cattle in the city boundaries.

The family's pet Subbotka was sold, the first television set was bought instead. In the evenings everybody gathered by the set and listened and watched the new TV programs: nine o'clock p.m. news, KVN shows, blue-sight parties with the prominent actors and actresses, popular singers.

The rise of Alla Pugacheva, a Russian variety solo-singer, who had started in 1965 when on a - program "Good Morning" to the whole country was sung the song "Robot" in her performance. She was only sixteen then, she had been studying in the Musical Secondary School named after Ippolitov-Ivanov, worked in the circus as a musician.

Red-haired, slim, Alla burst into sleepy Soviet variety stage shows where zombies like workers were moving, these were show-men of the Brezhnev epoch (well, sure, there were exclusions, always and everywhere). Frankly speaking, she was still not that Alla of the tough temper in which grew up, the incredible rumours whispered about her. It was a pretty, red-curled teenager in a mini-skirt, very nice and leggy, with a strong voice, remembering and retaining all her fans.

Her creative individuality was visible from the first glimpse and resented by her masters as a collective brain. Under the conditions of the Communist collective style of life, she began fighting against it, a tribute to her as an individual is that she rebelled in her mind. In nature, there is no such thing as a collective brain.

There is no such thing as a collective thought.

An agreement reached by a group of men is only a compromise or an average drawn upon many individual thoughts. It is a sec-ondary consequence. The primary act - the process of reason - must be performed by each man alone.

She was alone in her battles for freedom and independence in the arts, in creative activities. Nothing was given to Alla on earth free. Everything she needed had to be produced. Here a person faced the basic alternative: she could survive in only of two ways - by the independent work of her own mind, yes, or as a parasite fed by the minds of others, no.

The creator originates. The parasite borrows.

The creator faces hardships alone; the basic need of her was independence. The reasoning mind cannot work under any form of compulsion. It cannot be curbed, sacrificed or subordinated to any consideration whatsoever. It demands total independence in function and in motive.

Alla Pugacheva's motives and functions were still the same - creativeness. The brightest pop-star in Russia, a rarely gifted personality, such opinions were expressed by Eugene Evtushenko, a great Russian poet, by Janna Aguzarova, a pop-singer, by Michael Zvanetsky, a writer and a performer, by Bulat Okudjava, a poet and a singer, by Innokenty Smoktunovsky, Margaret Terehova, Oleg Jankovsky and Alissa Freindlich, the prominent in-land actors and actresses, published in the independent daily newspaper "Bulgar" by Igor Faber.

At last Alla Pugacheva could say about herself, "I am free and happy". Is not it a real Russian aftermath result nowadays?

That could not be said about simple poor Maria. Every time she had no money for housekeeping, for foods, for clothes. For many years she forgot how to wear a nice coat or a pair of nylon stockings. She simplified her life to one dress for summer and one - for winter, the same - about shoes and one coat for all seasons of the year.

She could not afford more. The only luxury was left to her - to work hard and to earn money and she did her best in this way; she sold ice-cream on hot summer days, cigarettes when it was getting cooler. All her life she fought against poverty in the name of her children. Oh, she loved them with all her heart and her children respond to Maria the same.

The children never noticed her heroic efforts to overcome the poverty because everywhere in the country everyone was poor and equal in dammed bloody poverty. The Propaganda told the people: it was nice to live in such a free country like the Soviet Union where everyone is equal to everyone else; everybody had the equal rights for education, medical assistance, work, rest.

Everything was free, all farms were collective and that meant everything was everybody's. Such a nominal brotherhood of equality, poverty and drunkenness.

Her Nick did not drink vodka, as many others around, but he did not make money, either.

In spite of his wife's pushing and attempts to motivate him, Nick was not promoted in his job, still he remained a very good executor. His salary never changed, except when the money reform came. He stopped resisting the circumstances, and lost all the hopes for a better life style.

The life stream caught him and transformed him into a small pin of a great mechanism which was called the Soviet state. Nick was an average normal citizen by the name of "homo soveticus".

Like all homos soveticus he got up very early in the morning, with breakfast or without it, went to the plant, did his work, communicated with his fellows at work, came back home, occasionally helped his wife in housekeeping, ate supper, read newspapers, watched TV and went to bed.

In the dreams he was a free man, brave and pronouncing the lofty words, holding speeches. In life Nick was not an orator at all, shy and hidden by nature.

Facing him, Maria was talkative, she could not hold any secrets at all. Her children's secrets were not secrets very long, she bragged about their love affairs to anyone who would listen to her because she was proud of them.

Her children became adults, having jobs, earning their own money and still lived together with Mom in the same post-war studio apartment.

Her room-mate once said to her, "Maria, have you ever heard about the cooperative housebuilding committee?"

"For the life of me, I can't imagine that one exists. It's something new after Khrushchev's policy of cheap dwellings, isn't it?" answered she.

A flicker of interest snapped in Maria's eyes.

"Hell to Khrushchev, bloody piggy guy! I'm inclined to see things purely from the viewpoint of common sense. Do you need a new comfortable flat?" he continued.

He was an ordinary man, neither well-dressed nor shabby, neither tall nor short, neither dark nor quite blond; he had the kind of face one could not remember even while looking at it. He was frightening by being so totally indifferent, he lacked even the positive distinction of a half-wit, however, pretended to be a commander.

"Well, I sure hope so", she answered to her neighbour.
From that moment on, the only thought grasping her mind was

how to manage to get money for the first deposit in the building-house cooperative. Her husband was beyond her calculation. "Look, you, poor, little rascal" Maria addressed Nick, "You've got sense enough to realize that you should work harder to earn more money, damned fucking money, so we can move to another flat".

"Good Lord, man. You've lost your mind! I've never heard of such a thing as a cooperative housing", he answered, bewildered.

"Ask anybody in the profession. See what they'll tell you. It's preposterous!" the wife attacked.

"Probably."

"Listen, Nick, won't you please listen?"

"I'll listen if you want me to, Maria. But I think I should tell you now that nothing you can say will make any difference. If you don't mind that, I don't mind listening".

Maria went on speaking for a long time and Nick listened without objecting, explaining or answering. At last he said a word, "The children will help with money".

In practice, it meant: Val had started to work as a school teacher, having her own wages, she could help, Emma had been saving money for her private flat; Gen, a student, whose stipend was so small just enough to buy one pair of shoes. He had a feeling of compassion for his parents' project but could not help at all.

Maria's strict policy of economizing was having results. As spring approached she knew the family money could last much longer. She paid the rent on the studio promptly on the first of each month.

She wanted the feeling of being thirty days ahead, during which she would save some more money for the future flat. She found only that she did not want to look at the calendar when it began to grow dark and she knew that another day of the thirty had gone. When she noticed this, she made herself look at the calendar. It was a race she was running now, a race between her saving money and... she did not know the name of the other contestant. Perhaps it was every man whom she passed on the street or her insistent desire to live better than she lived.

The necessary sum of cash was brought into the bank; the house building got started.On a spring day, eighteen months later,

41

Maria took her family for a walk and to observe the construction site of their future home.

They looked at the fields surrounding it.

Dandelions rose from unexpected spots, out of the low plain lines. They had a kind of startling suddenness, as if they had sprung the second before they saw them and they caught the last thrust of the motion; as if they were to turn away and look again fast enough, they would catch them in the act of springing. The first spring flowers in the fields reminded Maria of her first meeting with her first love Boris among the dandelions. Where is he now? What is he doing? The unheard pain touched her heart again, and the consciousness turned to the vast cleared tract.

Machines were crawling over the torn earth, grading the future yard. From its center the skeleton of house-building rose, completed to the sky. The top part of the frame still hung naked, an intercrossed cage of steel. Glass and masonry had followed its rise, covering the rest of the long streak slashed through space.

Maria thought, "They say the heart of the earth is made of fire. It is held imprisoned and silent. But at times it breaks through the clay, the iron, the granite, and shoots out to freedom. Then it becomes a thing like this."

"Marvelous", she whispered.

This construction house building miracle had been extended for seven long years, as among the folks called "dolgostroy" which meant "long-long term building".

Between the expectations, meanwhile, Maria's Jewish neighbour proposed to get a vegetable garden just beyond the city limits, closer to her home.

"My dear," she said some day, "What a long unnecessary discussion that would take, and how involved, I've always told you that we should be good friends. We have so much in common: husbands - failures, you - three children, me - two, sufferings. We started, as usual, from opposite poles, but that makes no difference, because you see, we meet at the same point."

"What are you driving at?" asked Maria. "For instance, it was interesting to discover what sort of thing appears nice to you, a vegetable garden, perhaps."

"Honey, Raissa Abramovna, I'll think about it and inform you by all means. Thanks a lot. Bye-bye, dear."

Maria agreed. The most popular vegetable garden plants to cultivate were cabbage and potatoes. The family planted potatoes early, middle, and late season varieties to get continuous roots from mid-July to mid-September. They could be protected from freezing by insulating them from the winter cold, and this could be done by covering them with enough hay to keep the ground from freezing in the climate of Russian middle zone areas of risky earth conditions, it was one of the difficult tasks.

As with so such gardening, there were a lot of different ways to get good results. Cabbage was the transition vegetable from unprocessed storage to process. Winter cabbage lasted three to four months in cold high humidity, just the same as root crops. The only real difference was that root crops usually lost their goodness by getting dry and limp. Cabbage usually rotted.

Therefore, they wanted to fill the sacks with potatoes in their cellar, but cabbage needed checking every now and then to make sure none were rotting.

The beauty of cabbage was that it was the only green vegetable that could be stored for any length of time without being processed if you were trying to eat as much as possible from your garden, which was a very important feature. Cabbage was also one of the vegetables they processed, for example, with Sauer-kraut recipe "a la Russ".

On a beautiful crisp fall day one brought some firm heads of late cabbage in from the garden, outer leaves removed, the cores to be cut out, cabbage leaves and carrots to be chopped and mixed with salt, pepper, "Antonovka" - type apples and cranberries. Everything to set into a wooden bowl, covered with an oak lid. In ten days the family got started eating the delicious dish: mashed potatoes with Sauer-kraut. From these vegetables, Russian borshch can be cooked as well as many other wholesome foods for ordinary people.

Besides Raissa, Maria chose for her friendship Sarah Smirnova, an enthusiastic "petite, but intellectual" neighbour woman. She was wearing dresses of size ten and shopping in the junior departments. She wore high-school garments and short socks in summer, displaying spindly legs with hard blue veins. She adored gardening, Maria felt always comfortable in Sarah's presence because she smiled at her and used to say, "Darling, Maria, you look lovelier every time I see you. One wouldn't think it were possible".

"Thanks, Sarah. Have you finished your job on the beds? If so, welcome to my table and have a meal after work. And then, let's go for a walk to the warm Desna river," suggested Maria.

Sarah agreed. The two friends ran fast along the path leading to the nearest lake, deciding to have a snack on the bank. The two talked and talked expressing the opinions of year-round residents and seasonal inhabitants, on all the current events, debating some news from local trials, judging about raising children and many numerous topics. Then Maria said to her friend,

"Have you ever heard that Christians had been cautioned by Jesus about making judgments: "Stop judging, that you may not be judged yourself".

Sarah gazed at her in astonishment, "Where did you know this phrase from?"

"From one wise peasant who had been helping me with the hay-stacking", Maria answered.

"I wonder where he knew it from", meditated Sarah.
"Probably from his parents", commented Maria.

They embraced, pressed to each other closer and thought over deeply.

"Can you sing, Maria?" asked Sarah.
"Certainly. Why?"
"Let us sing my favorite song by Leo Oshanin's words and Raymond Pauls's music."

They started to sing a beautiful, extensive refrain:
> "Oh, kindest Lake,
> The Lake of Warmth,
> Why did you touch
> My love with frost?
>> Oh, Lake, the warm and blue,
>> In the quiet greenish wildness,
>> Little fur trees rose above you,

44

As if the sisters of same likeness.
At each of them and underneath,
In day and when it's getting dark,
As lot we kissed under the trees,
As many needles you can mark!
    Smiles're laying on furs the dews,
    The birches stood of white -'e -stem,
    Close to the Lake of Warmth aroused,
    Danced, enjoyed and mocked at them.
The raindrops hung the fate above,
Under each of those pretty birches,
As lot of tears was poured of love,
As lots of leaves had their branches!"

It was Sarah who brought Maria good news, "Your house building has been completed. Dash for keys and move as soon as possible."

Sarah was a person who adored celebrities, and Maria in her eyes was such a person. That was Sarah's mission in life to contact celebrities. Sarah hunted them grimly; she faced them with wide-eyed admiration and spoke of her own insignificance, of her humility before achievement; she shrugged, tight-lipped and rancorous, whenever one of her friends did not seem to take sufficient account of her own views on birth control and the movies.

She had a great many poor friends and advertised the fact. If a friend happened to improve his financial position, she dropped him, feeling that he had committed an act of treason. She hated the wealthy in all sincerity. She considered Maria her best friend and wished her luck in her new apartment. Maria invited Sarah to a celebration party.

A government decided holiday was ordered the week-end after the family's move; it was without Emma, she had got the keys for her own flat; she got married and lived on her own.

Maria's husband did not have a bad habit of drinking vodka or other strong alcohol drinks like most of the Russian men.On that special holiday Nick got drunk as a skunk and dancing with Sarah some pretty tricky dances, laughing and making fun of his mistakes. His friend Kuzin, no one knew his first name, could not help but dance, with half-bared hairy chest, and very deeply set spectacles, ten-twenty times magnifying. His eyes seemed to be extremely large and frightening but his widely extended mouth was always smiling.

The trio performed an Argentinean tango. One was wondering how in these genuine Russian souls there could be such an unbelievable knowledge of overseas' dances, tapping and incredible bent knees, swirling, banging of boot heels etc. etc.

Kuzin was the king of dancing. He sat tiredly on the chair and proposed,"Nick, would you like to play a couple of games of chess with me?"

"I hardly can play chess", Nick shyly told to his friend.

"It means nothing for me. I'll teach you", replied Kuzin.

That chess lesson lasted from that moment on for the whole of Nick's life.

Throughout our lives, we were told that creativity was rare and mysterious, that only artists were creative, and that it was a "right fine brain" function, whatever that meant.

No, by no means. Two new friends, Nick and Kuzin, unleashed their creativity in chess games, convincing that creativity was within everyone's reach. New chess puzzles and ideas were fleeting like rabbits streaking through their consciousness.

If they didn't grab them quickly, they could be usually gone forever. The two used to explore their creative side and have learned ways to head and preserve their new chess solutions.

They had "capturing" skills. Capturing was easier in certain settings and at certain times. For them, the three B's of creativity - bed, bath and bus - were particularly fertile.

Sometimes they led "uncreative" conversations.

"Nick, do you remember how I used to be so fat and flabby?!"asked the first, "Well, I've been on an exercise program for a few months, and now I run the marathons."

"That's great!" replied the latter.

The first friend continued, "Do you remember how I used to be shy and a poor student? Well, I took a course in public speaking, and now I am brave and got a good job."

"That's great!" came the reply.

"Oh, what about you?" Kuzin inquired, "Have you changed at all?"

"Not at all," answered Nick, "except the job."

Really, he had not changed himself with all his years of service. He was like a monolith blowing around with the winds, but he was calm and unmovable, the day came when Nick was fired without any notice or explanations.

He knew his rights as an employee determined by the legal restrictions placed on the employer as they were few in number.

Essentially, employers cannot discriminate in hiring, firing, or promoting employees on the basis of race, colour, national origin, religion, sex, age, or disability.

But otherwise, the employer-employee relationship was a matter of contract law. Poor little thing Nick felt that in his case there was a breaking of the labour law.

He went to the Soviet Court, sueing the administration staff of his office. He wrote many documents and papers, studied the books about the Soviet law,"Legal problem solver", consulted the experienced attorneys, his trial was postponed. Two long years had passed before there was appointed the date: August, 12, 1965.

A crowd filled the local courtroom, witnessing the trial of Nickolay Filin. Nick sat at the defense table. He listened calmly. Maria sat in the third row of spectators. Looking at her, people felt as if they had seen a smile. She did not smile. She looked at the leaves in the window.

"The motive which the Administrative Staff proposes to prove", the prosecutor was making his opening address to people, "is beyond normal human rights. To the majority of us it will appear monstrous and inconceivable. A ruthless, arrogant egotist who wished to have his own way at any price - to draw the buildings accurately and methodically precisely, without being late to work, Comrade Filin had been fired without explanations and dared to appeal to the Court".

Unprecedential! The Soviet Slave dared to complain at his Employer, as Master. The people had come to witness a sensational case, to see the celebrities of Bosses, to get material for conversation, to be seen, to kill time. They would return to unwanted jobs, unloved families, unchosen friends, to drawing rooms, murdered hope, desire left unreached, to days of efforts not to think, not to say, to forget and give in and give up.

Everybody listened, their faces attentive and emotionless. People had whispered that the judge was tough-looking and stubborn.

The prosecutor introduced the opposite side, a representative of the Administrative Staff. It was a tall, blond-haired woman Comrade Ivanova.

"Comrade Ivanova, will you state under oath that Comrade Filin has possessed such a bad character that it was enough to dismiss him without reason?"

"Yes, I will".

"What kind of character? Could you explain it in details, Comrade Ivanova?"

"I am not capable of doing it myself. What was written in documents that was the truth", answered she.

"Do you know Comrade Filin personally?"

"No, I don't".

There was no sound of honesty in her voice, because there was no sound of effort to pronounce a truth of such nature; no tone of truth or falsehood; only indifference.

The prosecutor handed her a sheet of paper. "Is this the conclusion you signed?"

"Yes."

"Will you please read it aloud?"

Comrade Ivanova read it aloud. Her voice came evenly, well drilled. Nobody in the courtroom realized that this testimony had been intended as a sensation. It was not a Communist Party leader of the office, it was a woman, reciting a memorized lesson. People felt that were she interrupted, she would not be able to pick up the next sentence, but would have to start all over again from the beginning.

She answered a great many questions.

The prosecutor introduced in evidence Comrade Filin's last drawings fulfilled with extraordinary skill and mastership.

"The prosecution rests", said the local Attorney.

The judge looked at Nick.

"Proceed ", he said. His voice was gentle.

Nick got up. "Comrade Judge, I shall call no witnesses. This will be my testimony and my summation."

"Take the oath".

Nick took the oath.

"Why do you, Comrade Ivanova, so hate me? Why? Because I'm not a Communist Party member like you, or I have not got a diploma about Higher Education, haven't I? But I'm an experienced draftsman. Look at my drawings! I've been working here for more than fifteen years", his voice trembling, he was about in tears. He was a bad orator, could not hold speeches and least of all he could defend himself.

Nick sat trying not to show the tears running fast against his cheeks. He sat by the steps of the witness stand. The audience looked at him. They felt he had no chance. They could drop the nameless resentment, the sense of insecurity which he aroused in most people.

And so, for the first time, they could see him as he was: a man totally defenseless who faced fear.

The fear of which they thought was the normal kind, a response to a tangible danger.

It was the chronic, unconfessed fear in which they all lived. They remembered the misery of the moments when, in loneliness, a man thinks of the bright words he could have said, but had not found, and hates those who robbed him of his courage. The misery of knowing how strong and able one is in one's own mind, the radiant picture never to be made real. Dreams? Self-delusion? Or a murdered reality, unborn, killed by that corroding emotion without name-fear-need-dependence-hatred?

There hung the grave silence and suddenly the silence was broken by a furious voice from the third row. It was Maria who could not help crying in a very high tone.

"I'm the wife of this man. I know him as a very honest man, hard-worker and a good-hearted personality. Who gave you the right to discriminate my husband? Because he is not a member of the Communist Party of the Soviet Union. But he tried many times to join it and it was you who did not allow it, he was not ready enough, as if better to memorize the theory of Marxism - Leninism which you are grounded on. What sort of bloody theory that one simple worker could not grasp?

What sort of damned Communist Party government is it who threw out an ordinary hard worker to the garbage? What fucking people are responsible, who gave them the right to decide the destinies of others? Or, maybe, because he has no diploma of Higher Education? But his skill is higher than all those who had graduated from a great many Universities and Institutes, even if you added all together?"

Maria sat down and looked around, watching some people - who looked at her with delight.

Each of them, Maria thought, had known some unforgotten moment - a morning when nothing had happened, a piece of music heard suddenly and never heard in the same way again, a stranger's face seen in a bus -a moment when each had known a different sense of living. And each remembered other moments, on a sleepless night, on an afternoon of steady rain, in an empty street at sunset, when each had wondered why there was so much suffering and ugliness in the world. They had not tried to find the answer and they had gone on living as if no answer were necessary. But each had known a moment when, in lonely, naked honesty he had felt the need of an answer. People moved, preparing to depart, without haste, in expectation of many hours of waiting.

Nick stood by the defense table.

Those who bad been on their feet remained standing, frozen, until the judge returned to the bench.

"The Petitioner will rise and face the Court", said the clerk. Nick stepped forward and stood facing the judge. "Comrades, have you reached the verdict?"

"Yes, we have".

"What is your verdict?"

"The Petitioner Comrade Filin Nickolay Alexeevich to be reinstated on his job and to be paid the seven-months' salary for the forced lay off because of the fault of the Administrative Staff of his office".

Nick decided to be absent from work, however, because the

Administration was so vindictive against him, in a hidden nature and as soon as possible he changed his place of work.

Later he had graduated from the Bryansk Building Secondary School attending extra-mural classes for five years, together with his step-daughter Emma.

It was his second life victory to get a diploma in which he so needed; the first one was - the opportunity to live in a new, comfortable flat with a bath, shower, toilet.

"Turn the knob on and enjoy yourself as long as possible", thought Nick, and up to the last days of his life he enjoyed being in the water in his bath, splashing and lying there for long hours. "Darling, are you fallen asleep?" used to ask him his wife knocking on the bathroom door. "Why are you so quiet? An hour and a half has passed, and you are still in the water. Sweetie, it's high time to get out. Rush, rush, my dearest".

Very often he got thought over the origin of his name Nicholas. One book writes "Nicholas (a.c.). Probably born at Patara, Lucia, Asia Minor, of wealthy parents, became known for his holiness, zeal and miracles. One of the legends spoke that after his parents' death he devoted himself to the conversion of sinners and his wealth to the poor and to charitable works. One such was the story of three poverty-stricken girls whose father was about to turn them into prostitutes, since he could not afford to keep them.

Nicholas on three occasions threw bags of gold into their house, and all three were married.

He was the patron of storm-beset sailors, of prisoners, or children (on some accounts the story of the three bags of gold and the three girls became the heads of three murdered children restored to life by the Saint Nicholas), which led to the practice of children giving presents at Christmas in his name and the metamorphosis of his name St. Nicholas into Sent Klaus, into Santa Claus by the Dutch.

He thought to himself and used to repeat in whisper, "In our family there are neither mariners nor prisoners. But a lot of kids! I should help them all my life with all my forces up to the last seconds of my life ".

The words sounded as an oath. In fact, he was very faithful to

51

the children: a new stage had started for them, they became adults, grew up and wanted to live on their own, to get married, and to bear children. It was not the easiest time in the country - the end of nineteen sixties, the beginning of the seventies.

The Propaganda told everywhere: in the USSR there are the best successes in steel production, in iron production, in oil and many other areas of production, really in life ordinary people had hardly money enough for food, for clothes, for goods of basic needs. Again and again the Propaganda was feeding the people with the promises for a better life in the future.

The present life declared peaceful attitude to the drunkards, dishonest people, and the hidden criminals in the national economy. Under such circumstances there must be born baby-girls, the three granddaughters came to the birth almost at the same time, two Larissas and one Marina named after grandmother's name Maria and in her honour.

The three babies suffered since their birth badly: Larissas - because of fathers' lack of attention, Marina - because of the severe illness of her mother and vodka drinking of her father.

Maria and Nick helped as much as they could: for one year and a half they brought up Marina, while Emma was saved in hospital from heart disease. Maria remembered the doctors' words, "Emma, we don't recommend you to bear a child. You can die - your heart won't hold the stress. In that case we guarantee you the lethal end".

Emma did not obey and had born Marina - so great was her desire to have a baby, and her age of thirty three was also critical. It was the age of Christ who volunteerly had gone to the Golgotha accepting the suffering of the people. But the Lord did not end the tortures of Emma.

She felt fatigue, shortness of breath, dizziness, nausea, vomiting or heartburn in the chest. Pain here radiated to the arm, neck, jaw or stomach.

In her, less collateral circulation developed. "If a blood vessel was suddenly blocked, especially without collaterals, it could be shocking to the heart", the doctors added.

In hospital, the risk of dying dropped to one out of ten.

She was happy, survived, but since that moment became disabled and never worked, getting from the government a little pension, to live on and bring up a child. That was why Maria had fulfilled her mother's debt helping her eldest one to overcome the hardships. Practically, for other kids Maria had no time.

The Propaganda at that time cried on all the corners, "Party and Lenin are twins-brothers. We must be thankful to the country that there is no more war".

Oh, Maria remembered very well the lessons of War: bombardments, ruins, hunger, lack of everything. Now the post-war children went on carrying the same destiny of their parents -very hard life with lots of sufferings. Both daughters' husbands were drinking much, appeared at home mad drunken behavior, putting mess and arranging scandals. Police visited their home very often.

"Did you call the police?!" asked a young policeman gazing curiously at Emma, standing with the hammer in her left hand on the kitchen stool.

"Yes, I did."

"Is that your husband?" pointed he to the lying man with the blood stain on his cheek.

"Yes, he is", answered she.

"But you've committed your deal very quickly. He's very quiet now. I wonder how fast the things ran around the houses. In one family the husband hit his wife, in the second - the wife knocked out her husband. Really, it's your personal life, how difficult to judge who is right, and who's wrong", the policeman smiled at her.

"I have warned him many times not to approach me because I was hitting the nail into the wall. But he came over cursing and got his own".

When the policeman went out, she was scared as if it were not a joke. Her husband lay on the floor without moving. She took a cloth out of the kitchen, washed his face and listened to the heart beating. Everything was normal, he slept disarmed in vague consciousness what had happened.

Such scenes were repeated endlessly, in such case Maria's helper was Nick. He, shy and calm by nature, grew up in her eyes, attempting to fight with drunkards: so he hated the people who were drinking vodka and all sorts of liquor and then scandalizing with using cursed bad words. From that disgustful guy, his son-in-law, he knew a pretty great number of Russian fucking tough expressions which could not be translated into a foreign language and which ones were so loved by the men throughout the world. Nick never used these idioms in his speech and he could not fight either. The only thing to do in these critical situations was to punish and grab the law-breaker, then to call the police. It was good for Emma to live in the same house which had two entrance halls, one - for Maria's family, another - for her daughter's.

Nick was devoted to his oath to help the children whenever it was necessary, gave his credit to his step-daughter and did his best as he could.

Val's and Gen's marriage affairs were fixed up poorly. Maria's nerves and brain could not bear it any longer. The disaster knocked at the door by the mid-seventies.

A stroke! Sometimes called cerebrovascular accident (CVA) was sudden neurological disorder due to interruption of the blood supply to that part of the brain. Partial paralysis of the face and then arm and leg (hemi paresis) and loss of sensation or ability to perceive the environment correctly.

The fight for her life continued. Maria stayed in bed for longer and longer periods of time. Nick sat at her bed and forgot, at times, to turn on the lights in the early dusk. It was as if the heavy immobility of all the hours that had flowed through the room, of its door, of its air, were beginning to seep into the muscles. He would rise and fling a book at the wall, to feel his arm move, to hear the burst of sound. He smiled, amused, picked up a kettle and laid it neatly back onto the table.

He turned on the wall lamp. Then he stopped, before he had withdrawn his hands from the cone of light under the lamp, and he looked at his hands, he spread his fingers out slowly.

Then he remembered what Maria had said to him long ago. He jerked his hands away. He reached for his coat, turned the lights off, locked the door and went out of the flat.

Sleepless in the night he wandered around the headquarters. He was warned by the doctors that no recovery could be expected.

He was in despair; he did not want to believe it. He felt no hope because he saw that Maria, lying still in bed, looked serene and - almost happy, he had never found possible to associate with his wife. His wife, his the only treasure Maria, remained motionless without any hope for recovery.

For twelve long years be took it upon himself to help her, to feed her as a child, to wash her, to dress her, to take her to the toilet and many other life tasks. The doctors said, "If the stroke occurred in the left half of the brain, the dominant hemisphere, results might include speech impairment and paralysis of the right side of the body".

Her illness obtained for her a higher pension as a handicapped person of the first category, to have the telephone connected in case she needed to call for emergency help. Shortly Nick also felt breathlessness, an unpleasant sensation that might be a symptom of a number of diseases, ranging from asthma and bronchitis and other respiratory disorders to heart disease and defects in the lungs or chest wall.

He never came to the doctor's. Just he had no time for that. All this time he was involved with Maria.

"Hey, you, in the kitchen! Hurry up! Hurry up! Bring me boiling water, please!" she used to command addressing nobody special.

She guessed that by all means somebody would be in her kitchen and listen to her words in the very early morning about five a.m. "Boiling water" meant her favorite drink - tea with sugar.

That person who appeared to be in the kitchen at that time dashed for a tray and brought her a nice cup of tea. Nick happened to be there at the moment.

"What have you been doing for almost an hour?" questioned Maria.

"First, I looked out of the window to observe a nice morning, secondly, put the kettle onto the conformer and waited for it to be boiled."

"Musinjka, be quiet, dear. It took no longer than ten minutes", replied he patiently.

"Shut up! Shut up! Do you know the difference between men

and boys?"

"No, I don't."

"The difference between men and boys is the size of the toys. You are like a big kid. All the time you are either playing or dreaming", explained she.

"Musja, dear, but without a dream one cannot live, life looses its interest", he noticed philosophically.

They both started their day with early morning tea, sitting at her bed.

He had counted, thirty times a day she was nursed, served and changed her clothes or sheets. Thirty times a day she demanded his constant attention to be paid to her, including strolling inside the room, at length outside, standing with her still-shaky leg propped up by walking sticks. Suddenly throwing them aside, she took a few hesitant steps, and then continued through the doorway, shouting "Look at me! I'm walking!"

And then she fell down. Nick helped her up.

Once in his absence Maria had wished to feed her favorite pigeons flying daily by her window. She stepped slowly with the help of a stick, took bread crumbs and pulled herself towards the open window but could not reach it without help.

"What a square you are, Musja!" grumbled Nick peering at her and grabbing her at the same moment when he came back home.

"Why did you not wait for me? I've dropped into a shop just for a second. Why are you so impatient?"

Really, the more the disease progressed, the more impatient she became. Her character had been slowly changing for the worse, witnesses judged. Maria's eyes got weaker and weaker, and instead of reading she was eager to listen to the radio.

So her head had been stuffed with lots of international news, Communist Party leaders' speeches. She memorized everything and on the evenings reported about them to her close friends, neighbours and children.

"Do you know that Brezhnev visited America, and had organized the signing of the peace treaty with Northern Vietnam?"

"Do you know that the Soviet troops have invaded Afghanistan?"

"Do you know that Kohl arrived in Paris yesterday?"

"Do you know that Khrushchev 's celebrated shoe-banging exercise at the United Nations shocked all the Russians and the entire world as well?"

About the last event she had beard it from a man, not by the official radio-set, and its programs were mostly dull and monotonous. Sitting-and-lying-Maria was translated into a "walking political encyclopedia", everybody listened to her and was astonished.

Not so astonished was Nick. He knew his wife very well and worshiped her.

The world became simpler and society seemed to be more in touch with the values of family responsibility and faith for the Virgin Mary, whose name was as his wife's. His lady in his life was the central being in his pilgrimage through the roads and ways of this world, often he called her "My Mother" and "My QUEEN".

For him, compassion was vital to Maria's care, especially at a time when the USSR society was in the throes of a debate of Stalin's cult and its consequences.

"All sick people need emotional support, which means we have to give ourselves to them", said he to himself.

"Compassion is having the ability to feel something for the sick woman's predicament and to assure her she will not be abandoned", he added.

It is often that the sense of abandonment, along with depression and other feelings, drives a sick person to ask for help in dying.

"We must communicate somehow to her and tell her she is not dying alone, she's dying as a member of the human race, she's dying in community, and I'm with her always", he said.

Nick was the first of those two who died in March, 31, 1985. He sacrificed his life for her and after his death she was holy and meek, she did not want to live any longer.

Days and nights through, in secret and aloud, she pronounced the same prayer: "God, only you are in the whole world, I ask you to take me to my Nickolay. For sake of Jesus Christ, I am begging you to take me to you, my Lord, to my Saint Nicholas".

Around nine months after, in December, 13, 1985, the Christ heard her prayer: Maria had died in a Christian way, as it usually was in Holy Mother Russia.

God bless them, poor little Russian Souls, Maria and Nickolay!

They were buried in one grave, under one monument symbolizing the eternal law of the unity of two beloved hearts, in the little town of Bryansk, in the modest cemetery.

Let the soil be a feather for them!

PART TWO

EMMA

A seven-year-old-child with crutches under her armpits, Emma looked around to a green-yellow sunflower field so startling as to be almost electric, as if bright summer were simply a matter of flipping a switch. Hills, sky and forest revealed their blues, orange, grey mixed like the wash of an artist paints on a canvas before the masterpiece.

She stopped and she was astonished with the beauty surrounding her.

"Shorty, are you crazy? Stand still, and watch. If you see a guard, whistle three times and run away as soon as possible", an older boy of around ten instructed her. And a team of brave youngsters spread out in the sunflower fields in search of the best plants to twist the heads off and filling their shirts.

"Yes," answered little Emma, eager to follow their example, running as fast as they could, squeezing as skillfully as they could between the plants, jumping as high as they could, to reach the sunflower heads.

Poor little thing was Emma, she could only envy them, standing on guard and looking at the sky dreaming. Sunflower leaves sparkled under the sun, goldfinches, swallows were flying and the plants were fighting their way heavenward.

Then her thoughts returned her to the old apple tree near their home. It belonged to no one and therefore to everyone. The tree's dark, twisted branches sprawled in unpruned abandon. Each spring it blossomed so profusely that the air became saturated with the aroma of apple blossom. When somebody passed by that magnificent miracle of a tree, one could not help stopping at it, praising mother-nature and its good harvest of apples.

The teenagers used to get together under this tree and solve their children's problems although the war was rattling somewhere far and far from that place. They hardly realized that their game-mate was injured because of the damned war; they scarcely could understand the tragedy of the tiny, round-pink-faced girl with crutches...

Oh, these bloody crutches, Emma cursed them to herself, they disturbed her to play hide-and-seek in the sunflower field of the collective farm, a field which was under the protection of the collective farm ward. In a moment she saw him approaching the children, she whistled three times warning them of the danger.

Everybody was scattering in the fields save Emma. She was frightened to death, the bloody crutches prevented her from escaping. She was caught by the ward and questioned by another old man.

"Child, who is your mother?" he asked with compassion looking at her crutches.

"Maria Yakovlevna Filina."

"Oh, that woman who is managing the nursery school here, isn't she?"

He recognized her immediately.

"I know her. A very good woman. And you are her daughter. How could you run away from home, it's so far with only your crutches?"

"The boys helped. Some of them were carrying me on their hands, sometimes on the turned-over-crutches", replied she.

"What were you doing here?" the old man grumbled.

"We played with sunflowers. Look! How nice it is around here!" continued the cute girl, beset by the same concern all the time that the summer might not come this year. It was just like old apple tree, but in her winter bound neighbourhood community, it was appreciated.

"Just go home," said the guard, "Oh, no. I'll take you home, " he changed his mind looking at her crutches with compassion.

"Don't be scared of anything, you'll wake up one morning, and war will be over, and many happy springs will come in your life", added the old man, again and again gazing at her crutches. He accompanied little Emma to her home.

When she saw her favorite tree, she got so glad: it gave her the feeling of moving in another element, like a kid on a bike, her present dream. Until the last moment Emma thought she was the only one aware of this tree. And then all of a sudden, in a fit of summer madness, she set out with pruner and hopper to remove a few dead branches.

No sooner had she stepped under its boughs than neighbours opened their windows and appeared on their porches. These were people she barely knew and seldom spoke to, but it was as if she had come unbidden into their personal gardens.

Soon half the neighbourhood had joined her under the apple tree. It struck her that she had lived there for many long months and only now was learning about these people's names, what they did for a living and how they passed the winter.

It was as if the old apple tree was gathering them under its branches for the dual purpose of acquaintanceship to share the grief of war, the personification of which was the girl and her crutches.

The majority of the village population consisted of women, children and very old men who had helped each other with all their hearts and physical forces. Nobody complained at their illness because everybody knew there was no doctor around, nobody cried because there were no more tears in their eyes - the faces were trying to listen to the moaning of the killed husbands, brothers, and fathers.

Every now and then, gathering at the old apple tree, the folk shared their sufferings with each other.Maria, the wounded girl's mother, happened to be close to them, telling each woman a story of her Ivan, or Peter, or Michael, about his feats in the war, reading cards about their future and when their returning men would be home, or the men suffering from wounds in field hospitals. They believed, poor simple Russian souls, in everything they heard, in the coming victory, in the better communist life in the future.

In fact, they lived in one community as one family, sharing all they possessed. It was brotherhood in unhappiness, they were just equal in poverty, misery and the only right for death. Among them it was Katja who one day rose up decisively and proposed, "To hell, the sorrows, let us sing our favorite song "Katjusha", and above the old apple tree and damaged roofs raised the words and sounds:

> *"Pear trees and apple trees fall in blossom,*
> *And the river fogs about to swim,*
> *On the steep bank favorite Katjusha,*
> *Came out and began to sing.*
> *Pretty Song about her beloved,*
> *Steppe eagle, proud and on high,*
> *Whom she loved with her soul, scarlet,*
> *And to whom in letters she did sigh".*

The actual war law read, "For stealing from the collective farm property penalty is death by shooting". The guard did not report on Emma, her salvation was her crutches.

At nights the little girl used to recollect,the deep gouge had exposed torn muscle and shattered bone close to the ankle joint. Severed flaps of skin lay around the leg. Several days had passed since the accident, increasing the risk of infection.

Emma remembered that her leg was saved when the bomb shrapnel was pulled out, once the bone chips and blood clots were flushed from the wound, one could see that no nerves or tendons had been damaged. The red-haired young surgeon stitched up the muscles and put the bones back together with pins and bolts, under field conditions, when the damned bloody war continued, without anastaesia.

Every so often the people gazing at this child could barely hide their compassion for Emma, their eyes became wet and filled with tears. "What is your name?" they asked her as a rule.

"Sitnikova Emma Borisovna", she answered very seriously.

"How old are you, Emma?"

"Seven. "

"Where are you from?"

"From Bryansk."

Bryansk was rising in her dreams - she was returning home, her leg had been healed, she like everybody would go to school. Sometimes she was in the image of a princess.

Like magic the tiny princess appeared on the stage with her lacquered blond hair and ice-blue satin gown. A young prince took the hand of Emma, a tiny girl undergoing bouts of severe treatment intended to go further. He lifted her up onto the stage. As Cinderella talked to her, Emma stroked her long white gloves, piped through the large speakers. There came Cinderella's theme song: "A dream is a wish that your heart makes".

Her dream Number One was about the prince. Sometimes she saw his face very vividly: the traits of her father's face whom she met once in her young life. He gave her then as a present lollipops and a doll. It was a small package in cellophane, a naked puppet figure. But Emma remembered that event for her whole life.

Frankly speaking,to give a doll while raising girls, plays a great role in the children's life. A doll!? Whose daughter has ever played with this toy?

For a girl, that is not an unusual toy to be entertained. Not at all. In her eyes it is transformed into a living being, her favorite pet, with which she shared all her childish cares, troubles and thoughts. She names her beautiful names, has long conversations with it, and nurses her pet for long periods of time.

Emma did instinctively understand: her doll is a child, and wants to be held and cuddled. She started touching her as affectionately as if she were a fiancee during the courtship.

Her doll transported the little girl into the feeling of motherhood, of a future wife, or a nurse. When she recollected memories about her parents during the Second World War and the postwar years that followed, her Mom was not accustomed to worrying about romantic and emotional needs. Later, her mother was too busy to bring up three children without revealing her innermost feelings to them. A tough prsonality in tough time.

Under the conditions of the absence of a husband, or of his small financial role in the family's budget, her Mom would have been confused and defensive if someone suggested that being a good provider was not enough of a contribution to the family's happiness.

The kids were growing up emotional, close to each other, frank and open in their hearts and dreams.

Emma's dream Number Two was about the school.

Oh, how many children were like her, she had been dreaming about regular classes, school desks and blackboards where one can write, about school text-books and note-books?!

Gladly, that dream had become true: after a long two-years-evacuation, Mommy with her children went back to her native town of Bryansk.

The little girl's independence of character increased more and more because of her awareness of being the eldest among three children's society at home. She tried also to realize the current events happening around her.

From the adults' talks she heard that the Russians launched a sudden counter-attack, supported by an immense tangle of artillery and "katyusha" rockets and, of course, T-34 tanks.

She heard that behind the German Sixth Army 200,000 shattered troops were isolated from the divisions on their flanks. The German Sixth Army surrendered.

The news summaries on the Russian radio 'Inform Bureau ' announced that, "The Red Army recaptured all the territory it had lost."

The cute mind of Emma grasped the main clues: the main Soviet war leaders: Stalin, Zhukov, Konev, and Rokossovsky were very good. The German General von Pauls and Hitler were bad and evil.

As the war neared its end, and Nazi Army sank slowly to its knees, the Soviet armies were bloodied, but rampant, stronger than ever despite terrible losses. In every Soviet citizen's mouth was the name of Stalin associated with the remorseless necessities of victory in battle. Next to the name Stalin stood the name Lenin. Both names were mentioned at all school lessons which Emma started to attend.

At school there were Lenin's rooms, Lenin's corners, Lenin's lessons. The biography of the Communist leader Vladimir Ilyich Ulyanov ("Vladimir" in the Easter Orthodox Church means "ruler of the world") was taught in details, which there were put marks for to be discussed later at the school committee meetings. Everywhere there hung the portraits of Lenin and Stalin connected together by the Propaganda machine.

"At school Ulyanov," wrote his schoolmate Naumov , "differed considerably from all of us, his comrades. Neither in the lower forms, nor later did he take part in the childish and youthful games and pranks, always keeping to himself, busy either with his studies or some written work. Even when walking, between classes, Ulyanov kept to his books, reading as he walked up and down past the windows. The only thing which he liked as a distraction was playing chess, a game in which he usually came out victorious, even when playing against several opponents.

He was a walking encyclopedia, extremely useful to his comrades and the pride of his teachers who considered him gifted, keen, possessed with insatiable, scholarly curiosity and an extraordinary capacity for work".

That Lenin's main trait was put to Soviet schoolchildren as an example to be copied, and his "Testament" to be forced, to learn by heart and passed as a test.

"Kolobok, do you know of Lenin's lesson? Can you answer me?" the teacher asked Emma.

"Yes", and she began reciting this lesson of comrade Lenin testament as, " the first thing was to study, to study and once again to study".

"Further? What else did Great Lenin say to us?" asked the teacher.

The more she had been pushed, the more her face got red. Emma was in despair. The necessary words rushed out of her brains.

She dropped in and out of the school for the next couple of days. Whenever she was half-alert, she was torn with anxiety. She knew for certain she had to learn tasks at home for longer time.

But her memory was shaky. She was slurring words, if anything had happened to the language centre of her brain, Emma was through.

A few days after, she spent two days trying to memorize the "Testament" again. She tried to write it down. She picked up a piece of newspaper (there were no note-books at those times) and a pencil with an effort that sapped her strength, she got a few lines down on the blank margins.

The next day she wrote more.

When someone looked at her scribbles they read like Croatian. She was dejected. Then she told herself, "If I know it's lousy, I can still think enough to do it right". And she started again.

The subject was her during-war-leg-operation without narcosis. Her physical weekness and being overweight was to cause as a progressing heart desease. She did not know about it yet.

Now she was glad, exhilarated, having passed at length the Lenin's Testament exam and gained the "satisfactory" mark.

At that moment she wanted to thank Mommy for letting her being alive. For letting her have everything which all other children had. She wanted to thank her own brains for remembering Lenin's words.

It was a composed "Testament" by members of the Communist Party Central Committee.

Its original contents became known in only after sixty years .

It read, "Comrade Stalin, having become Secretary-General has unlimited authority concentrated in his hands, and I am not sure whether he will always be capable of using that authority with sufficient caution." This part was hidden from the nation till 1969.

"Stalin is too rude and this defect, although quite tolerable in our midst and dealings among us, Communists, becomes intolerable in a Secretary-General. That is why I suggest that the comrades think about a way of removing Stalin from that post and appointing another man in his stead who in all respects differs from Comrade Stalin in having only one advantage, namely, that of being more tolerant, more loyal, more polite and more considerate to the comrades, less capricious etc. " wrote Lenin in his real "Testament" in January, 4, 1923.

Emma was not a lazy girl, she committed her energy to all work in housekeeping while her Mommy was at work. She could even handle to milk a cow when it was needed, other times she swept and washed the floor, warmed up the meals for her younger brother and sister, took care of them, singing to herself the same song over and over:

> *"Very early in the morning,*
> *I'm getting up,*

Everything in our lodging,
I'm tiding up,
Dishes washed be-not -forgot
As well as
The flowers in the pots,
I'd be watering!"

Results at her classes were very poor, she tried to do her best, everything was in vain. School teachers reproached her more and more, pointing out at her rosy cheeks and fresh complexion, plump body-building, hinting her mother at her daughter's laziness.

"Kolobok"(ginger bread girl), it was her nick-name among her school-mates, resembling a round pie in the Russian fairy-tale "Kolobok".

"Kolobok, did you not learn your home task again?" asked Antonina Ivanovna strictly.

"Yes, I did," answered Emma in embarrassment.

"If you are so brave, come in front of the classroom. Retell the famous Jack London's story "Love of Life" which Great Ilyich had loved very much".

The girl began describing how a gold prospector struggled to survive after straining his ankle in the Canadian wilderness and finally did so by strangling a wolf that tried to attack him, and then drinking the wolf's blood.

The teacher was pleased this time, gave the schoolgirl a "good" mark and allowed her to go to her place. Antonina Ivanovna, was a great Lenin's successor, continued telling the stories about Lenin. According to his wife Krupskaya, he liked that story enormously. Then the teacher told about the meeting of the members of the Eleventh Congress of Soviets in the Moscow Bolshoy Theatre when Kalinin without warning asked everybody to rise before announcing,

"I brought you terrible news about our dear comrade, Vladimir Ilyich. Yesterday he suffered a further stroke of paralysis and died".

The emotional Slavic temperament reacted immediately. Sobs and wailing from all over the huge opera house came, not loud or shrill, but pitifully mournful, spreading and increasing in volume.

Kalinin could not speak. He tried in vain to motion for silence with his hands and for one appalling moment a dreadful outbreak of mass hysteria seemed certain.

Antonina Ivanovna spoke so vividly that the tears appeared in her eyes.

The pupils listened to her story motionlessly. Emma loved her stories. Her spirit was high, her personality responded the lofty words about love of Lenin, Stalin, and the Communist ideals.. She as everybody else in the country was a Pioneer, a member of the Young Communist Organization. They wore pioneer red ties around their necks with great pleasure, participated in all their meetings and marches with enthusiasm.

She could not march very well: her ugly left leg disturbed her; one foot was shorter than the other, and the fibula area being abnormal shape. All the days of the year, winter and summer, she did not take off the stockings which were covering the ugly scars to prevent people from mocking at her.

To tell the truth, she was considered a real, grown-up without any little pussy-childish nick-names, "Emma" was pronounced always seriously and challenging at home. Because she was the eldest of the family kids, and ought to do this and that, managing to go to and fro, no seconds to relax or sit quietly and have a rest.

Meanwhile at school Emma was examined by doctors and they stated the fact - her heart disease and the rheumatic fever was once a major cause of overweight, particularly among the young.

Emma who needed great attention to be paid to her, did not get one because of Mommy's daily efforts how to make up living. The doctors warned insistently that many forms of cardiovascular disease included congenital heart defects, rheumatic heart disease, disorders of the heart valves, heart muscle disease were possible. Abnormalities such as congestive heart failure or disturbances in heart rhythm (cardiac arrhythmias) which resulted from heart disease, also may become life-threatening.

Emma did not understand a word of such scientific terms, but did not feel any thing wrong apart from the overweight which both her neighbours and school teachers were constantly driving at.

"Kolobok-Kolobok, sit at my mouth tip and I'll tell you a funny fairy-tale", used to mock her schoolmates.

"Why are you so fat, nobody will love you, you'll never get married, you, ugly duckling", said the neighbours' kids and their mothers.

It seemed to be no end of mocking. Emma reacted in one and the same way when she was offended, she ran away quickly home and there when nobody was at home, she burst into tears covering her face with the pillow to dampen the screams. Everybody wanted to humiliate her, most of all, the History teacher, Antonina Ivanovna, an old spinster wearing dark eye-glasses and always in black dress.

"You, Kolobok, do you know your lesson?" she addressed Emma in a provoking manner, peeping at her eyes mockingly.

"Yes, I do", answered the latter.

Emma told about the successes of the country from 1928 to 1934.

In 1928, the school girl told, nearly all peasants were individual farmers on small holdings, State Farms and the Collective Farms represented only three per cent of Russian agriculture. By 1934, State and Collective Farms accounted for 86,5 per cent, with individual holdings reduced to 13,5 per cent.

"Everything and everybody was collectivized and the greatest emphasis of all was on heavy industry, without which a modern nation could not make provision for its own defense or even independence", concluded the pupil getting as always her "good" mark.

Emma continued being frightened of and adoring her teacher at the same time. Because Antonina Ivanovna knew a lot of interesting things which were not written in their text-books. For instance, the avant-garde such as Malevich, Vladimir Tatlin, and Alexandra Ekster in the graphic arts, Meyerhold in the theatre, Mayakovsky, Blok and Yesenin in poetry, Eisenstein and Pudovkin in the cinema, tried to operate and florish at the moment of the Socialist Revolution in Russia.

A style of Socialist realism was devised in the description of various aspects of heroism. The teenagers liked to follow her stories.

Many of them, including Emma, for the first time in their lives had seen the colored pencils and brushes, she got a note-book for

71

drawings and had been fond of painting.

What a happiness to appear in the wonderland of paints: green, red, pink, yellow, blue, black-and-white to mix them up and get quite another one, for example, yellow plus blue turned green. Little childish discoveries led to astonishment and amazement in the kids' eyes: the competition to be arranged at Emma's home.

"Who is the best artist in out flat? Who can imagine what certain kinds of flowers look like?"

Most of all Emma liked to draw flowers: camellias, forget-me-nots, apple-peach blossoms, golden-and-scarlet poppies, red hibiscus, roses, native violets, peonies, showy lady-slipper, magnolias, haw-thorns, purple lilacs, scarlet-blue-red carnations, dogwoods, lilies, Indian paint-brushes. Really, under her paint brushes everything came alive: the simple flowers transformed into painted miracles.

The ultimate miracle for Emma contained a variety of paper dolls and their clothes . Here it was exact as in the motto: "Fortune smiles on the bold and frowns on the timid". Her fantasy was not limited, her paper-babies were each more beautiful than the others, with blond-dark-brown hair, eyes of different colours from hazel to bright blue and greyish shadow; dresses of the utmost splendor from the old-fashioned up to the modern vogue. She supplied her lovely creatures to all her neighbourhood friends and anyone who had been asking her about them. Among them was a girl in a dashing hat, covering much of her red hair and another one, wearing a brightly decorated straw hat. Her creatures were so picturesque that one of the adults once said, "You've let me have this doll of yours".

Emma, "I'm giving you a fair warning. Nobody of adults wants it".

Lady, "What difference does that make? We have to put something on the walls to hide these patches of damp".

Emma, "If only all doll lovers were like that!" and allowed her paintings to be taken with her.

Emma was a very kind person and very responsible as well. Responsible for her two younger relations, Val and Gen, pondered this scenario: as the eldest sister of the children, aged nine and seven, she thought she'd done her best to help them develop their minds. She started reading to them as infants, she took them to the library. Now they're doing well in school. But should she be taking all credit?

Not at all. Her brother and sister would have done just as well without her zealous efforts. Little Emma understood that the children even in one family grew up and developed in different way.

"Why?" many times she asked herself and many times she could not find the answer. She puzzled.

Some years later, her teacher in biology explained: "There seems to be such a curious science as genetics plays a bigger role than environment does in creating Intellectual Qualities (IQ) and differences. But Marxism-Leninism indicated that the dominant role of developing the human being is the socialist society which influences him basically and totally.

Not only genetics, cybernetics were forbidden at that time in Russia. There were certain changes of attitude which came with the undoubted stabilization of the state, and a feeling of growing power of the Communist Party at home.

The past was examined with greater thoroughness. Tsarism was no longer summarily dismissed as being a bad thing. Even men like Ivan the Terrible were re-examined, and the positive contributions of his reign to the greatness of the nation highlighted, a past time which was curiously apt during the hegemony of Stalin. But "bourgeois" was still the dirtiest of words. Domestic life gravitated around potted palms and table-runners in the shadow of dull streets..

And divorce, once so easy in the bohemian atmosphere of the early revolutionary days, was now made extremely difficult, and abortion, that final liberation of the woman from the doctrine of religion, was forbidden altogether.

It is a curious European phenomenon that on three occasions, important nations have fallen victim to the dictatorship of foreigners, always coming from the south, and dominating more industrious people to the north.

Napoleon began the trend when, as a Corsican, he waited for the bright flame of revolution to bury itself out, and then deflected the new spirit to serve his particular gifts. Stalin, from Georgia, had the mind of a tycoon, always one step ahead of the fiery Jewish intellectuals, with their grasp of abstractions, and of the Russians, who merely wished that things that were going well would go better. He had a cynical disregard for theory, although he paid it lip service when necessary. He was more of a god-father figure than a father figure, and finally the only of the three to know real, if horrible successes.

Hitler, the third of the trinity from Austria, was too shrill in his courtship of destiny, and never gave himself a chance to rise to any kind of heights as a Prince of Darkness. He lacked Napoleon's style and impertinence, and Stalin's smiling detachment. He merely looked to the heavens, inventing intuitions when none were forthcoming, and dragged half the world with him in an orgy of death and destruction.

None of the three did their neighbours much good, but Stalin was certainly the most casual in his betrayals, the most secret in his fears, and the most soft-spoken in his outbursts. On Russia, he had the effect of a Tartar army, but he was more demanding in the collection of the tributes due to him.

A notorious series of Five-Year-Plans were his official legacy, which projected the future progress of the nation in Draconian terms.

Nothing was left to chance. The individuals who had operated so successfully under the New Economic Policy were snuffed out of existence, as were the richer peasants by prohibitive taxation. Collectivization.

On the kids' level there were pioneer groups and Young Communist League Membership of all the schoolchildren without exclusion of any. Then it was reported to the Central Committee of the Communist Party of the Soviet Union: 80 per cent of membership rising to 100 per cent. Everybody must join the Communist Organization; in fact, all were the members of the Communist society. The same happened to be when a person of 28 years old, leaving the Young Communist League, educated, convincing in the future achieving of the Communist ideals, and by all means agreeing with the policy of the native Communist Party and Government, automatically joined the members of the

Communist Party of the Soviet Union.

Emma joined the Communist Party after finishing 8-years-secondary school when she went to work at a construction site. There she heard the tragic news about the end of Stalin through a series of massive strokes.

Stalin was associated with all successes of the nation and therefore earned his immortality by having been at the right place at the right time.

It was the right time for Emma to enter a High School to go on with her education. She remembered her parents who were unable to afford groceries or buy clothes, and the heat being shut off when it was minus 25° because they could not pay the bill. But through it all, her only Dad - Boris, refused help. At that moment when she was eighteen, it was an official refusal on his part.

Her Mommy always stressed the importance of presenting yourself in a professional, respectful manner, and Emma thought this advice helped her get a job. She started as a dispatcher and then worked in the drive-through window at the building site. She learned to be patient, on time and always to provide service with a smile.

After work she was attending the Building Technical High School in the evenings. Her step-father Nick did the same, helping Emma as much as possible.

Working and going to High School was hard, but Emma never considered quitting or complaining. Learning a good work ethic at an early age instilled a strong sense of self-confidence. That could take her a long way in life.

"Long way, long way", repeated the young girl thoughtfully.

One midsummer night she bumped into one young boy, taller than her, with perfect almond skin, soft features and fluorescent white teeth. Honey-blond hair hung in strands past his shoulders. His sleeveless white shirt glowed in the strode lights, setting off arms that were brown and strong from swimming, perhaps, athletic exercises and weight lifting.

They began dating. As passionately as she could she returned some of his kisses that summer, for her, he was part of the interlude between childhood and the more serious endeavors of adulthood to come. Emma was in love with him, and she had a bad habit of also saying so. One night, when Emma and he were together, out of nowhere he decided to end this relationship.

"Emma," he said, "I think we should just be friends".

She was very upset. For a long time they did not meet.

At length, they ran into each other occasionally. By this time she had learned her lesson. No more moony eyes. She could be as detached and aloof as the next guy.

It worked beautifully for a few weeks. Finally he asked, "What's wrong with you?"

"What do you mean, what's wrong?"

"You're not yourself ", he said.

"You haven't seen me for a long time", she answered.

"No", he said.

Then she proposed a deal: "You will be who you are and I'll be who I am. You don't love me, do you? I won't go to your dates any longer".

It was a bargain he quickly accepted. She was as good as her word. One day, by nightfall, Emma still hadn't arrived home from her school.

"Where can she be?" her mother wondered. Her younger daughter followed her. They both worried more and more, taking to the streets, they ran in the direction of the Desna-river.

To all appearances, they looked like two shot birds flying in search of the third one. They found her naked preparing to commit suicide. Psychological problems, depression, troubles at school, lack of future prospects, the crumbling of moral values - all contribute to what is called teenage suicide syndrome.

"Sweetie, what are you doing?" cried out Mother.

"Be quiet, be quiet", repeated Val, helping to pick up Emma's clothes and dressing her elder sister.

"Not a word about the accident," said Val, "to nobody". The three embraced each other, kissed and slowly wandering home.

Some people say if parents are worried, they should ask children directly if they are thinking of killing themselves. And if parents can't, they should ask someone who can.

No, no. Nothing of that kind must be advised to a person at

risk. Nothing directly. Intuition must and will help always. Although girls make many more suicide attempts than boys, the death rate among boys is much higher. Part of the explanation is that boys choose more lethal means such as hanging or guns; more than a third of boys who kill themselves use firearms.

"And what about our boy Gen?" asked the three women "'Where is he?"

"Oh, here he is, he's at home, such an intelligent pal," all of them were so glad.

Emma also was a clever girl, starting to save money for her future separation, a one-room-flat was all she dreamt of. It was under conditions when the differences in salaries between skilled and unskilled workers became far more marked, as did the differences between the upper bureaucracy and the lower, and the lower and the worker.

A new hierarchy was rapidly developing, and in a way, a new aristocracy of the Communist Party members was not based on heredity of any sort, but was purely a matter of merit, and acceptance of the prevalent grey discipline.

Emma was a very disciplined worker on the construction site "SMU-4", taking an active part in the Communist Party meetings, fulfilling its errands and being a very convinced follower of Stalin's policy.

She did not admit any criticism of Stalin, relying on his statements as dogma. For instance, about "Socialism in One Country", as early as 1924. In his view, Socialism had to be constructed in Russia, without reference to potential Communist uprisings in other countries.

She did not like theory, being a very good executor of Stalin's ideas.

"Daughter, have you ever heard about Stalin's cult?" asked her Mommy.

"Yes, I have", answered Emma.

"What's that?"

"It's made by Nikita Khrushchev, Mommy, who summoned up the courage to denounce the consequences of Stalin's cult in Russia and his mistakes in the foreign policy. The "Iron Curtain" is over", she explained. Stalin had no experience of foreign countries, and no great desire to acquire such experience.

Despite all the terrors of his reign, the disappearances and barbarous trials, he can also never be forgiven for the suffering he caused to thousands of individual cases. However the communal conscience accepted it as an evil which had become necessary once the Nazi invasion had been launched.

That communal conscience had been utilized skillfully by the Propaganda. Propaganda confirmed in all the mass media. By that moment the first Soviet TV programs had appeared, including, "That the fearful frustrations of the Cold War were over." Peppery Nikita Khrushchev did not give distinct relief from the dull facade of Stalin.

The colourless Malenkov had added or subtracted nothing to the sum total of Russianness, and he was easy to overlook the events after the Stalin era.

Brezhnev was a more substantial figure, even in appearance, with his astonishing eyebrows, raised in a permanent surprise looked like wild windswept hedges above the cool dispassionate eyes. It was not an unfriendly face, ready to express warmth within a general framework of misgiving.

Emma's Mom used to love Brezhnev very much. His speeches and smiles influenced on ordinary people a lot, touching their hearts. "We shall overcome all the hardships, just as if it would not have happened again the damned bloody war. We need the peaceful life for us and anybody in the world", thought Emma's family after Brezhnev's speeches.

One day in one of those troubleless Brezhnev's times, there appeared on Emma's horizon a young man, three years younger than her, he was neither handsome nor ugly, just of simple appearance, named Victor Prokofyevich Detkov.

They met and soon decided to get married. The wedding reception was not going to be very big, a little banquet with Russian folk band strumming balalaika-like instruments playing the traditional Russian dances of the kind "Barynja", while solo-dancers tapped and the other wedding guests clapped all together.

"It was wonderful," Emma recalled.

"The wedding band, organized by the future husband's relative, serenaded us as we walked in. They played all night, and we danced and danced".

Everybody was happy at this wedding, the future looked promising.

"It is ridiculous," used to say Emma's husband, "for someone of any generation to hate another for deeds committed by his grandfather. It's not a crime to be punished. A child is born innocent, and it's the family that teaches to hate. This has to be stopped". Nobody wanted to hear any more complaints about the younger generation.

Some days later it became clear Victor liked to drink vodka often, repeatedly.

It was like a thunderstorm in the clear sky. In Emma's family none was fond of drinking vodka, opposite, her husband's family cultivated this old Russian tradition of heavy drinking an alcohol. This was helped by the government's policy of tolerant attitude to the any drunkard as a fish.

"In vodka veritas". Drinking played a predominant part in the Soviet life. Among the majority of Soviet population there was a proven conviction that vodka, the clinking of glasses, not only sealed the friendships of an evening, but loosens the tongues in the night.

It was noticeable in Russia that the drunks tended to be benign and overflowing with a sense of universal brotherhood, perhaps for that very reason that they were so stiffly impassive when sober. Russians drink without sandwiches, no snacks, that's why they are getting drunk very quickly. There must be a certain culture in drinking alcohol.

Problems of alcoholism and of what is known as "hooliganism" are the products not only of the severe Russian climate, but of boredom, the rigor of life, on one hand.

On the other hand, it used to be a bad habit since the grandfathers' generation of drinking vodka and boasting in front of their neighbours, "Well Ulya, I could drink more than one liter of samogon (moonshine), couldn't I?" grandpa Kuhovan used to say.

In other words, on one of other days, Kuhovan after a series of drunken nights said to his wife,"Well, I could roll a cigarette from the three-rubble bank note, could I not?" The same character as old Kuhovan, Victor Detkov had, exactly the same boast.

The rigors of the Detkovs' couple had started.

Poor little thing, Emma, she resisted the hardships of their life as she could. "My husband taught me", she said, "that in building a life together, you can't let other people colour your ideals and values. You can't let outside influences tear you apart. You couldn't find a more perfect half for me. We are very compatible and love each other so much. And that comes first".

Oh, love, such an unpredictable thing as it was!

Over the months she complained to her Mom that her husband was no longer as attentive or interested in her as he was early in the relationship. The two women wondered what had happened to the man Emma fell in love with, and Mommy used to repeat to her that he was still there, and with a little effort and understanding everyone had the power to bring the romance back into a marriage.

In the beginning Detkov held Emma's hand in public, stroked her hair, hugged her, and wrapped his arm around her when they walked together. But once, they started having sex, he touched Emma only when he was in the mood. What she did not understand was that when Detkov caressed her during their courtship, it was because he was not allowed to touch her intimately.

When a man is dating a woman, he has to practise physical restraint. Once he is given the green light to touch a woman in a sexual way, however, his impulse for affectionate touching may wane. After the intense pleasures of sexual touch, a simple caress can pale by comparison.

Detkov didn't instinctively understand Emma's need for a non-sexual touch. As children, both boys and girls want to be held and cuddled. When boys hit puberty, the desire for sexual contact becomes stronger than nonsexual. Women, the opposite sex, may never lose that strong need to be held and loved.

As Detkov began to understand why nonsexual touching was so important to Emma, he started touching her as affectionately as he had during their courtship.

Emma encouraged him by letting him know how much she liked it. Even in time, touching became an enjoyable and sensual experience for Detkov, too.

The "honeymoon" lasted for several months, mutual understanding was reached and they were both happy.

Soon Emma got pregnant.

"Darling," she said to enchant Detkov, "it's marvelous, it's my life's dream to have a baby".

"Oh, yes, and mine, too," replied he looking at his wife's eyes full of tears.

"Why are you crying, darling? Why? Why? Do open your heart to me", he asked her.

"My doctors don't allow me to bear a child. Because of my very weak heart", said Emma simply.

"It's easy to misinterpret the motives the doctors said. Maybe, you didn't understand anything in their very scientific medical terms", assumed Detkov.

"Here is the medical document". It read that all doctors were under the Hippokrates' Oath to help the people to live, never to terminate life. The doctors were not responsible for the lethal end of Emma Borisovna Detkova if she gives birth to a baby.

"Look! And the seal of the medical hospital and signatures of the whole medical commission are here, you read it! " she said.

"It's up to you, Emma. You have to decide, darling", he answered. He got upset.

Emma remained alone face to face with her dreadful thoughts rebelling the doctors' collective advice, concentrated on a small sheet of paper.

Again, and at which time, she could not count, her opinion was ignored. Why? For no reason. Such acts never have any reason, unless it's the vanity of some secondary doctors who feel they have a right to decide everyone's fortune: to bear or not to bear a baby. They do not want to help a patient without radically destroying her. Who permitted them to do it? No particular man among the dozens in authority. No one cared to permit it or to help. No one was responsible. No one can be held accountable. Such is the nature of all collective actions.

It was an ancient conflict: an individual and a collective mind of a group of people. Emma had come close to the truth be or not to be alive after the baby's birth, as her sleepless night had passed she took the hardest decision in her life - to bear the baby.

The doctors explained and explained her that the heart was one of nature's most efficient and durable pumps. Throughout the life, it beats an average of 60 to 80 times per minute, supplying oxygen and other essential nutrients to every cell in the body and removing waste for elimination through the lungs or kidneys. They said about the weight of the heart of an adult heart and how it worked.

Soon Emma spoke to a professor of medicine in heart diseases. She acknowledged that the classic chest pain identified with heart attacks in men wasn't as common as in women. Instead, they were more apt to have tightness or discomfort in the chest area which occurred mainly with exertion or strong emotion and disappeared during rest. Fatigue, shortness of breath, dizziness, nausea, vomiting or heartburn can signal trouble. Also, worrisome was the chest pain that radiates to the arm, jaw or stomach as a warning.

Emma felt sometimes all the symptoms, sometimes - not at all. She risked the pregnancy. Her baby-girl, Marina, came to birth in December, 15, 1968, a pinky, good-looking kid, and very healthy. Since that moment, Emma spent one year and a half in hospital. The doctors fought for her life day-and-nights, there were many risk factors in her body: her blood cholesterol level, even by a small amount, reduced her heart-disease risk; secondly, monitoring triglycerides blood fats the body uses for energy was especially important; thirdly, hormone-replacement therapy was safer and more beneficial than doctors realized.

The doctors also could not realize what a feat was being performed by their patient's mother. Emma's Mommy, with her soft-spoken manner and a lined face that bespoke, years of experience was a reassuring presence. She worked on two fronts: raising up a tiny girl Marina artificially with the help of baby's food and rescueing the dying daughter. Daughter's husband Victor did not concern himself; the only thing he could do was drink vodka and somehow earn money. He right now found out that he got married to a sick woman and she was in great danger.

He became a father, and discovered what he should do with that baby, as he also did not know very much. Detkov realised that the first evening he dropped anchor in Emma's family harbor he was very happy with those kind people. That night he decided to go through with the family, tied firmly to the marriage ties to Emma for good.

"Now, the damned bloody death is threatening", thought he to himself. Detkov, managing a smile, got drunk as a lord. He was upset, and had banged on his window to attract the attention of some passers-by outside; the glass had broken and slashed his wrist. Peeling back the towel, his mother-in-law saw that the radical artery supplying blood to the hand was almost severed. It took no time to call the emergency ambulance.

Detkov got taken to the hospital.

"The wound would have to be stitched quickly or he could get gangrene, even bleed to death", said the doctor on duty. At the clinic the wound was sterilized and injected with a local anesthetic.

The damaged artery was saved. Emma's mother was exhilarated. Because of the great load on her, she felt like a young lady again, with a whole new career on the horizon to save the three of them. Emma's family stayed in the same apartment with Maria and Nick.

It was clear enough that Detkov was not a reliable person. Once in a blue moon he was sober, and it was at those rare times that his behavior seemed to be childish, needed to be conducted, to be shown the right way. His mother-in-law's daily schedule was written in details by hours:

6 a.m. getting up and cooking some food for Emma and herself;

7 a.m. feeding the baby; feeding the men;

12 a.m. feeding Marina;

2 p.m. feeding Marina;

6 p.m. feeding Marina.

Between 7 a.m. and 12 a.m. - visiting Emma's hospital and feeding her - she was very-very weak;

Between 2 p.m. and 6 p.m. - visiting Detkov in hospital and

walking with Marina in her baby pram.

In the evening time she got busy with shopping, buying every day fresh products for her menu; she did everything walking on foot without a car; nobody helped; her husband worked and the kids also were busy working and arranging their new-married lives.

The idea of organizing a new family was like passing the first driving lesson. When you are trying to downshift around a curve on a gravel country road when you hit the brake instead of the clutch. This sent the car sliding, killing the engine and jerking to an abrupt halt. The parents and the kids sat in surprised silence as a cloud of dust sifted down on the car. You waited for an angry reprimand, but instead your parents took a deep breath and suggested that you restarted the engine.

What was the parents' secret of remaining calm with their kids? Struggling for their kids' lives, and of their grandchildren, Emma's mother Maria kept the patience on a daily basis, many times she wished her daughter were here to give her a piece of advice or to solve the next problem.

Tired from her long, hard day and lulled by the baby's song, Maria appeared to nap in the armchair after Marina had been asleep for only a few minutes.

Marina grew up a very active baby,starting to walk at eleven months and always being on the go. Maria used to think that it was a non-stop baby, simply very independent.

Marina was climbing out of her crib at all hours of the night. Put to bed regularly at 7 p.m., she would stay awake until 1 a.m. and be up again at five.

The one year and a half of Emma's illness had gone quickly for Maria and seemed like one day. She really could not have any free time for watching after her other grandchildren.

Nobody of that family noticed then how fast the Soviet Government was changing: in 1964 Khrushchev was boosted and replaced in a coup by Brezhnev and Kosygin, who headed the Soviet Union from 1964 until 1982, increasing military strength and ordering the invasion of Afghanistan in 1979. Nobody of the family knew that although the Soviet Union and the United States of America had fought together to defeat the Germans, from 1945 onward the two super-powers became rivals. The Americans and other Western people were worried by the spread of communism across Europe, and by the new Soviet nuclear weapons program.

After 1945, Europe was divided by what Winston Churchill called an "iron curtain". To the West were Britain, France, West Germany, and the United States.

To the East was the group led by the Soviet Union, a military alliance called the Warsaw Pact, made up of Poland, East Germany, Hungary, Bulgaria, Czechoslovakia and Romania.

This period of rivalry between the Soviet Union and the West was called the "Cold War".

Nobody knew in the family that in 1956 there were riots in Hungary against the Communist government. The Soviet Army led the Warsaw Pact troops that halted the riots. The same happened in Czechoslovakia in 1968.

Everybody was involved in their own problems, within the Soviet Union also there were a lot. Shortage in everythng, despite massive efforts there was never enough quality milk, meat, fruit or bread in the stores. Eggs may be unobtainable in some big cities, but within a few kilometers, elderly people were trying to sell masses of eggs on railway platforms.

If fruit is suddenly fairly plentiful in a super-market, it is not surprising to find it due to a form of private enterprise, in which the profits go to those with the initiative to have brought the fruit to market. Hungary was known to point a way in this direction, as indeed was the case with the New Economic Policy, responsible for the rapid economic recovery after the Revolution.

The Russian Revolution early survival was a miracle: her youth was a torment, her adolescence merely dangerous; her maturity gave a series of challenges. As it may seem strange exactly at those times of the "thaw" as Ilya Erenburg wrote a novel with this symbolic title, every now and then appeared a great number of humoristic anecdotes among thousands of the Soviet people. Such was typical,

"Stalin, Khrushchev and Brezhnev are crossing the country aboard the Trans-Siberian Railroad. Suddenly the train stops with a terminal sign. Then all is silence.

Stalin strokes his moustache for a moment of reflection. He smiles, and announces that he will deal with the problem. He alights, and comes back after twenty minutes. "What have you done?" the others ask him. "I have shot those responsible", he replies.

Not unnaturally, the train shows no sign of reanimation. Khrushchev's impatience grows. He suddenly blurts out a few wild accusations against Stalin and leaves the compartment with the announcement that he will settle the matter. He returns after twenty minutes.

"What have you done?" the others ask him.

"I have rehabilitated those responsible", he replies.

The minutes tick by, and the engine shows no sign of life. "My turn", says Brezhnev without any visible intention of rising from his seat. The others stare at him for a while.

"What are you going to do?" they ask.

"I'm going to draw the blinds and pretend the train is in motion", is Brezhnev's curt reply".

On the face of it, anyone in Russia had a perfect right to express doubts about whether the Communist system worked and how, since there were many indications that there was only a scant appreciation of how to achieve equitable distribution.

As remarked the American politician, Harry Hopkins, the most Russian authority Joseph Stalin said, "Even if the Russians are a simple people, the West often makes the mistake of regarding them as fools".

Really, Emma's Mommy was no fool when saving money for her separate flat, helping and saving for Emma's family, under the severe conditions of shortage of money, food, clothes, economizing on what was possible, she did her best.

Emma alive but handicapped returned home to her sweet one-year-and-a half-daughter. Up to the end of her life she was to be given a small pension for disabled, without the right for work.

Oh, poor little thing, the Russian soul Emma, again, she had to learn walking physically and live without work mentally.

How hard it was, for her the science of life was very difficult!

How to live disabled when she was only thirty five? When she was very socially active, when all Soviet Propaganda was aimed at the working people. Physiologically it was the disability that hurt her more than heart disease. She lost friends whom she worked with, she lost favorite Communist Party activities which she actually enjoyed, she could not move very much in her own home. The only light at the window was her a diamond Marinochka, her daughter.

She got started to educate her, to raise her Marina politely in that rude world.

"Marinochka, our family rule is that elbows don't go on the table", repeated the young Mom to her child with patience, and persistence, believing that her Marina was the smartest beauty in that world full of beasts.

Meanwhile, Emma's husband said, "Marina, you're such a slob. Get your elbows off the table", and his tone of voice was so rough. For sure, Marina preferred Mommy's words rather than Daddy's. Criticism, name-calling and orders only make a child angry and defensive. Because incorrect behavior in children is more often the result of thoughtlessness than deliberate aggression.

"Get off my table!" Detkov yelled calling his daughter an obscene name.

Emma raced to them, "You've no right to talk to your daughter like that", she scolded.

Of course, all the training in the world won't persuade a child to behave gallantly if her parents become aggressive, demanding and rude at the slightest provocation. That's why the best way for parents to improve their child's manners is to improve their own first.

Parents need to be especially vigilant not to say something casually, that they may be alarmed to hear later in the mouths of their children.

A wife who tells her husband to shut up and a father who calls a neighbour a jerk are likely to hear their children repeating the same way to them.

To be a model to the children was very difficult for always drunkard Detkov, vice versa - for Emma.

She did her first steps of learning the science of motherhood where she was generously helped by her mother, and above all, financially.

Because, you know, Russian drinking husbands are not reliable, all their wages are sufficient only for their hobby - vodka. No practical assistance to their families, neither fiscal nor moral.

Wives, indeed, raise up their children alone and hold their husbands as their second kids.

In Brezhnev times, even, there ran such an anecdote about a Russian woman that every day walking from her work she was holding in one hand "setka", in another -"Swetka", and in front of her a drunkard husband.

For example, "setka" was a very heavy bag with food products for the next day; "Swetka" was a figurative female's name for her daughter.

Emma herself like a child enjoyed playing with her daughter different sorts of games.

"Mommy, sweetie, let's play "hide-and-seek", begged Marina.

"In a second", answered Emma. After some while they were on their way. Can playing hide-and-seek really teach a child about manners?

Yes. Because it tells the child that her Mommy cares enough to spend time with her, she is loved and can learn to love others.

Manners, good behavior are about being kind, team playing, making tiny sacrifices. Children learn that through their parents. Marina's parents were the best in the world for her, even Daddy, whom she could not understand at first, as had no sooner grasped him, than she got started commanding him, occasionally bitching at him.

"Detkov, why are you again so late?" Marina asked him as if she were not a daughter but his wife.

"What time is it?" asked he questioning her in his turn.

"Look at the clock. 9 p.m. All the descent people have already come back long time ago", grumbled she as an eighty-years-old woman.

"Okay, Okay", agreed Detkov.

"I've just drunk a little with my pals", replied he in a guilty tone.

In her free time, Emma was fond of reading a lot of political stuffs about the Soviet Union and the United States of America who began a space race after the Soviet Union put Yuri Gagarin into space in 1961.

There was then also a great competition between the two countries in building up their powerful nuclear missiles. Each country wanted the newest and best weapons. The economy had been weakened by overspending on weapons, and agriculture was in poor state, with food having to be rationed as a result.

To be distracted from the bad reclusive thoughts, she loved reading love novels having bought them at a bookshop.

"I am wondering if I can help you in the best choice of a book", habitually asked a young saleswoman from the bookshop.

"Oh, yes", readily answered the latter. "It's high time for new books here, I'm looking for love stories."

"We've just got a new interesting novel "Happiness Keys" by Anastasia Verbitskaya", went on the former.

"I'd like to read the annotation to this book."

"For the first time after eighty years' silence, one of the most scandal novels of the XX century is returning to the reader - it is "Happiness Keys" by Anastasia Verbitskaya.

It is about love of a woman to several men at the same time, passion and love, and tenderness, arts and love... Freedom of creativeness and a prisoner of love. That is far from the completion of the list of subjects to be touched in the "Happiness Keys" by A. Verbitskaya."

"The style of writing is the best I've ever met. The story of growing up, life, the way to the fame and fortune of the eternal love of the prominent bared-foot-ballet-dancer - that's what is the "Happiness Keys", said the young lady.

"Yes, you're right. The passion story is simultaneously the way to self-demolishing, so to the death," said Emma.

"Have we really been changing so much since the beginning of the century? Is it so very far from us the sound of words and topics of that most famous book of Russian pop-literature?" the saleswoman concluded philosophically.

After reading her book Emma's thoughts were back to her

wedding time. In Russian tradition couple has crossed the married time get for weddings:

after one year - gauze wedding;
after three years - chintz wedding;
after five years - wooden wedding;
after ten years - tin wedding;
after twenty years - silver wedding;
after fifty years - golden wedding.

She dreamt of golden wedding, of course, remembering her Detkov - husband-lover vowing his fidelity to her with the words: "I will love you 'till the white birch'".

She asked him at that precious moment, "What does it mean 'to white birch'"?

Detkov explained with patience, "Why would the people say so? Because the faithful husband or a wife is going to love the mate until death comes, and by Russian graves the white birches usually grow as a sign of fidelity".

"Aha, honey. Now I got it", Emma said thoughtfully.

"What a smashing guy my Detkov was", pondered she gradually changing her opinion about him for worse, because during her illness her beloved had not visited her in hospital as often as she wished.

"What are my happiness keys? Where are they?" she sadly anticipated the future.

"In toil and a peaceful life. But what about my husband? That is my fate, why did it give me that man? This one is a drunkard, and I am handicapped. We're both unhappy. The great Russian writer Leo Tolstoy once said in his book 'Anna Karenina', "Happy families are happy in a similar way. Unhappy families are unhappy in different ways".

"No, that's incorrect. We are with my husband unhappy equally, and it's got to be our happiness keys", Emma saved her happiness keys slyly as a box of paper dolls.

Her vicious Detkov as a steam-roller was meek being drunk after policeman was called. She suffered, fought and survived.

In 1973, when her daughter was five, the family roles had changed. Her mother, her biggest friend, got ill.

To tell the truth, Maria had been broken at length under the burdens of unlucky circumstances in her family's heads. Her ill nerves could not stand any more.

Emma's Mommy got Bell's palsy, the term used to describe paralysis of muscles on one side of the face. It occurred suddenly when Maria woke up one Sunday morning. Normally there was no pain but a slight discomfort in the region of the jaw.

The paralysis resulted from temporary damage to the facial nerve. Although the cause was unknown, the disorder occurred when she was 64.

She recovered completely without treatment. Three months later the stroke had happened, called CVA, sudden neurological disorder, which she had suffered from for the whole twelve years, not twelve months or twelve days, but a long-long disabled 12 years. CVA had happened after her one-month-rodon-bath-treatment of her leg near Kiev. As she confessed to one of her daughters, CVA occured after her sexual intercourse with her husband. As usual she was an initiator: "Honey, you are a man, aren't you? Is it not the time to play in bed?"

"Oh, yes, dear Musinjka. With great pleasure", answered her Nick with readiness, kindness and gratitude in his eyes.

Maria, you might feel desire, but you don't take the trouble to make yourself desirable, is it really fair to ask for sex?

Really, it was not fair or right to present yourself to a husband and say, in effect, "Here's my body, see if you can figure out what to do with it".

Maria knew how to be desirable in their long time marriage life and that is why she was certain that a man's sexual responses are like a light bulb. When you turn it on, and it goes from cold to hot almost instantly. When you turn it off, it cools down right away. But a woman's responses are more like an iron, you turn it off, then wait and wait and wait until it cools off.

As Nick got older, his sexual responses slowed down a bit. The instant, unstoppable erections of his teenage years now roused themselves more slowly, more reluctantly, and usually required more manual help in order to become fully rigid. In other words, the aging Nick began to need more foreplay.

In many ways, Maria knew all about this, it was a blessing, because his sexual arousal cycle fell into closer sync with Maria's - the light bulb began turning into an iron, at length.

Foreplay for Nick did not only mean touching. It might also take the form of visual stimulation, like watching X-rated videos. Maria, who might feel uncomfortable or even offended by steamy movies, could perhaps bear with her Nick on this. "Musinjka, you are a queen of sex, such a beautiful more marvelous woman I've never met in my life", said Nick in ecstasy.

"Darling, you have a habit of exaggeration all the time. I'm as simple as other women. Only I love you very, very much", she answered in relaxation. They both enjoyed the afterglow, for Maria, the wind-down part after intercourse, the hugging and kissing, the feeling of closeness was the nicest part. At those moments she forgave him everything - financial disabilities at home, absence of his physical man's aid in house holding.
Nevertheless he remained to be her beloved man whom she respected and appreciated very high.

"Oh, my love is like a deep ocean, my Maria!" said Nick.

Sex and sexuality, for them, were bathed in the faint mist of erotica. Nick was for her like a candy man, he smells of honey. Their honeymoon had passed long-long time ago, but they fell in love with each other as if it were their first romance date. Romance fed desire, and desire was immensely important to a good sex life. For Maria, it were getting back to the dark days of her life illness, her disability.

Now it was the daughter's turn.

"Mommy, dear, what can I do for you? Say only a word and I'll do something in house-keeping. Going out far away I myself cannot, you know", Emma used to say.
"Honey, cook for me my favorite chicken soup, and Nick will go shopping", she replied sadly but decisively.

Everybody in the family fulfilled her orders or wants, without hesitation at once, never showing his or her own displeasure or irritation.

Because of their disabilities two women Maria and Emma were transformed into two commanders. The others did not object by the only reason of great compassion to them.

The circle closed, their grief and sufferings cemented a great friendship and mutual understanding which could always exist in the world. Their home world was decorated by Emma's four-legged pet, whom they found not far from their house. Every few steps, the dog would collapse in paroxysms of coughing, then struggle to get up.

There was no identification tag, not even a collar to suggest that someone had once loved and cared for her, Emma was hooked the minute she saw her, though. She had the dearest face Emma had ever seen. As the young lady patted her head and scratched under her chin, the dog nuzzled up close, as if they were long last friends. She named her Chapa.

Chapa was two years old, and although her dark-gold coat was dull and dry, they could tell she had once been a beauty. Now Chapa looked old and haggard. Her gums were pale, and her hacking cough signaled the severity of her condition.

Emma began treating immediately. Day by day the dog improved. After about one month, her cough had gone, there was brightness in her eyes, and her coat had the beginnings of a healthy sheen. As Emma leaned over to hug her, Chapa let out a couple of boisterous barks, wagged her tail and slobbered her face with kisses. From that moment on she came alive, and the sweetness and warmth that had drawn everybody to her in the first place took on a new dimension. Chapa seemed to possess an unlimited capacity to love her hostess Emma.

All her free hours, minutes, days she devoted to her Mommy although the social life went on without any penetration in the family's troublesome life circle.

Communism at work meant at the beginning of the seventies the Russians had over four million men under arms in peacetime, simply because "peacetime" had not been peacetime for half a century now. The counter-standing of two military blocks - Warsaw Pack and NATO.

The Propaganda told to Emma and, as an echo to everyone, repeated after it, "The Soviet Union is the strongest country in the world, and the noblest one in the history of men. The country of

93

greatest achievement, greatest prosperity, greatest freedom. The country is based on selfless service, sacrifice, renunciation or any percept of altruism. It was based on a man's right to be able to pursue happiness." Her own happiness. Everybody's happiness, she concluded, was the peace in her country, and in the world.

But if there was little to eat, little will be eaten always. Look at her small amount of pension of her disabled Mommy's pension, and pension of her poor step-father, who had been retired in 1972. Only all together they could survive. It was noticed that the Russians are deeply attached to their miseries as well as to their joys. Their literature and music had made an artistic pleasure of sadness. The well of melancholy is bottomless and laughter is a close relative of tears. Russian exiles suffered more from the absence of this pungent perfume of sorrow than other exiles who seemed to miss whatever they had left behind, and they tried to recreate it wherever they went.

In order to understand the Russians, it is worth knowing that no other people speaks so shamelessly of the soul, not for want of a better word, but because it is a correct description of that aching void which is not a void at all, but a nerve sensitive to everything. Emma's sensitive soul belonged to the membership of the Communist Party of the Soviet Union, which she was very proud of.

She didn't notice the double standards that became the order of the Soviet day. One moral life standard was for the Communist Power authorities, with their closed buffets for distribution of the first-class-food products and clothes, another - for all the rest of the people who were the majority of the society.

She did not watch or, maybe, did not want to, because also was a user of Mommy's privileged distribution shopping bag, assume, it was little but valuable to her.

Emma did not know, perhaps, did not want to, that in 1979 the Soviet Union sent its troops into Afghanistan. For what reason?

In recent times the Olympic Games were disrupted, and the tone of the Propaganda became shriller all round. Mark you, it could well be that Russia was anxious about her Muslim minority, nineteen per cent of her population and increasing faster than the Slavic element, as the wave of religious fundamentalism spread elsewhere like a forest fire, obeying no borders and appealing to allegiances much more ancient than the Soviet power. But nobody looked for reasons in this case.

Emma did not do, either. Nobody of her surroundings understood what the reason was for a great Russian scientist, Andrei Sakharov, to be a political prisoner.

Why were so often changes in the Soviet government? In 1982 Brezhnev died and was replaced by Andropov. In 1984 Andropov died and was replaced by the elderly Konstantin Chernenko.

In 1985 Chernenko died and Michael Gorbachev replaced him. Gorbachev began policies of perestroika and glasnost. He inherited a country in crisis.

Crisis time for the country was translated into Emma's family's crisis. In 1985 both of her parents had died, first Nick, second Maria. All the funeral preparations were committed by her sister, as she was working at the plant and had an opportunity to use the plant's service help in this respect.

Emma was scared of death's images. She struggled with them in the mornings, at noons and at nights.

She had nightmares about their visions. At the start she refused even to go to the cemetery. After Maria's death she saw a vision of a kind of lightning in the daytime. Emma was on the hill. Arriving more or less half-way down the slope, at the level of the top of a large-holm-oak which was situated there, after walking a few more steps she saw another flash of light. On a small hollow-oak there stood a lady, all dressed in white, more brilliant than the sun, radiating a light clear and more immense than a crystal glass filled with clear water pierced by the most burning rays of the sun. She stopped, surprised by the vision. Emma was so close that she found herself in the light which surrounded the Lady, or rather which emanated from Her, perhaps, a meter and a half away, more or less. Then Lady Maria said to her,

"Do not be afraid. I will do you no harm".

"Where is your Grace from?" Emma asked her.

"I am of Heaven", answered Lady Maria.

"What does Your Grace want of me?"

"I have come to ask you to come here for twelve months in succession, on the ninth day, at this same hour. Later on, I will tell you who I am and what I want. Afterwards, I will return here yet a seventh time".

"Shall I go to Heaven top?"

"Yes, you will".

It was in pronouncing those last words that Lady Maria opened Her hands for the first time, and communicated to her, as by a reflection which emanated from Her; a light so intense that, penetrating Emma's heart and even to the depth of her soul, it made her see herself in Heaven. Who was this light, more clearly than she saw herself in the best mirror.

Then, moved by an interior impulse which was communicated to her, she fell on her knees and Emma repeated: "Oh, Most Holy Trinity, I adore Thee, My God, My God, I love Thee in the Most Holy Sacrament".

The first moments passed, and Lady Maria added: "Do not be afraid to go to the cemetery and do not forget me".

At the second funerals Emma overcame her fear and went to the cemetery. She overheard from her neighbours that if everything in the funeral procedures must be done to the best of Russian Orthodox traditions, then she would be praised by Christ and be blessed to an easier life.

Surprisingly, Emma, a Communist by her strong convictions, had committed the last debt to the parents according to the Orthodox customs, however, without a priest.

The family, itself, individually organized the nine-days and forty-days memorials with feasting and drinks, which Emma's husband liked most of all. Always he was cursed for drinking, and now there was an official and legal excuse to have a free booze.

He did not ever stop drinking, adding extra-sufferings to Emma's life and making it very hard for her.

It seemed the light at the end of a tunnel - her growing daughter Marina finished the Technical Secondary School of Light Industry. By that time she could sew very well, had many friends, and among them was a boy-friend, who invited her one day to a theatre.

Oh, a theatre! Everywhere theatres play the important role in

96

the country's culture. Everywhere the names of the famous play-wrights, directors, producers, actors and actresses are widely known. For example, the name of Peter Ustinov, of Russian and French origin, he produced many dozens of plays, including "Billy Budd" (1961), it was Emma's favorite one. In Russia there were widely known the names of such producers as Sergey Bondarchuk, Eisenstein, Pyryev and many other ones.

For young people like Marina and her boy-friend the theatre visit was a holiday, because this place was a concentration of all cultural and national traditions.

The theatres were as a rule full, the foyer and balconies being over-crowded. Everybody wanted to show oneself and to observe every-one. The girls had their dresses specially done for such occasion.

"Marina, what's on to-night?" her fellow asked.

"Just a second, I'll have a look at a program."

"'A Man with a Rifle' by Pogodin", she answered.

"What is it about?"

"It seems to me the play is about Lenin, when the October Revolution had begun, how he had met a man with a rifle and their conversation", Marina read.

"Oh, really?" he was astonished. "Do you know, Marina, that Lenin's living expenses in emigration were low? He paid only twenty-eight francs a month for the little room and kitchen where he and Krupskaya lived. It was lighted by kerosene lamps and Krupskaya cooked on a spirit stove or the gas range in the Kemmerer' quarters across the street. They had written their sophisticated books for money but not for simple people like us.

There was so much blood while that Revolution began. Even their close friend, writer Maxim Gorky said about them: "The reform-ers from Smolny do not care about Russia. They are cold-blood-edly sacrificing her to their dream of world of European Revolution".

"Oh, that's interesting!" she exclaimed. "Let's read this book together. I've never read such things before", and they dived into the book which stated: "As long as I am able", Gorky said, "I shall tell the Russian proletariat again and again, 'You are being led to ruin, you are being used as material for an inhuman experiment, and in the eyes of your leaders you are still not human beings. There is no poison more foul than power over people'". On the next page Gorky simply described a street scene of Petrograd in 1917.

A group of people was standing at the Fontanka. On the bridge was a dense crowd.

Gorky listened to the people talk. "They're drowning thieves!"

"Did they catch many?"

"Three, they say!"

"They beat one, a youngster".

"Killed him?"

"What else did you expect?"

'They've got to beat them to death, otherwise they'll make their life a misery. .."

"Hey, he's howling!"

The crowd, Gorky said, became silent, straining to better hear the screams of the dying. Nowhere, Gorky commented, was a man beaten so often and with such zeal and joy as in Russia.

"It looks", he said, "as if these people brought up on torture have now been given the right to torture one another freely ".

"Who gave you this book?" asked Marina. "Nobody", said the guy, "I've found it near the City Park".

A note of distrust sparkled in her eyes. Such books were forbidden in Russia, the Revolution and Lenin were praised, to be described in lofty words, poetry style at a time.

"The rumours say", continued Marina, "the role of Lenin could not be given to just any actor having a wish to play it. There was to be organized a contest for acquiring this part. An actor, a Communist Party member, of high morals, faithful to the Communist idea and to his own family, had to fetch it. Really, a great sweat as far as I'm concern. Now who is playing the Leader?"

"Smirnov. Let us see this stuff, the curtains fell down, the show is starting".

"Aha," agreed the youth.

In 1993 Marina got married to another man, a short, stocky figure and with big eyes and a snob nose, a worker by profession who had by that time the only one suit for all the seasons of the year and two working hands. A real proletarian!

Frankly speaking, he was without any 'kopeyka' in his pocket because he drank a lot as it is accostomed in Mother-Russia, for whom the Great October Socialist Revolution had been accomplished, for whom the old Revolutionary people used to sing the "Marseillaise" through tears:

"You have fallen in the fatal battle,
 For the Love of the people,
 You have given all,
 For Life, for Honour, for Liberty".
And the "International":
    "You fell in the fatal fight,
     For the liberty of the people,
     For the honour of the people ..."

74 years had passed since first Lenin's decrees about peace, land and bread but a proletarian still started his family life from level zero.

The newly-weds settled in Emma's huge three rooms' apartment, everything was at their disposal, everything was for the happiness of the young ones. Emma's family increased to double its size, but salaries were still too small, insufficient to make ends meet.

"They seem to be crazy in the government", thought Emma at nights, "they don't think about the simple people but of their political debates".

There came the time of perestroika and glasnost.

1987, Arms reduction treaty signed between Soviet Union and USA;

1988, Soviet Army withdraws from Afghanistan;

1989, Yeltsin elected as a leader of Russia;

1991, Coup to overthrow Gorbachev fails. Yeltsin gains influence;

1991, Eleven republics form the C.I.S. (Commonwealth of Independent States),

1992, A Federation Treaty is signed by fifteen Russian republics.

What is happening in the country?

"Glasnost opened all the doors to speak aloud. Everywhere debates, in the parliament, in the shop lines, in the streets. It has not become easier to live when everybody can have the right to talk", Emma thought to herself and aloud, discussing the country problems with her neighbours.

"Emma, you are among us the only one who is literate, explain to us whom is Michael Gorbachev for, whom is Yeltsin for?" asked one of them, a blue-eyed, seventy-five-years-old woman. And Emma tried to do her best as she could.

"On August 20, 1991, hard-line, old-style communists tried to stage a military coup in the Soviet Union. They arrested President Gorbachev at his vacation home in the Crimea, and declared an end to perestroika and glasnost. They feared that the Soviet Union was disintegrating and that the central power of the Communist Party was being destroyed. Boris Yeltsin and the newly elected Russian parliament led the opposition to the coup. When military leaders refused to order their troops to fire on civilians the coup failed, and its leaders were arrested. A shaken President Gorbachev returned to Moscow on August, 23".

"What is a strange word 'coup'?! What does it mean?" questioned her curious women.

"Coup" means "take-over". It accelerated events that were already underway. The leaders of the republics were eager to destroy the power of the Communist Party, which was banned in large parts of Russia in September 1991. The fifteen republics agreed to formally end the communist Soviet Union in December 1991.

The communist state, established by Lenin in 1917, was thus formally destroyed. There was organized a new state - a Commonwealth of Independent States (C.I.S.), led by Russia, which would have fairly limited powers over the rest. Lithuania, Latvia, Estonia, and Georgia chose not to join, retaining complete independence".

"Bullshit! What on hell do they need that damned independence when there is nothing to eat in shops and markets?!" concluded the people scarcely grasping any of her words.

Really, the economical crisis was increasing, facing the great hardships of the country's transition to a market economy. Nobody understood what was in effect.

Everyone knew that Russian people want to see some positive benefits from all the changes, especially more goods in the stores. There appeared such a new word as "inflation".

What on the devil was it?

The damned "inflation" was currently surging toward 1,000 per cent per year, and previous food shortages have now been replaced by soaring prices. Wages, however, were not and are not rising at the same time, threatening a large-scale descent into starvation.

Compared to the previous Brezhnev time, when Emma's family lived basically close to her parents, they added up three pensions together although it was so small, reckoning on the old people needed not so much in their life, Emma managed to change a small apartment for a bigger one, furnish it properly, feed her daughter and husband who never helped her financially at all. Mother and daughter Emma lived in separate flats but shared everything: food, money, clothes.

After her parents' death, times changed for Emma in direct and figurative senses. Directly, because Emma felt immediately a lack of money, food, basic life products, even the medications. Figuratively, because the events happening in her country puzzled her. Somebody called those years "Time of Troubles". She remembered from her school history lessons it was the period of 1604-1613, the pastime of Ivan the Terrible, when so often the Russian throne came from one false Dmitri to another one.

When the Russian sky began to glower, the possibilities were as endless as the horizon, and there would be ample time for every single possibility to show itself.

Fate has no need to hurry. The fate of Russia in 1990 - 1997 was rushing with such speed that to be impossible to realize.

Russia has set out to establish itself as the logical successor of the Soviet Union. However, serious problems remained. There were continuing disputes between the states over control of Soviet nuclear weapons, the Red Army, and the Soviet Navy.

Many Russians as well as Emma did not like the sweeping powers. Yeltsin had been given to carry out his reforms. A break-up of

Russia itself was prevented by Boris Yeltsin when all but two of its constituents signed a Federation Treaty in 1992. Chechnya-Ingush and Tatarstan, however, had yet to sign, highlighting the dangers facing the entire territory of the former Soviet Union.

What is the price for nuclear energy or weapons? Nuclear accidents and waste had made parts of the Russian territory uninhabitable for decades to come.

Nobody could forget 1986 Chernobyl disaster, and the dumping of waste was covered up by the former Soviet communist government.

Public debates continued in government, and everything in the country and everywhere was open to public with the help of mass media coverage. Now the Propaganda of one communist voice was substituted with many voices and speeches, these were discussed in every person's kitchen. It was the impression as if the country has gotten ill with political discussion fever. Even divorces got started on the grounds of political disagreements between a wife and a husband.

Husband, "Do you know that Michael Gorbachev, born in 1931, President from 1985 to 1990, won the Nobel Peace Prize for his contribution to world peace, becoming internationally famous?"

Wife, "Yes, of course. So what?"

Husband, "I want to say that he was a good President, very close to the people. He understood the needs of the ordinary people".

Wife, "Yeah, yeah, yeah. Your beloved Gorbachev was yapping and yapping all the time and doing nothing. I am tired of his promises to reconstructing, rebuilding but there are empty store shelves and spiraling food prices. I hate Gorbachev."

Husband, "And what is your Democrats' proposal? Your favorite Yeltsin. Who's that? Eh?"

Wife, " I love Yeltsin, born in Sverdlovsk in 1931, joined the Communist Party in 1961, in 1990 resigned from it. In 1976 he became head of the Party organization in Sverdlovsk, and built two poultry plants there, people there were very satisfied with his administration. Our neighbour had visited her sister in Sverdlovsk at that time; everybody loved him there because their stomachs were full and kids grew up normally. Had your Gorbachev done any thing useful for the country, except yapping?! "

Husband, "Your Yeltsin was removed from his posts: as the Chief of the Communist Party organization in Moscow and was a member of the ruling party's Politburo in 1987. In 1989 Yeltsin won a seat in the new Soviet government, but his bid for the leadership was opposed by Gorbachev. In August 1991 he led a popular opposition against Gorbachev and became powerful and famous at home and abroad".

Wife, "The Soviet Union is cracked up, and the new state of Russia appeared and you must understand and not underestimate this fact, my darling".

The similar or almost similar debates had taken place in each Russian family.

The population was divided again into the reds and the whites, ours and not ours, into the communists and the democrats.

Emma cursed the new democrats or how they were called among the people as "the new Russians" with the dirtiest of words as often as she could, she got angry about the delay of two-three months of her pension delivery, delay of her husband's salary, the sudden absence of a job for her daughter and her son-in-law.

How to live without money, to pay the rent, utilities, groceries? Her shopping box decreased to the minimum of bread and milk. Potatoes were picked up from her vegetable garden and some fruit.

How could we continue? In this transition period she could not find a place for her, she could not reconstruct herself because of her disability.

The new powers, however, seem to have forgotten about these unprotected layers of the society.

Earlier Emma's family was helped immensely by her parents, now - 'finita la comedia.'

Everything had finished.

At length the pensions were given to the population, for Emma started new problems: the serious illness of her daughter who was getting overweight, as doctors concerned, it was because of the hormonal destructions and, perhaps of, her husband's disease.

In our times the difficult and often frustrating struggle with many details of our daily existence was bad, we often would end up fatigued or depressed or run down. Or we develop chronic headaches, sleeping difficulties, or itchy, persistent skin rashes or a host of other troublesome symptoms.

Those symptoms had appeared in Emma's husband's organism very long ago, at first usually mild and transitory. Then they could be overbearing and completely consumed the sufferer. Likewise, the symptoms could last for several evenings and be relieved by a glass of vodka or something like that. Or they could be so severe as to require a significant change in lifestyle.

Emma's husband could not change his lifestyle, drinking alcohol was his second nature. In such a way he got free from stress and life troubles. It was impossible to conceive of a stressless environment. But Emma's partner who complained of undue fatigue denied any extra or excessive stress in his life at that time.

Indeed, he was incapable of dealing with particularly stressful situations simply because he knew he had no alternative. Several years ago, when he was younger, he rarely developed fatigue, probably then he could afford it.

It's more accurate to say that these symptoms were due to Detkov's inability to adapt well to the normal stresses that were part and parcel of daily life, to his unhappiness with his situations and his lifestyle.

Detkov began counting the years and days left before he retired. In 1997 he was given a small pension and was allowed to live without work in full retirement.

Meanwhile the second elections of Russian President in1996 showed vividly that the Communists reorganizing their Party on new grounds, kept their influence on the simple people such as Emma's family.

She as well as her native Bryansk region had voted for the Communist Party who formed part of the red zone, facing fearlessly the possible complications and more suffering in their sad lives.

All of us experienced a type of sadness related to short winter days. We call it the winter blues, or flash, or winter doldrums. The psychiatrists have now come along to tell us that there are people to whom the sadness is really a sickness. They have named it seasonal affective disorder, or SAD.

The Detkovs remained sad because they were more depressed than expected from a simple change of seasons or political events in the country.

PART THREE

VALENTINA

"0, wondrous moment! There before me,
A radiant, fleeting dream, you stood,
A vision fancy fashioned for me,
A glimpse of perfect womanhood",
which was recited by Nick in front of his decorated with a pink
flowery chintz baby-girl's cradle.

One late afternoon in March on the seventeenth of 1940 his
daughter, the first child of his own, was born in Bryansk. He
seemed to be very happy and in very high spirits. You bet, not
every day there came the birth of such a beautiful tiny creature
who was named - Valentina. It seemed to him that twelve angels
had been flying over the skies to bless her.

"Love, poetry, romance, wisdom, joy, peace, long-suffering,
kindness, goodness, faith, mildness, self-control, - all of these are
invaluable qualities that will help her to endure", said the angels
and disappeared.

The baby cried like anyone else's child. When she opened her
eyes wide for the first time they were filled with tears and bleary.
She could not see anything in detail. She could not tell what was
near and what was far. Thus did she confuse the sunset rays gazing
at her through the window, a picture of three mighty men hanging on the wall just opposite her place in the bedroom, with her
Dad's face, leaning over her and smiling.

The night was approaching.
A crescent moon arose.
Lots of stars glistened in the skies.
The points of Your star dropped off.
These were cries of dismay.
There were thumps.

The moon shone on the forehead of Nick, who with great love looked at the baby. Nick held his daughter. Nick so adored the infant that he had allowed himself to forget about the time. Only one minute old, and cradled in the hands of Nick, Val has witnessed the first human accident.

The falling points of the star were beads as on a necklace of beautiful Maria. The thumps were made by Nick's feet as he stamped out of the reflection of Maria's necklace creating the little fires on the floor.

Nick begged for happiness for his child, closing his eyes tight, expecting to return to all-knowing darkness. The baby learned that perfect darkness would not be hers again for so long as it chose to live and keep its eyes closed. Human eyes, she learned, imagined that they saw things even when they are closed. They showed Nick all these imaginary stars.

Nick opened his eyes wide again. This would be the second time. The sky was now a dazzling chaos. It was nothing but an exploding March night sky full of stars and reflections from the full moon.

His wife Maria and their neighbours stood for the amusement of seeing a baby, born. Maria wished to show the baby something wonderful at once, and so had removed the crystal necklace from her throat, and now dangled those prismatic chips of quartz, back-lit, before Nick's eyes.

The necklace was not his present. Only the memory of its glitter was Nick's to keep. All the stars fled as the necklace was hastily withdrawn. And the full moon began to rise.

The baby Val was given into the arms of her mother. Maria, in her joy, after all the pain was gone, looked herself like the seeming rising moon; she was glowing with motherly pride. The pale skin on her face was electric light, switched on in the night by Nick, who wished to look at the sleeping Maria as if she caused the full moon to wane. What could be the explanation? Nick looked at Val. The baby's eyes had closed. He looked out of the window: now he saw the moon and a star came together in an impossible cosmic tangle, his brains connected them to one triangle: Maria, Val, the moon and Val's leading star; let them be lucky and happy for ever, he thought. In his thoughts there was such a great force of creativeness which was inherited by Val since that moment on and led her for her whole life.

On long winter evenings Nick used to investigate the poetry rhythms, anapest and amphybrahiy, chorey and white verse. Designing the musical, poetic lines which deepened into the wells of images, gradually he came to his own verse composition. It was easy for him because by nature he was so close to such stuff as romance, especially Blok's type. A genius Russian poet Alexander Blok started his poem "The Twelve" with:

> "Cherny vecher,
> Bely sneg.
> Veter, veter!
> Na nogakh ne stoit chelovek.
> Veter, veter
> Na vsem bozhem svete!"

> "Black night,
> White snow,
> Wind, wind!
> A man can't stand.
> Wind, wind -
> All over God's world!"

Nick liked this image to twelve Red Guards appearing out of the night, the cold, the snow. A soldier slept with Katya, a prostitute; she was killed by an angry shot from Petrukha's gun; Petrukha filled with remorse; there was a glimpse of Katya's dismal history; a glimpse of a bourgeois standing on a street corner, his nose hidden in his collar, looking like a mangy dog.

The Twelve marched on through the stormy night, the whirling wind filling the down trodden streets, their clothes in tatters, their destination and duties unknown.

> "So they march with solemn tread
> Behind - the hungry dog.

109

Ahead -with bloody flag,
Unseen by the blizzard,
Untouched by bullets,
With gentle steps above the storm,
In a white crown of roses.
Ahead - goes Jesus Christ. "
(translated from Russian by Ibid)

Nick shared his poetic feelings with his friend. "Have you ever happened to walk in the city on a dark night?" he asked.

"No, I have not", he responded.

"In a snow storm or driving rain it is better to stay at home ".

"That image of the storm is the Russian Revolution headed by Lenin, that was the Revolution which trudged the "dark people", the remorseless force of the Russian storm, sweeping over taiga and city slums, destroying everything on its way. As it had been from the time of Pugachev and the terrible rebellions of Catherine's days."

On every following birthday Val and Nick recited his new-composed verses dedicated to his Princess Valentine, so by the end of his life several block-notes had been filled up, never shown to anybody and never, therefore, published. Funny?!

Funny how the mind summons random memories of long-long ago passed days, of which Val began to be aware of herself, starting with the age of seven.

When she went to school for the first time, school was divided into girls'- and -boys'.

The separate education of males and females was the norm of Soviet upbringing the children of the post-war time of 1947. The girls were daily dressed like some proletarian workers, forbidden to use make-up, sophisticated hair-does or hair-cuts, or body ornamentation. There were Feast Days and May Processions requiring a uniform, brown dress and a white apron. There were flowers and music, and slow walks down the aisles.

How natural, then, it must have been for Val to mount the stairs of Bryansk school Number One wearing a usual school uniform, her neck set off by a scoop of tight pleats.

That's her in a line of debutants decorating the facade of school building like song birds. Her first teacher, Nina Nickolaevna Ledneva, stood behind them. What a miracle teacher she was, being their class leader during straight eight years. Thanks to Nina Nickolaevna the lessons were transformed into fascinating journeys into different parts of the world of knowledge.

Now, when she died many years ago, just looking at her photograph which was browning, her face seemed so strict and kind at the same time, gazed at the pupils with curiosity. She was clutching a big bunch of lilacs. She loved children and each of them did write her a thank you note:

"Dear Nina Nickolaevna,

Granted, I'm a few years late, but it's been on my mind and remembering how crucial the note was to the smooth operation of the social system into which all of your pupils were born. Because neither of us knows at this point whether either has escaped the worst results of all that you taught us.

We wished you had remembered that we tried to turn into extraordinary polite people. Though your steadfast politeness was what I think of now and something that, of course, I never appreciated when we were young.

Now I'd like to thank you for everything good you did for us and may I tell you it was Wonderful. Marvelous.

Sincerely yours
Valentina Filina."

It was Nina Nickolaevna, who started her pedagogical ccareer in 1947. She taught and learned simultaneously, developing the kids' best skills in arithmetic, reading, hand-writing, spelling. "Today, dear children," addressed she to the new-comers, "you are not simple children, you become schoolchildren, and the main task of yours, is to study. 'To study, study and study', so said our great Lenin".

"Shall we draw? Shall we dance? Shall we do physical exercises, including acrobatics?" questioned the pupils one by one and sometimes in chorus.

111

"Certainly", responded the young teacher, "and even we will try to compose verses. Everybody is capable and must develop one's own creative abilities. Everyone possesses them, only they are not always revealed, it is pity." she continued.

As soon as the kids learned to read and write, she brought a brilliant big album and said, "Now, pupils, I shall give you a task: to write down in the note-book the verses,which will be composed by each one of you. It will take you not very long, I guess".

Poor little things, the kids were!

Their teacher apparently overestimated their potentialities because not all of them could compose verses. Half of the class, around twenty girls, were helped by Val, who found it easy to carry out the teacher's requests. Those were for example:

"Dear Teacher, dear Lenin,
You're buried in the coffin,
As I'm soon growing up,
Join your Party - be the top!"

Or:

"You, blessed and miracle, my pen,
As much I love you as I can,
In sleepless night awake I you,
For sake of God write a line anew."

Or:

"Me was writing in a rush,
Off the chair fell down, Oh, hush!
Feather -pen and my inkpot,
Happened be under the cot."

And so on and so forth.

Nina Nickolaevna was thorougly convinced that environment played a bigger role in creating intellectual qualities than genetics. Genes, she considered, play not a dominant role. The brain of a child in the yearly years is still taking shape; it needs the great attention of adults to develop children's activities, in equal amounts for all of them.

Parents were excluded because of the demands and long hours of their jobs which were required to supply families with dwellings, food and all the basic necessities. All of her youngsters were from lower income families, the main emphasis of education could be done on school which tried to open in the young brains "windows of opportunities".

Next time Nina Nickolaevna entered the classroom and said, "This morning, my dear children, there will be a task for you to draw your impressions from your summer vacations. I am giving you coloured pencils, and you will try. After that we'll organize the exhibition of your drawings and we'll see who the winner will be".

"And if I cannot", someone said from the school desk in the corner.

"Good", answered the teacher enthusiastically, "Look! There are different colours: this is a yellow book", she pointed to her class register, "and there are brown, black, red, and orange pencils. What can we do with these colours? Let us together draw a picture on the blackboard as an example", and she began drawing a big fish, peeping out of the river water.

Nina Nickolaevna came over to each pupil, encouraging them for a better accomplishment, praising one, cheering another. Really, she could explore the creative atmosphere around her. After the lesson all the drawings were picked up and hung on the wall. They are raising curiosity which was satisfied by watching, touching and even tasting the things to be depicted about.

Actual intellectual quality scores might not change dramatically as the children grew older, but academic achievement could. These were the years in which the brain was fine-tuned and environmental influence continued to count. The teacher's attention did not necessarily create a Repin or Picasso, but it remained a vital ingredient to the children's intelligence.

Like this Nina Nickolaevna's school girls danced touched with rhythm and melody; piano and group-singing lessons greatly improved in their spatial-temporal reasoning, important in understanding math and science.

She spent a lot of after-class-time with her favorites, visiting the cinema, walking to the forest or to the townwoods named "Nightingales".

"What is this? What is that? Why do the ferns grow in the shadow but buttercups under sun in sunny spots ?" one hundred of whys and whats poured out of her wise head. She explained and explained without tiredness, herself discovering the world for her in quite new dimensions, proving a known saying that a good teacher was not only a teacher but a pupil for all her life.

The teacher comrade Ledneva entered the Pedagogical Institute, the Mathematical faculty, which she graduated from successfully at this post-war time, allowing her not only to be a teacher of elementary school, years later as a math teacher going on to teach in senior classes. She was awarded with a Labour Order and entitled as a Deserved Teacher of Russian Federation, by the way, as her mother and grandmother. She was a teacher of the third generation in her family. Family tree's teaching traditions gave influence on her, from her to her pupils.

Once they saw together with Nina Nickolaevna a movie in a small movie theatre named "Newsreel". Before the ten-o'clock presentation, their teacher instructed them to sit quietly. Except for an occasional whispered question, they sat in rapt attention.

The sound track, however, was inaudible because two strange children. Bounced on their seats, talked loudly and raced up and down the aisles. Never once did they see a parent with them. The only reaction of Nina Nickolaevna was to this behavior:

"Look! Their manners are worse than just saying "please" and "thank you".

They are egotists neglecting the opinions of other people. They are impolite".

That was a very special lesson in politeness taught by these rude strange children, on the one hand, and the reaction of their teacher, on the other.

Later she met those children's parents and said: "My kids were having a hard time watching the film with your children running all over the theatre".

"Do you think if they're not interested in the movie you could keep them out here and under control?"

The father regarded Nina Nickolaevna coolly.

"We've paid for the tickets. Our children can go anywhere they please". Val heard this conversation and was dumbfounded.

114

What could make a seemingly rational couple condone this behavior that was so obviously rude, even to a child's opinion? Here they become so consumed with their own needs and the impulses of their children that everyone else's rights were ignored? "It is a very pity that you behave yourselves like this, that your teenagers cannot grow up politely, I'm sorry for your children", said thoughtfully Nina Nickolaevna. For Val, it was the continuation of the lesson of politeness and social activities.

Everyone in class was involved in class-and-school activities, everyone had a duty to do an errand, Val was responsible for the sanitary conditions of her mates and the room.

Every morning she stood proudly in front of the entrance of their classroom, inspecting the dirty hands, and dirty nails, and the palms, ears and hair. If someone was found out having something suspicious, the school medical nurse was called and the pupil allowed to attend classes unless she was healthy.

The break of sanitary norms was considered to be unhealthy, that rule was written in the class register.

In the third grade there appeared the pioneer groups with Lenin's meeting corners in the classrooms. Everybody must be a member of this young pioneers' organization. Val became a leader of a pioneer team of her class, and later of the whole school.

The same was with the Komsomol Communist Organization - everybody was ordered to participate, everybody was automatically prepared for the future to join the membership of the Communist Party of the Soviet Union.

What were the advantages and disadvantages of the Pioneer - Komsomol Russian movement?

The advantages seemed to be in developing the social activity of everyone's personality. For instance, Val became braver and expressed her own thoughts and formulated the collective opinion of her fellows, they helped each other in fulfilling their home work, stimulating their social interests and broadening social horizons.

None of the pupils ever dared to think about disadvantages of such sort of activities, everything became a "plus".

Shortly everyone realized that in Russia everything was centralized and there existed only one opinion, that of your leader.

The criticism of the Communist system was regarded as anti-Soviet Propaganda without reference to the personal predictions of an individual.

All Soviet individuals were developing in one unique direction, the Soviet thought and required results. The Soviet State was dumb-founded by Stalin's death in the spring of 1953.

Val's teacher, sitting in front of her pupils, gazed sadly at the window and cried with tears just like a baby.

Her girls were giving her strange looks. So far so good the understanding of gist of the current events, appeared in Val's first publications with the dedication to Comrade Stalin. She was thirteen at that time.

Following Adrienne Rich's, a great American poetess, poem "The Rain of Blood" we could say:

"In that dark year an angry rain came down
Blood-red upon the hot stones of the town.
Beneath the pelting of that liquid drought,
No garden stood, no shattered stalk could sprout...
And every dawn we woke to hear the sound,
And all men knew that they could stanch the wound,
But each looked out and cursed the stricken town,
The guilty roofs on which the rain came down."

This very great image of the rain of blood needed to share our animal passion for existence characterizing the dark atmosphere of Stalin's epoch which happened to be over together with the moaning and tears of Nina Nickolaevna.

The young pioneers' motto "Be ready!" and the reply "Always ready!" was symbolizing the mentality of the young generation.

"You, youngsters, are you ready to explore the virgin lands in Kazakhstan?" was the question.

"Always ready!" was the answer.

The song appeared in those days, to that was what the Party had ordered, the Komsomol answered "Yes".

"You, youngsters, are ready to pick up the harvest in the fields?"

"Always ready!" was the reply.

If you answer in any other way, you will be immediately expelled from the Komsomol, or from the Party.

Val's conscience since those memorial days of Stalin's death started formulating a new concept of thinking. On the twelfth day after that, to be precise on her own birthday, the young teenager asked herself for the first time in her life, "Why are you living in the world? For what reason? What to do?"

The last question repeated the title of the famous novel, "What to Do?" by the Russian philosopher Nickolay Chernyshevsky.

This question - what to do? - had preoccupied the generation before. Indeed, it was essentially the question that had preoccupied Russia since the early nineteenth century and was to preoccupy it into the twentieth. What to do? Everyone asked the question. Alexander Herzen's question, "Who is to blame?" Or Tolstoy's, " What are we to do?" All the writers have asked the same question and when the time came, so did Lenin, paraphrasing Chernyshevsky and calling his pamphlet, "What is to be done?"

Questions, questions, questions. Where were the answers?

Poignantly and persistently one generation of young people after another debated, talking to themselves of self-examination, of moral inquiry, of self-flagellation, in which every question was asked and every possible answer was advocated, and but nothing was ever agreed upon. What to do? What to do with themselves? The eternal questions of the Russians, which they put to themselves.

Val's school friend Mary Fomina asked her,

"Would you like to go to the public library?"

"Why?"

"To borrow some books from there. To write a composition our teacher had asked for", answered the first.

"Oh, yes. I've forgotten about that, let's go".

Russian public libraries looked like huge palaces of knowledge with a great book storage place for more than one or several million volumes.

Having shown up there for the first time, the girls were greatly impressed and from now on they often attended the Bryansk libraries. The atmosphere was so friendly and the service - excellent. It was the library where Val discovered for herself a great many interesting works, such as: "The Esthetical Relations to the

Reality"(N. Chernyshevsky's theses), the poetry of Anna Akhmatova who was depicted on the portrait as a beauty in a tight black silk dress, a large oval cameo on her belt , such verses as:
"We are all sinners, we are all whores,
How sad we are together".
And Mayakovsky's rhyme:
"For you who only love women and food,
Should I give my life for your pleasure?
I'd rather serve pineapple juice
To the whores at the bar".

It was in a Petrograd cellar called "Stray Dog" where the famous poets began to spend their nights.

It was somewhere very far from her home, Valentina's thoughts whirled and spun thinking about the adventurous life out there, however here everything's quiet like in a chapel. Meantime, there happened several changes in Val's life: according to the higher authorities' decree, the males' and females' schools were reorganized, the combined education got started bringing with it certain problems. The girls could not stand the boys; the boys hardly accepted girls.

"What are you doing, Val?" asked her schoolmate.

"Nothing. It's none of your business", answered she.

"Yes, it's mine", continued Symon Bederov, playing with a little pocket knife in front of her eyes while she be sitting at the desk and reading the text-book before the anatomy lesson.

"No, it isn't ", replied she.

"I won't let you read ", he went on.

"Yes, you will ", answered the latter.

She was not scared of boys and pretended to protect the book against the stabbing knife pulling forward her hand over the book.

The knife cut into a spot a bit above the wrist of the girl's hand. It was her vein which squirted blood onto his face.

Symon Bederov was frightened, he grasped Val on the hand and rushed with her to the emergency. The pain vanished, some weeks later; the scar only remained as a memory of stupid childhood pranks.

Symon Bederov had drowned that summer. All the class was present at his funeral. Val was crying and so bitterly with lots of tears that Symon's Mom came up to her and asked, "Dear girl, what's your name?"

"Val", she replied.

"Why are you crying so greatly?" asked the beautiful Jewish woman. "It's your son, I miss my friend terribly", Val retorted.

"Don't cry, darling. We both have to be strong now more than ever", she continued.

"Yes, sure. We ought to go on living", Val calmed down and looked around.

The Bederovs lived in a big wooden house with many rooms. The coffin stood on the large table in the master bedroom, through its open door Val saw the angel's sculpture figure on Symon's desk. It was Val's last present for his birthday, his sweet, childish face, blond hair and a sky-blue robe which was so vivid as if in the picture. Val dashed into the room, carefully took the angel, wrapped it in tissue paper and put it next to Symon's face as if he were alive, sleeping, and only looked strangely taller than usual.

"Now you're at home, too", told to him Val and left the room. It was the first contact she had with the Jewish people, who lived in a richer way compared to the Val's poor family members, but they still suffered nonetheless.

For the first time Val tried to answer the question, "Why do so many people dislike the Jews? Why and what was the reason?"

She read in very old, sometimes ancient and antique books that the anti-semitism of the Russian state set up its own reaction within the country. As early as the reign of Elizabeth in the eighteenth century, Jewish traders were barred from the Empire despite the ardent pleas of Russian merchants that such additions to the Russian market place were good for business.

Behind every restrictive practice lay the usual villains of the peace, the Church, and the nobles at Court. The Church wished to convert the Jews from their faith to Orthodoxy while the Court dealt with the problem in a secular and generally obnoxious manner. Further decrees by Alexander the Second opened up higher learning to the Jews; these were contradicted by the bestial pogroms under Alexander the Third. Restrictive legislation with occasional discrete concessions, such as a quota of Jewish students in secondary and primary schools as opposed to a ban, continued until 1917.

In the annals of the Communist Party, Jewish names occur with astonishing regularity. Long ago as 1883, the first Russian Marxist group was composed of Plekhanov, Vera Zazulich, both Russian revolutionaries, Akselrod and Lev Deutsch. Among the most influential early Bolshevik leaders Lenin (Ulyanov) was Russian, Dzugashvili (Stalin) was Georgian, and Trotsky (Bronstein), Kamenev (Radomyslsky) were Jewish.

In 1930, Litvinov (Wallach) took over the Foreign Ministry from Chicherin, and at one time the ambassadors in London, Paris and Washington were all Jewish.

Val felt a great sympathy with these suffering people because they were intelligent and determined to overcome, the same as her. They had a determined spirit - a will to survive.

As a member of the Young Komsomol League Val was given a direct order to be a leader of the junior pioneer group, they were having classes in the same room, as senior Val had the first morning shift, juniors did the afternoon. For many years Val and her wards did not separate for very long.

They made friends, having spent a lot of time together. More and more children were lured on by the social activities and sports programs and a homework club, complete with prizes for the best students.

Unforgettable was one party before the New Year's Eve. Somebody read the last lines - the bedroom scene, the end of Christmas Day, "Looking through my bedroom window, out into the moonlight and the unending smoke-coloured snow, I could see the lights in the windows of all the other houses on our hill and hear the music ringing from them up the long slope, snow fell steadily that night. I turned the gas down, I got into my bed. I said some words to the close and holy darkness and then I slept ".

The romantic atmosphere was created, and the miracle-dancing-singing-party got started: on the school hall floor there appeared the kids in scary thrilling costumes as a warrior and evil -witches, classic clowns in costumes and angels, princess and even a snow-lady; "trick or treat" sounded the commander's words followed by an ugly scarecrow on an imitation bale of hay, then a shrieking ghost with a cat in boots, Ali-baba and forty robbers.

All costumes had been designed and sewn by their own hands with the aid of parents. The competent jury valued very high them, especially, the skull warrior was one consisted of a chest piece with attached epaulets, an oversized mask, cape, shirt, waist sash, arm and leg guards plus realistic-looking wooden skull warrior sword. All the drawing designs for these costumes were made by Val. Since that moment on she was fond of designing clothes for herself and sewing them at home.

The numerous prizes to be given to the costume-parade-carnival winners included a great amount of home-baked cakes and candies.

Imagine! Five-kilos-of-sweet-cake was given to all the participants because in this competition there were neither losers nor winners. Only friendship among the young good people was given to each other.

Val was friendly and communicative not only with pioneers but also with her classmates. Mary Fomina, her best school friend, wanted her to think about the future, how to continue studying after high school. Both were dreaming about the pedagogical carreer, the first - in the foreign languages, the latter - in Russian history and literature. Both had good marks in their High School Certificates.

They were both seventeen, to be preparing for the entrance examinations at the Orel University.

At last that day had come.

The University Professor asked at the exam:

"Can you remember, comrade Filina, the description of the ball scene when Natasha Rostova danced with Andrey Bolkonsky in the famous Leo Tolstoy's novel 'The Peace and the War'?"

Val: "Certainly", and started describing.

Professor: "What can you say about the method of socialist realism, which a Soviet writer composed his works with?"

Val: "But Leo Tolstoy wrote in his own manner and could not know about this modern method. The latter was invented later by the Soviet writer Gorky and implied into the Soviet literature nowadays".

Professor: "Well, tell us, please, about the historical epic of Tolstoy's times. What was he mistaken in?"

Val: "With one word it is impossible to answer if you mean Tolstoy's point of view in respect of non - resistance against evil by violence that was criticized by Lenin. We can discuss it in details and we'll see who was right and who was wrong".

Professor: "And your opinion?"

Val: "To my mind, Tolstoy was right from his point of view, Lenin - from his. The history will judge them." Val was refused entry into the literature faculty because of the high competition that year. The passing examination criterium was 'excellent' in all four subjects. Val had got three 'excellent' and one 'good'.

The 'good' mark was given for the written examination and in an unusual way.

It was habitual at Soviet entrance exams to pass the written compositions first, and then unsuccessful applicants' last names were hung on the announcement board, thus on the second day after the exam everybody knew who failed.

The others did not know for sure how high they were appreciated, just during the next oral literature exam the teen would know both marks, including for his or her written composition.

As Val finished with her oral answer, she got interested in her mark for the written composition. One of the three teachers was scrubbing thoroughly 'excellent' for her oral exam and "satisfactory" for the written one.

Val became pale, got shocked with this "discovery", she did not expect such a low mark as 'satisfactory' because of a simple reason: she had been already writing the theme of her composition 'The Image of Lenin in the Poetry of the Great Soviet Poet Vladimir Vladimirovich Mayakovsky' for the third time.

So it happened to be the same theme at her own school as a home composition, Val was given an 'excellent' mark for it, and two months later that theme was repeated at the finishing school examination with the same 'excellent' mark.

The little girl knew this topic by heart, from the very beginning up to the end, every comma and every paragraph of it.

And now what an occasion!

'Satisfactory' mark!

Val possessed an outspoken character because of her developed social school activities, she could express her thoughts frankly and open to the adults, she was not scared of either teachers or principals of schools.

It took her, perhaps, a few minutes to concentrate her attention to this problem - the biased attitude to her composition. Then she said,

"Excuse me, comrade Professor, could you possibly show me my written composition, please?"

"What for?" asked one of the angry teachers.

"I'd like to look through it in order to see my mistakes. I doubt if there are so many of them", the brave girl answered.

"The students' compositions are now in the teachers' room, it is locked, and nobody is allowed to touch them without a special permission of the Chairman of the Entrance Examination Committee", explained the other one.

"But I insist upon showing me my written composition, and I have a right to look at it", Val did not give up.

"If you are so insistent then I'll try to do my best for you", the third one said reluctantly and went out.

In a few minutes the teacher came back bringing in her hands the five white sheets of paper.

That was Val's composition, she recognized it at once. She looked through it hastily, noticed three mistakes: two were her spelling and one comma after the introductory word "however", which can be separated from the other words in the middle of the sentence, and not be separated when it is at the beginning of the sentence.

Valentina grasped quickly that two mistakes were marked with the special purpose to underestimate her composition.

Very politely she proved to the examiners that they were mistaken without noticing Val's correct spelling with the Russian letters "a" and "o" in the fast handwriting spelt in the similar way. The picky teachers agreed at long last.

It was left the only mistake with comma after "however" which was really disputable - it can be written in both ways, with comma and without.

The examiners preferred to leave it as a mistake. So the 'satisfactory' mark was transformed into a 'good' mark, and on Val's examination card had appeared the note, "Corrected to be believed", and the signatures of all three teachers with the official Orel University seal.

Unfortunately, this 'good' mark did not help to enter the literature faculty, opposite, perhaps, it disturbed, who knows.

The Examination Committee offered Val to transfer her documents to another faculty; she chose foreign languages where the youngster succeeded extremely well in.

She had however to get a permission of the highest authorities of the Orel University for doing so.

"What do you want, comrade Filina?" asked the rector dryly.

"I'd like to ask your permission, comrade Mikhalev, to transfer my documents from the literature faculty where I could not achieve enough points to enter, to another faculty - of foreign languages", said Val daringly, without the apparent hope for success.

"Well, really? You cannot do this. Come to us next summer, try again to pass the examinations and then obviously you'll be luckier," answered he without even watching who was sitting in front of him.

Valentina understood immediately that her "vis-a-vis" was a Soviet bureaucrat of Communist type and to persuade him meant to win a great victory.

Val was like a soldier who stood before a Field Marshal. She decided it has to be all or nothing, advancing all her chess figures at the same time to the front positions.

The battle continued.

"Comrade Mikhalev," she said, "I cannot come to you next year and have the exams, because of a simple reason: the whole year will pass by and I doubt if I will get the brilliant marks I am having now, just with fresh knowledge after school.

Secondly, have you ever noticed the reference letter written by the principal of my native school Number Four, in which the deserved teacher of Russian Federation comrade Stepan Ivanovich Bondarenko characterized me as a prospective teacher after three-years- pedagogical experience with the pioneer group of grade 5."

"No, I have not", honestly exclaimed he, nodding with his grey head negatively.

"In that case,may I ask you to read, please. It is in my file, I'll wait for a while".

While he was reading, slender Valentina increased *crescendo* in her attack.

"Thirdly," she said insistently, "if I were your daughter of only seventeen years old, who loved studying at school all kind of subjects such as literature, history, Russian and foreign languages. For her, it was a very difficult choice of what faculty she would prefer to. Perhaps, you would converse to her in a quite different manner, wouldn't you?"

It was the last argument which comrade Mikhalev had given into.

So Val entered the University, her friend - not. The student life began with picking up the spuds. All first year students were ordered to go to the fields to save the harvest for two months before the frosts arrived.

Val was assigned to be a monitor for her group.

In the fall of 1957 the peasants practically abandoned their villages, nobody of local population wanted to work in the fields, the Communist Party policy was all citizens of towns, soldiers, students, workers of the plants had to take an active part in the agricultural life of the country. It was not of their concern whether a person is able to do this kind of work, he or she was involved in the hard slavery labour: just to lift and carry, pick up potato roots out of the earth, fill in the pail and bring it to the common pile, then load a lorry.

It was a tedious twelve-hours'-work in the hot sun in September, it was cats-and-dogs' rain in November.

When such weather started, Val's fellow students asked her as a monitor to go to the chairman of the collective farm and ask him to supply them with the overalls and rubber boots, if he could not, ask his permission to go home for a day or so to take warm clothes with. Really the students wore sandals and light summer saraphans at that time.

The chairman was very rude and cruel to Val.

"You simply don't want to work in the fields at all. You are looking for excuses to avoid work. You are sabotaging the schedule of picking up the potatoes. I do not allow to leave the working place and I'll report on you to your University autorities."

And he did.

As soon as Val returned to the University she was called to the dean's office and the dean told her, "You, comrade Filina, personally misbehaved at the collective farm, spoiled the discipline among your fellow-workers. You are to be punished by denying you the students' allowance for the whole semester".

In such an unlucky way Val's first steps as a student were to be, for five months without student's stipend, which was twenty nine roubles a month. Comparing to her father's monthly wage of around seventy roubles, it was a great sum of money. Part of it, she used to rent a studio for seven and a half roubles a month.

There was her first economic lesson how to survive under the harshest of conditions: at home, she knew, her mother attempted to make ends meet with two children and a husband to be taken care of as well.

Mommy sent some money to support her daughter, who was trying to economize on everything: food, drinks, never thinking about new clothes and shoes. That's why Val never told her Mom about her misery.

Sometimes she through starvation fainted, this had happened before the winter examination session. Once she stole a few products from her room hostess's cupboard so she had something to eat.

Alla Romanovna Lyakh, the hostess's name, an elderly, short woman, 75, with curly, grey hair and blue-eyed, told her new tenant about her husband, an academician by education with a widely known name in the scientific world, who was caught by "black raven" (the name of the KGB lorry which came habitually to people's homes in the middle of dark nights when everybody was sleeping and could not witness anybody taken away) and since that time on her husband never returned home and nothing was heard from him. Her fate was as a "straw-widow", who was neither wife nor a married woman, frightened even to know or enquire about the fortune or future of her husband.

Alla Romanovna was scared of everything and everybody. From the government she got nothing for her husband: simply he disappeared, and that's all. She worked as a nurse and getting only fifty five roubles a month' pension as a senior, Val's hostess, as a rule, sent the whole pension sum to her only son who had a wife and two children. She herself lived for the little rent money Val gave to her, and a few roubles she earned by giving injections to the sick people.

Alla Romanovna's sacrifice in favor of her kids was understandable to Val: in front of her eyes was a bright example of her Mommy's life.

One sacrifices his or her life in the name of some other people, but not an idea, that is why life continued. Thus Alla Romanovna always needed money badly. It was proposed to her by a new acquaintance:

"Dear, do you want to buy sixty volumes of the Great Soviet Encyclopedia, or thirty five ones of the Smaller Soviet Encyclopedia?"

"I saw the high wall stand stuffed with books where I am sleeping. These are your husband's and you lost the last hope of his return, and so you want to sell them, don't you?" guessed Val.

"Certainly", the sad old woman answered, "I am tired of expecting him for all my life, not being married again. I feel he's dead, and I don't know even where he has been buried, or maybe, he is not buried but thrown away as a stray dog to the garbage", and she burst into tears so bitterly and pitifully that her tenant began calming her down, reciting to the old lady her favorite Shakespeare's poem:

> *"When to the sessions of sweet silent thought,*
> *I summon up remembrance of things past,*
> *I sigh the lack of many a thing I sought,*
> *And with old woes new wail my dear time's waste.*

127

Then can I drown an eye, unused to flow,
For precious friends hid in death's dateless night,
And weep afresh loves long since cancelled woe,
And moan the experience of many a vanished sight.

Then can I grieve at grievances foregone,
And heavily from woe to woe tell o' er,
The sad account of fore - bemoaned moan,

Which I new pay as if not paid before.
But if the while I think on thee, dear friend,
All losses are restored, and sorrows end."

The old lady's face was pleased; she could read and speak fluently in three foreign languages: English, French and German. She had graduated from the old Russian gymnasium having possessed a very good memory and good capabilities for a few subjects.

"No", concluded Val, "I can't afford those superb books, I myself am in great need of money, but I like your library very much, and I hope to use it, if you allow me".

"Sure", answered Alla Romanovna.

Later there was declared a student competition for the best translation of any poem one liked at random into the Russian language. Val got the first prize for the thirtieth Shakespeare's sonnet beloved by her room hostess. In the linguistic exercises she was assisted by her permanent love for her original Russian language, about which a great Russian writer Ivan Turgenev said as following:
"In the days of hesitations,
In the days of second and third thoughts,
About the destinies of my Motherland,
You, had always been the only helper
and support of mine,
Oh, the great, powerful Russian language!"

Besides the linguistic thoughts, Val's mind was occupied with the meditations of the social society progressing.

In the Lyakh's archives she found Maxim Gorky's, "Untimely Thoughts", (his paper was finally closed down in July, 16, 1918) when he declared:

"Everything that I said about the Bolsheviks' savage crudeness, about their cruelty which approaches sadism, about their lack of culture, about their ignorance of the psychology of the Russian people, about the fact that they are performing a disgustful experiment on the people and are destroying the working class - all this, and much more that I said about "Bolshevism" retains its full force".

Val read in secret the notes of the Russian philosopher Berdyayev, in the reasoned opinion of whom, "Lenin, who had made the cavalry from belief in Karl Marx to belief in Jesus Christ, he was not a vicious man. There was a great deal that was good in him (Lenin). He was not a mercenary and absolutely devoted to an idea; he was not even a particularly ambitious man or a great lover of power; he thought little about himself; but the sole obsession of a single idea led to a dreadful narrowing of thought and to a moral transformation which permitted entirely immoral methods of carrying on the conflict." Lenin, Berdyayev believed, was a man of fate. Without Lenin, it seems entirely clear, the vast insurgence of the Russian people would not have taken the turn it did. And without the raw turbulence and cruelty of the people Lenin's course would not have taken a turn so brutal and inhuman.

That was the explanation of the cruelty undertaken in the relation to Alla Romanovna's husband.

Why? Many times repeated whys were not really coinciding with the official Soviet Propaganda and everything which was taught at the Universities, and at schools.

The double moral standards were getting more and more visible: one - for the simple people, and another - for Communist Party leaders and their close relatives. The slogans of such type as: "The Communist Party is the mind, the honour and the conscience of our epic" (Lenin's words) were hung everywhere, in the auditorium's halls, corridors, and in the streets, on the roads, railway stations, generally speaking, in every possible place so as to be noticed. In word these slogans were pretty eloquent, in deed everybody followed the Party's orders.

After the first year all students without exclusion were directed to raise Kazakhstan virgin soils during the summer vacations; they were transported in cargo trains for cattle, and lived in the vast field barracks constructed for horses, lying on straw above the ground without any accommodations, no toilets, no washing basins, no soaps or things necessary for hygene.

It was a great casual order: there were all together thousands of young people from all the Technical and High Schools, from all over the region.

The field kitchens were coming to feed them three times a day, the food was ugly and impossible to eat.

Female and male barracks stood next to each other, in the night time there started "love" games, continuing till dawn.

Kazakhstan dawns in lake Triushorye were unforgettable. To imagine, the open wild fields, far away, three blue salt lakes, and above was the huge red disk of sun raising slowly and lazily as if not understanding what is happening around and what on hell has been awakening him. The Kazakhstan sun was very severe and burnt the young generation in a few moments.

Val emerged to illness after cleaning the dusty grain elevators which were of the closed type, having fainted once and transported to the little town hospital which was overcrowded with lots of people.

So far so good the students nevertheless had earned some money and were very glad. The first honestly earned money could ever not be forgotten, everyone dreamt of what to do with it. No one of young people was rich; they were poor and felt equal in poverty.

The government people, however, did not consider themselves poor, they dwelt in the big apartments with high ceilings in houses named of Stalin type, using luxurious cars and summer dachas for their families to have a rest. Many other privileges to be described later.

Double standards were the order of the day. One thing was told at lectures, by radio and the official Propaganda, office, but it was another thing - in real life.

130

For instance, among the young people there ran a myth of no prostitution, no houses of free love; but at the Komsomol meetings with membership of several hundreds and more at an open public forum there had been solved the problem of a poor second year student with a long Russian plait, how to behave after midnight in the hotel where she met a foreigner and got caught with him shortly.

Val's memory might well manage to contain a photograph of a Soviet prostitute adjusting her shoe after a tough evening on the sidewalk, and it might well be that she the whore would eventually report her pillow talk to the appropriate authorities.

This poor Soviet student called publicly a "whore" was expelled out of the Unoversity and the Komsomol because of the reason of moral depravity.

At the same time the authorities' morals were beyond their own criticism; they were having more than one mistress at a time; at home they left a wife with kids. The theme of moral priorities was interesting to Val as well as the duties of her whole day.

To prove that all time has value, a senior executive at the University asked everyone who attended the last meeting to "punch in". At the session's end she calculated the total price of the meeting in man-hours and converted these into roubles by estimating each staffer's salary.

The executive made her point.

Meetings seemed to be free, but they were actually very costly, because time really was money for students. Indeed, a single hour was worth one rouble. And if you could save just one hour a day, you would not only conserve thousands of roubles' worth of time each year but also give yourself opportunities to learn and do things that make your time even more valuable.

That was why Val started mastering the time-and-not-a study-tactics. Unless she had a sense of priorities she could work hard all day, but be further from her goal than when she started.

The time-table of a humanities student included a lot of reading: in foreign languages, Latin, English, German, philosophical works of the Marxism-Leninism trend, special disciplines of theories in phonetics, old English, linguistics, grammar of modern and

131

old English, semantics and semiotics.

From that moment on there were organized the students' scientific readings where they were holding the reports about the famous writers' lives and their works.

"Martin Iden" by Jack London was discussed by Val, who for the first time revealed for herself the philosophical points of view of Herbert Spencer and Fridrich Nitzshe with his "Twilights of Prophets". Those were official readings, but, in secret, very often in a written form passed by hand among the students there spread the readings of the forbidden authors, such as Balmont, Bely, Tsvetayeva, Akhmatova, Mandelstam, Esenin, Blok. Nobody knew why they were forbidden, everybody enjoyed their poetry style:

"It seemed to the poet Balmont that a white mist filled the air, blurring the outlines of buildings and dissolving the figures of passers-by. It was as hard to see the Russian city of Moscow as it was the future. It was too cold to stay in bed, too cold to stay in his flat. He often met the poet Marina Tsvetayeva in her cold flat as in his; still, as they huddled in their coats over a glass of tea, the words flew back and forth and soon the dark streets of the Arbat vanished, the frost melted, and they found themselves in the bright world of imagination of beauty, of golden images, laughter and dreams".

Balmont told his story:

"Once in the empty street he looked at the darkening sky and saw the pale ark of a young moon.

His thoughts were distant. It was a harsh moment for him; it was a harsh moment for Russia.

Suddenly out of the dusk appeared before him a woman dressed as a peasant, wearing a peasant's winter felt boots, along dark caftan, almost like a monk's robe, and a warm white shawl over her head. Balmont could not tell whether she was beautiful or not but he knew he could not take his eyes from her face and that she was young.

The woman spoke and Balmont halted.

"Uncle", she said, "where is my home?"

She spoke in the soft voice of a child who turns to an adult in absolute confidence that her question will be answered.

A strange feeling overcame Balmont and he started to go ahead but the woman came abreast and touched his right hand:

"Uncle, where is my home?"

"I don't know", Balmont said, his heart feeling full of despair.

"You do know", she said, her voice like a trusting girl's.

"You know, uncle, that it's right nearby. Show me where my house is".

The woman's face seemed strange and her question was strange but it did not seem strange to Balmont. They walked past a row of houses. No one appeared. Again the woman asked:"Where is my house? Where is my house?"

"I can't help you", Balmont said with falling heart. "I just don't know".

"Oh", said the woman, "you should be ashamed, uncle".

Balmont felt a blush sweep over his face.

"It's not", she said," where you are going".

Balmont's head whirled and his heart beat fast. Some monstrous desire arose in him - was it monstrous or holy? He could not be certain. All he knew was that he wanted to take this woman into a snow-filled courtyard, sit with her under the portico and embrace her passionately. To oblivion.

At that moment a man emerged from a gate. It was too dark to see his face. The woman ran to the man, spoke to him quickly, and in a moment they had vanished into the darkness of the courtyard, he with his arm over her shoulder.

For a moment Balmont halted, waiting for what he did not know. All was quiet. Then he went to the Cafe of Poets where Marina Tsvetayeva sat. She glanced at Balmont's shaken face and cried:

"Brother! What's happened?"

He told her of his brief encounter. A solemn look came over Marina's face and it seemed to Balmont that her eyes saw something deep within herself. She took Balmont's hand in hers.

"You should have brought her with you", she said, "You should have. She was Russia."

Balmont, a revolutionary who broke with the Bolsheviks, left Russia in 1922 and died impoverished and insane in France in

1943. Tsvetayeva left Russia in 1922, returned in 1939 and committed suicide in 1941, living in neglect, poverty and oppression in her homeland.

Not only the destinies of Russia preoccupied the young students' minds, by the fifth year all of them got troubled about their private own fortunes. One after another was getting married; even divorces happened to be frequent. Val was not an exclusion from that rule.

Her first love with a man to whom she got married was Michael Abramovich Agranovich, a second son of a Jewish family from town Pochep in the Bryansk region.

Everything were good if they would have had a place to live, both students having nothing in their pockets but love, strained to finishing their education. The newly weds soon said "farewell" to each other. He changed his partner for a new one in Kiev, she was a woman with a flat.

Val was alone again. Her ideal dreams about a good Jewish husband were broken against the severe reality.

She thought for a long-long time about all that had happened and came to the conclusion, she had made a bad mistake. Naturally the Jews have the exclusivity complex, germane to numerically small peoples, about what Shalom Aleihem did say in his novel "Tevye-Milkman" (here he is more famous for the musical "Fiddler on the Roof").

The Jews, like the Russians, gravitate naturally into communes. Because of historical pressures, the community feeling is very strong. Despite all the fears and hostility lavished on it, the word "Communism" derives from that simple source.

Collective farms may be a bad phrase in some places, whereas kibbutz captures all the glamour of a struggle against an ungrateful soil, but basically the two concepts are identical, The Jews, for so long the tragic victims of circumstances, are now for the first time in a position of authority over others. Perhaps with their natural sensitivity, at least some of them may realize that their experiences of Left Bank in sector Gaza are not much more praise worthy than the ugly manners of the Tsar in a period of far less general enlightenment. The existence of second-class citizens, be they Jews,

Arabs, Africans, Indians, Russian Dukobortsi, is always a disgrace, and worthy of unqualified condemnation.

After Khrushchev's Thaw, there appeared the first fighters for human rights in the Soviet Union.

If at those times there were demonstrations in the United States and elsewhere in support of Soviet Jewry, it was largely because of the creation of the State of Israel, and the reluctance of the Soviet government to allow an exodus in the direction of a National Home to the creation of which it was among the first to subscribe. This was a subject which was delicate, and which therefore had to be discussed objectively and unemotionally.

It was undeniable that among the gifts displayed by Jews were not only those of introspective, balanced wisdom, but also those of extremism and imbalance. Prophets invariably had and have a bit of both. Jews have been both stubborn in the insistence of their right to worship and, at times, violent in their abrogation of all mysticism. They had brought forth both Jesus Christ and Karl Marx and have, in most cases, indulged in the final luxury of following neither, while waiting for a third.

In Val's attempts of understanding the Jewish religion and their behavior she addressed one day to her mother-in-law,

"Dear Rahil, how did you instruct your son to grow up? To appreciate the family's values?"

"Oh, well", she answered. "But Michael is quite different from his elder brother; they are like the moon and the sun. Michael knows the success among women, spending a lot of money on them. He's a tough nut".

"It's a pity, dear Rahil. The first love is unforgettable for ever. But I'm going to divorce him. The only memory of him was left: my diploma is having been issued on his last name".

Val's pedagogical experience as a graduated teacher was kept on at the same school Number Four she left five years ago.

The teachers' staff greeted a younger collegue heartily; assigning her as a grade five as a counsellor, and teaching English and German languages - at High School.

In the evenings she was ordered to attend the Marxism-Leninism University, the esthetic faculty expanding her knowledge

135

in arts, movies, and culture.

Each spring for three years Val's pupils and her went to the woods in their spare time, visited cinema-and-theatre houses together, sharing their opinions after the shows, Val was very close to the children and they paid her back.

On one of the pioneer class meetings on the twenty third of February, a holyday of the Red Soviet Army and Navy, one pupil's parent was invited to tell students about the Second World War.

"When you're in a war", the old vet began, "your intense concern is your own misery and deep terror. In the immediacy of terror you have to learn to cope with it".

"Dear Comrade Colonel, would you like to tell us one episode of your military biography", asked the teacher Valentina Nickolaevna.

"Sure. For a year before final spring of the Second World War, I flew Pe-2 bombers. The Pe-2 was not a user-friendly aircraft. Rumor had it that more people were killed training in the Pe-2 than in combat.

Too many nights during that year I lay awake worrying that I might make a mistake at the controls and kill not only myself but the other two guys in the plane. My crew in the plane - a copilot, and bombardier/ navigator and a gunner - were all youngsters.

After my first bomb run, over a target in Germany, I started to shake and gave the controls to my copilot. A few seconds later, I was all right and took the controls back. Completing that mission taught me that no matter how scared I am I can handle anything while the crisis is right there, breathing on me. Afterwards I may be glown sky-high but that's afterwards. Combat gives you a perspective, feeling for priorities", continued the old vet, gazing at the sparkling eyes with warmth and curiosity.

"Combat gave you a sense of what not to choke up on. It gave the rationale of all agony. If you can live through the minute or hour, day or week - maybe the next one will be better.

Combat gives you antennae to find the funny side in the grim reality.

That's essential for survival - awareness of the ludicrous gives your beat buoyancy in any of life's stormy crossings.

I had a comparatively easy time in the Second World War.

I did not go through any of the private hells of infantry-men or men on ships. But I saw and felt enough to empathize with those men. And I learned one profound lesson. Don't panic. What I got out of the Second World War - and I am grateful for it - was a crash course in growing up.

Over a lifetime I might have learned what I learned in that violent war. But what I and others got in a short span twenty years ago was undying appreciation for every day, ongoing every day, ongoing and the resilience of the human spirit".

The human moral spirit of the class was on the top, excluding a pretty brunette girl, Valentina Stepannikova by name.

As a matter of fact, that pupil was not handicapped but depraved by her own mother who brought up her daughter alone, without a husband, daily changing the drinking sexual partners, she taught her junior a bad example of how to behave and live without honour, stealing money from her lovers.

The new pupil in the class, she did not get interested in school, missed lessons, did not want to learn home tasks, and obviously was inclined in quite different hobbies: guys and alcohol drinks, and money.

None of teachers' elite wished to deal with her. So she appeared in the young teacher's class.

"First", thought Val, "I need to separate this girl from her mother and settle her in my family's flat", and spoke about her intention aloud in the teachers' room.

"Do you have your father at home? Is he young? It will be him whom she will try to seduce first. Secondly, you have a brother, don't you?" put the ironical questions the French teacher Helen Lazarevna Borovskikh.

"Yes, I have a brother", answered the former in a dreadful mood, apparently guessing about the hints of the latter.

The things did not stay still for long, as Val soon found out, two days had passed, and the class leader comrade Filina was summoned to the court as a witness in the case of Valentina Stepannikova, 14 years old, accused for the depravity of another guy, 16, who were caught by the police in the school attic, to be

137

subpoenaed and sent out of town to the labour camps for severe regime crimes..

From there the girl wrote letters to her suffering teacher:

"Dear Valentina Nickolaevna,
I am doing well, making friends with the other girls and boys. I was a fool when I did not understand your great desire to making me study lessons and fulfilling my home tasks. For the one year and a half period that you were my class leader I realized that there were and there are true teachers in the world who were wishing me good and happiness. When I am free out of this camp I will drop in to you and tell you everything about my present life.
I love you very much and wish you to be healthy and energetic as you are nowadays.

With sincere love
Your pupil forever
Valentina Stepannikova".

She kept her promise. After a two-years-sentence at a labour camp she visited her teacher, introducing her husband, told about their plans to build up a new family, having a baby in the future. Val was glad for her. The young girl really seemed to be happy with her new mate. Happy are the ones you choose and love beyond approach.

The young people's friendship was indeed a precious gift, appreciated by Val and she was making more friends among the school children.

They in their turn behaved themselves not always in a correct way. One of the parents told a story about her daughter Svetlana Komkova, who was an excellent pupil with top marks and a brilliant memory, this she was praised for.

A group of girls was waiting for Svetlana in the ladies' room. The biggest one of the crowd gestured as though she had something important to say. Svetlana stopped.

"What are you, stupid!" the big one cried, spitting the words into Svetlana's face.

"Don't you know how stupid you are, damned bloody parvenu?! " an ugly girl continued, using a lot of curse words to characterize Svetlana's mind, and her heritage. Svetlana was shocked and could not understand anything.

They wanted revenge? For what? For her lucky top marks in all subjects?

She could not pronounce a word, she was afraid; the other girls joined the first, without yelling, started kicking Svetlana, beating her with fists, on the legs, and knees; they kept silence, being scared somebody could hear them.

The bell rang, everybody ran up to the classroom. The normal school life was on as if nothing had happened.

Out of fear Svetlana did not complain of being threatened. Her rude school "pals" were taking over. The cruelty of the society was evident more and more among children.

Unfortunately, Val was informed of this incident some months later, it was hidden from her for the same reason: fear. There was something to think about.

Rude, nasty people!

You run into them more and more often, in more and more places.

Recently Val watched the ugly scene in the food store. A woman went on her shopping expedition after breaking her ankle. There she was balanced on crutches, looking through a rack of dresses. She felt some pressure, then a push. Another woman at the same rack was trying to nudge her out of the way.

"Um", the former said, "I think there's room enough for both of us here".

The latter glared at her and said: "Get out of my way unless you want your other leg broken".

The former reported the incident to the store manager, pointing out that the store was about to lose a good customer on account of this bully. The manager said there was nothing she could do - not unless there was actual physical contact and a store employee witnessed it. "Rude people like that are just the type to sue", she told her.

Rude people seize all the power, normal, courteous people get none. This is what Val concluded as she tried to think of a way to combat the bullies.

She in company with her father at home imagined Laws against Rudeness. They considered mandatory tranquilizer prescriptions for rude people. They envisioned support groups for the victims of the rudeness, one of these Val supposed could happen in the school teachers' room.

Val substituted the English lessons of senior grades of the teacher Margareth Pavlovna Bashkatova as she was hospitalized for a semester.

After returning to her teaching duties, Margareth Pavlovna met her colleague Val in the recreation room and in presence of a great many teachers started an argument with her.

"You are a stupid, silly teacher! What have you done to my students? You have spoilt all discipline in my classes. None of my pupils is subordinating to me; nobody wants me as a teacher. Everybody wants you, stupid scoundrel", continued angry Margareth Pavlovna.

Val was shocked. She did not expect something of that kind and left the room. Val was about to brake into tears. She did not feel she had done anything wrong. She did not feel guilty.

However her only "fault" was to be a young teacher and preferred by school children, her "fault" was to be nice to the kids whom she loved with her great open heart. Comrade Bashkatova's rudeness was the result of professional jealousy, and attack committed because of the weakness and disabilities of her pedagogical career.

In fact, according to Val some students who score high on traditional measures of intelligence such as IQ tests become bored in school and won't put in any effort. They can wind up developing bad habits and fail to live up to their potential.

Strange as it seemed but some high-achieving students actually did fewer hours of homework than their lower-scoring classmates. The kids at the top of the class got their high points by mastering some basic techniques that others could readily learn if they wished to.

Here, according to Valentina Filina and the students themselves are some secrets of straight-A students:

1. **Set priorities**. Top students break no intrusions on study time. Once the books are open, TV shows are unwatched, phone calls go unanswered, snacks ignored. Study is business, business comes before recreation.

2. **Study anywhere and everywhere.** Do a little but every day at any time of personal preference. That keeps you on top of the subject and makes it easier in the long run.

3. **Get organized**. A special study or even a backpack or a drawer keeps essential supplies together and cuts down on time-wasting searches.

4. **Learn how to read.** The secret of reading well is to be an active reader - one who continually asks questions that lead to a full understanding of the author's message.

5. **Schedule your time.**

6. **Listen in class - and take good notes.**

7. **Clean up your act.** Neat papers make a better impression.

8. **Speak up.** It's a matter of showing intellectual curiosity.

9. **Helping others to help yourself.** Tutoring people is a means of review for a student.

10. **Test yourself.** Anticipating the questions that a teacher might ask, make sure you know the answers.

11. **Do more than you're asked.**

12. **Use what you learn in class when you leave.**

These and many other various clues were debated at Val's lessons together with her students.

"All education", used to say Val to her pupils," is self-education. A teacher is only a guide, to point out the way, and no school, no matter how excellent, can give you an education. What you receive, is like the outlines in a child's coloring book. You must fill in the colours yourself. I hope in these classes to give you an idea how you can travel in a big world of knowledge".

Two of her brilliant students entered the Moscow State University, eleven - entered different colleges, twenty five became students of High and Secondary Technical Schools according to statistics of 1966.

For almost all the students, the contribution of their parents was crucial. From childhood, the parents set high standards for their children and held them to those standards. They as well as the nation's Propaganda stressed the importance of education and encouraged their sons and daughters in their studies, but did not do the work for them.

In short, the parents impressed the lessons of responsibility on their children, and the children delivered.

Some teenagers went to work, choosing the way of combining the further education with a part-time job at the plant.

Val decided to get a new job as an interpreter at the plant, wanting to try something new; she explained how her skills, personality and goals were more suitable to the new career and that she wished to add something to her experience that would help her achieve a longer-term goal.

To quit her beloved children was not an easy solution; very often in the nights she awoke to horrible dreams and at times, dreams of her schoolchildren, the happy memories would remain forever.

They also missed her immensely. Later one of her pupils' mother told a story of how Val one day came by the school, a pupil saw her outside the window and shouted during the lesson aloud, "Look! Valentina Nickolaevna is passing!" Everyone jumped off their seats, rushing to the windows, crying something to attract Val's attention.

Everything was in vain. Their beloved teacher did not hear their voices, hurrying up to another destination.

Her technical translator (TT) career got started pretty well. Ultimately she would like to be a TT but she knew she's had more to learn first. The next logical step was to investigate the plant production to do a better translation from English, German, and French. That is why she thought she would be ready for that only in one-two years.

The greatest accomplishment of those years was a triumphal project of writing copies and supervising photographies and proofreading the layouts with the emphasis on the foreign countries' experience.

The policy of the "iron curtain" was gradually disappearing, in stead of it appeared that the respect now for new foreign technologies, including the productions of three enterprises Val happened to work: producing the tubes for old-fashioned TV-sets to be kept as a repair station; semiconductor and intergrated circuits technology; and the reflectometer and oscilloscope production.

Upon finishing the half-year-technical courses for her self-education, Val connected her main job as a translator to the additional one as a teacher of foreign languages for persons going abroad on business trips, who badly needed the knowledge of foreign languages.

Her twenty-five-years' experience of such a type of job allowed her to enrich herself with the professional translator-interpreter skills and to develop her own teaching course consisting of one hundred twenty hours' English lessons for Russian people and the same one - for foreigners.

Val always concentrated on her job and the results, and she was flexible enough to work with almost any boss she met. She was really happy with any job, but at home the events were changing every year.

Val's brother and half-sister got married, following them she assumed she could try to remarry and it was high time to bear a baby, she thought to herself.

Val's new acquaintance's name was Victor or Vikentij Illarionovich Kostin, a journalist by profession, 28, the same age as Val, tall, a good-looking man, who was very fond of his work.

They met in his office of the regional newspaper "Bryansk Worker" when she brought her next article to be published.

"Through my images", said then Kostin to Val, "I like to comment on the social problems of the day. I like to do documents in almost every aspect of life from politics to sports to the production of essays".

"Why do you usually speak in the first person 'I'? Do you love yourself best of all in the world?" noticed Val ironically.

"Oh, no, no. It's a wrong impression in the first sight. That will go away soon".

"Kostin has a tremendous feeling for Russia and its people", as his collegues were characterizing his job.

The journalistic approach to life was not surprising, considering Kostin's family background. Both his parents were school teachers, the only literate persons there at those times. Father did not return from the Second World War, mother had been waiting for him all her 54-years-old life as Penelope - for her Odyssey. With the only difference, Penelope had met her husband, but Kostin's mother had not, she died from cancer.

Current events fed the young Kostin's imagination. As a boy he would run to the neighbours' houses where widows lived to help in house keeping. They paid a little to the teenager just as an adult and he would receive a glass of moonshine ("samogon" in Russian), which filled him with wonder and pride. It was so gradual that day by day the young masculine body was poisoned by alcohol which soon became an addiction.

Kostin's nature was also to sing serenades in front of his new flame Valentina. He stormed her like an inaccessible fortress with daily telephone calls and visits.

Several months later, the "fortress" of Val surrendered, getting married in April, 1968.

By that time her two cousins baby-girls were born, on the 16th of December, 1968, - Marina, six days earlier - Larissa in Kiev, and on the twelfth of February, 1969, Val bore her daughter, Larissa by name.

The coincidence of the two Larissa's names was occasional. Val chose that one in the memory of Kostin's mother who dreamt of a daughter, saving such a name for her. Somehow we ought to remember our ancestors, perhaps, in names passed from generation to generation.

By that moment there could be related Val's joining the membership of the Communist Party of the Soviet Union, it had been done automatically after leaving the Komsomol at age of 28.

The country's Soviet bureaucracy came to its full blossom, the evidence of its inefficiency was possible to find by the groups of grandmothers mending a main road, doing a job which would more than satisfy ambitions of the most ardent women's fibers, while a few kilometers away, young men of near military age were idly spearing leaves enjoying the autumn beautiful weather. The era of double standards went on developing, which it was promised to tell later about.

Kostin was a vivid example of personification of this new order. Having joined the Communist Party of the Soviet Union, he received a better job than others had: a chief of the department, he had now the possibility of attending the closed buffets with fine food products provided for better price, on the ground floor was for average members and on the third floor - for superiors. He had an opportunity of freely visiting the theatres and concert halls while other people paid; in the summer time he attended better sanatoriums, which were houses of rest while other people had to pay a great amount of money or they had no access there, simply it was forbidden to go there. Of Kostin's type people had better hospitals, and drugstores, too. The privileges for that sort of people were not earned or deserved, they got them because of their pretty closeness to the authorities whom they served with faith and obedience.

They assisted with the flexible character of a person and his fondness for drinking vodka.

Even in those days was an expression "drink in a Central Committee way" meant drinking is allowable but in a cleverer manner: do not let some of the average people notice you; it was a hypocritical and a cunning way. Kostin did it with great success. His drinking behavior was kept out of sight, no one saw him, except his wife.

"Why are you drinking so much, Victor?" Val used to ask him.

"It's not your business. I drink, I drank and I will drink", he declared arrogantly.

"But you will ruin your health, won't you? Look at yourself in the mirror", she tried to persuade him again and again.

"Maybe you will tell me not to breathe, won't you?" he mumbled staggering a bit.

"For you, to breathe means to drink, doesn't it?" Val said.

"Nonsense. Fiddlesticks", he replied.

The wife stopped listening to her drunken husband's slurred speech.

To describe Kostin's behavior at home is enough to remember the popular American show of Sally Raphael, a lady from Costa

Rica, under the title "Men are behaving badly".

From the first day on, Val saw she was hectored by her bullying husband, the marriage was unhappy and he could not care less.

All her attention was concentrated on raising a child, the thought of which comforted the young mother who terribly needed financial help, moral and physical support.

As helpless as appeared Val's situation, she maintained outwardly as it was always expected and required strict decorum from Val as an example which was a facade that hid the reality of her private hell. At that period of time she herself happened to be feeble on her own, her mother Maria got busy with her other grandchildren, born at the same time, including the permanent care of her eldest disabled daughter Emma.

That is why Val went to work; early in the morning she had to bring her baby daily to Maria. In the evening after work Val had to take her child back home, to cook, take care of her husband, housekeeping, do laundries by hand et cetera, et cetera, et cetera.

It was the hardest time of Val's life.

How did she survive? Don't know.

How did her country survive? Don't know.

She was saved by her spirit in which she believed, she had discovered the secret of Russia. Following the Russian poet Andrey Bely in his novel 'The Silver Dove' who wrote:

"The Russian earth knows the secret. So does the Russian forest. The Russian soul is new-born; the Russian word is strong as pitch. If you are Russian there is your soul a 'red'* secret - how to live in the fields, keeping to yourself that one holy word, which no one knows except those who have received it and received it in silence."

'In the West there are many books; in Russia there are many unspoken words", added Val and unspoken fortunes as was herself.

In 1976 her divorce had taken place, again she was single, nobody was waiting for her at home, only her seven-year-old daughter to be taken care of. Oh, loneliness!

Val was sitting alone at the airport watching people in the final

---

* 'red' means 'beautiful'.

moments before their loved ones arrived or departed. They were pacing, nervous, looking at one another, touching and not touching. The emotion was intense.

A woman, speaking fast, was running in circles trying to gather family members together for a good-bye. Her voice was high-pitched. When the final moment came before boarding, she wrapped her arms around her son, giving him a powerful embrace that should protect him until he returned.

A grandmother and a grandson stood at the rail where Val was waiting; the people who were supposed to pick them up were late. Two ladies, unrelated to them, looked up and down the corridor as if scanning an open sea. A mother held a baby as she kissed her husband. Tears dampened her cheeks. The moment was charged. At gate 5 the arrivals were just coming in. "I see him. There he is." Just as poignant the arrivals fold into the mixture of people as if they had been the missing ingredients. There were tears and smiles, pure delight ringing in the laughter of seeing someone who had been gone.

Val sat, glancing at her book, waiting for her turn to leave, alone, because she wanted to be alone.

The book she was reading was not as interesting as the people leaving and coming, coming and leaving. A little boy about five was meeting his grandfather for the first time. He looked up and up at the face of a man, who was not that tall, except to a child. Joy shone down and up, and Val was wondering how one would capture that moment in words or on film. When her flight was finally called, she gathered her books and things. Since there was no one to see her off, she did not look back to see where she had come from. Instead she thought of her business friend Lucie in Moscow wondering if she had left yet at the other end.

Life needed to be this important all the time, Val wished all the people who went on a journey or a business trip, as Val herself, could come back to find someone waiting for them. She also wished they could leave with someone to see them off.

At Bykovo Airport Val was met by Lucie Novichkova, born in Moscow and very proud of her beautiful city.

She was behind the wheel of her car and proposed to drive

through the centre of the Red Square. Val agreed.

As a first-class-guide Lucie began telling:

"In front of you, Valentina, there is the Kremlin, the ancient fortress surrounded with a tall wall with guard towers. To the left is Vasilij Insane Cathedral, a monument of the Russian architecture of the sixteenth century".

Val asked, "Sorry, Lucie, what is our farthest plan?"

Lucie,"From here we'll ride along the quiet streets of Zamoskvorechya and its wide prospect to the Lenin (Vorobyev) hills. In 1953 there was being erected a huge building for the Moscow State University. From the balcony of the twenty-fourth floor there is the wonderful panoramic view of Moscow."

Val, "Oh, Christ, where is such exact information from, Lucie? Didn't you yourself enjoy it since you've been a student?"

Lucie, "No, I didn't. Let's go out and we'll see for ourselves."

Val, "Sure. Explain to me, please, dear friend, what is around us."

Lucie, "At the bottom, just in front of us, is Luzniki, the Central Stadium with one hundred thousand people capacity, the Palace of Sports, and a swimming-pool, our sports grounds.

A little to the right of the Stadium you can see a twospans-bridge over the Moscow-river for passers-by, traffic-and-underground vehicles. Behind the bridge along the embankment is a very green strip of the Park of Culture and Rest named after Gorky. To the right from the University is the headquarters of the high house-buildings which are visible. This is a new district of Moscow in the South-West where I live."

Val, "Lucie, do you have a comfortable flat?"

Lucie, "Oh, yes. After our seminar I'll invite you to visit my family".

Val, "Thank you very much. Let's drive along the Moscow-river embankment to the hotel "Ukraine"."

Lucie, "Sure. Look! Here is the Garden Ring; we'll pass the sky-scraper house building in the Rebellion Square, by the Chekhov's House-Museum, by the Tchaikovsky's Concert Hall. In the Mayakovsky Square we turn to the right, to the centre of the city past the Pushkin's Monument, the Monument of the founder of

Moscow-city, prince Jury Dolgoruky. We turn to the left and get out of the car. In front of us here is the Bolshoy Theatre, next to it -Maly Theatre and Central Children's Theatre".

Val, "Holy cow! How many theatres in Moscow! Have you visited all of them, dear friend? "

Lucie, "Of course, not. I have my favourite one. It's the Theatre of Satire. "

Val, "Thanks a lot for this nice walk through Moscow. But as it is said "time to work and time to play" - "Revenue a `la moutons", let's go to the seminar of technical translators".

Val participated in these and similar seminars in Moscow and other cities and towns of the Soviet Union and abroad for her whole life as a chairman of the Bryansk regional organization of technical translators working on the public grounds volunteerly.

The goal of such seminars and conferences was to keep the high scientific level of the technical translations, to exchange the latest news in the science as well as in practice of translation.

Some hours later Lucie took Val to her new flat where her twenty-one-year-old son Valery had been who shortly missed the classes of the Plekhanov University because of a skin abscess in the region of his armpit; it lasted a six-months-period before it healed.

All the time it was wet in his left armpit. Doctors had done their best, lanced, and treated with antibiotics. But the red swollen "spot" continued to be wet, Valery could not wear his shirts, nothing had helped him. His Mommy Lucie told Val this story with the tears in her eyes. Val sympathized with them both terribly, put her questions:

"Did you squeeze the sties?"

"No, we did not", answered Lucie." Why?"

"Did you soak them?" Val asked again.

"No, we did not", Valery responded.

"Have you got herbs at home and a Medical Encyclopedia?" asked Val.

"Yes, we have. Here they are," replied Lucie.

Both women pulled their noses into the thick scientific books, digging out the proper recipe.

Val boiled the poultice and then, all of a sudden, the crazy idea

149

came to Lucie's head and she said:

"Val dear! I beg you on bending knees, to do something as best as you can. I cannot stand any more my son's sufferings. I recollected when he was a six-month-baby, something terrible had happened to him. All the nights and days he, poor little thing, screamed from the pain. The doctors also could not do anything to him. They did not understand the reason. I was in despair. Then some woman gave me a piece of advice: to visit one village woman who could heal diseases in her own old - fashioned way with the words. I took my baby to her and two days later everything had gone.

I beg you, Val, you are a strange woman to him, do something to him, I am going out, leaving you alone, face to face with him". And she left.

She even did not ask Val if she could do it or not. She just left.

Val took the warm poultice of herbs and put it on a cotton pad, soaked all sties in the armpit of Valery so that they will rupture through the surface of the skin rather than spread inward. Then she got a look at him and, without talking, starting to massage around this spot, repeating all the time the words heard from her mother Maria since childhood when the latter wanted to help recovering the wounded fingers or toes of her kids:

"The little bones, the little joints, set into your proper places", and spitting to the sides all the time after those words, praying to the God.

Some minutes later Lucie entered the room, and all the three began drinking tea without either discussing or mentioning the event.

Soon Val was off to Bryansk.

After some while there came a letter from Moscow where Lucie wrote to her:

"Dear Val,
you even don't realize what gift you are possessing! As soon as you left, the wet abscess became drier and drier day by day and at long last disappeared.
More important was to realize that those of us who once believed that

150

*it couldn't happen to us are now aware of something mysterious in us
because it is happening to some of us all the time. Or as Queen
Victoria once put it, we are not immune.*

*My husband is kidding me why I did not write the words you had
used while you treated our son Valery who also is giving you love and
thanks for all. Looking forward to meet you again.*

Best regards from all my family.

*Sincerely
Yours Lucie"*

So Val revealed that she could do something different from her
professional skills: she possessed the inner intuition to find out
from the first sight that Lucie's son was particularly friendly with
the mother helping her around the house and yard with chores
such as carrying her groceries, and other odd jobs. It became clear
to Val that Lucie's son was a sensitive person. In that case, Val had
been in the right place at the right time and got caught in Lucie's
drive to put a thorny case to be solved. Also like Lucie, Val was odd
enough to appear to be a medicine woman - and hapless enough
to be unable to defend herself against the cruel powerful system
which was called "a society" of human beings.

She never confessed to anyone about her intuition in fear of
being mocked at.

The Communist fellows, however, gave her another public load to
be a lecturers' group leader with the obligatory participation on
every meeting and debate, conference or symposium.

All these public activities were not charged, but distract her
mind from raising a child which required more and more attention for her development. Val decided to finish the course for the
tourist guide so she could travel in her spare time with her daughter to different parts of the country.

On the one hand, it was not easy to take a group of thirty
tourists and supply them with the adequate rest, on the other
hand, it was the only legal possibility to involve her daughter with
traveling and show her the world.

So nineteen journeys were committed by Val at homeland.
While her daughter   growing up, she stopped accompanying

Mommy on her tourist roads. Those were really pretty various trips: Moscow, Leningrad, Kiev, Chernigov, Riga, Tallinn, Vilnius, Odessa, Simferopol, Yalta, Sochi, Krym, Zakaucasea, Batumi, Makhindgauri, Minsk, Brest, Novy Afon and the towns of the Golden Ring of Russia.

Later Val began traveling abroad. There was a special Communist Party Committee giving the permission to go abroad, instructing how to behave, forbidding contact with foreigners. In every group a KGB representative was included, dressed in a civilian suit whose duty was to watch everybody and then report on them to their bosses.

Everyone in the tourist group, heading for Czechoslovakia knew that somebody of KGB was among them, but nobody knew exactly who it was. That is why the fear settled in the people's souls and that poisoned the rest.

It was in 1979, Val recollected that the attitude to the Soviet people was, softly speaking, not very positive in foreign countries such as in socialist Czechoslovakia. Why? It was not understandable. Because the Soviet Propaganda cried in all the corners that the Soviet State is the most democratic, fairest and best in the world that every country who wanted to be friendly and had a good relationship with the USSR must be thankful for it. In reality, the tourists saw opposite, for instance, in Czechoslovakia. If they spoke Russian, none of the shop assistants was going to serve them. The Soviet people understood nothing.

If Val spoke in German, saleswomen smiling with cordiality were ready to serve her.

"Prepare a list of things you need", Valentina said to her fellows, "Point out the sizes and colours and step aside, and wait for me around the corner".

She came into the shop and speaking German, complaining that she had got a great family who asked her to buy a listed amount of goods.

The same frequented in other countries of the socialist camp, including Latvia, Estonia, Lithuania.

Nobody grasped what was happening. The foreign policy was hidden thoroughly, even for lecturers in foreign affairs; the events were given in a revised form, instead of raw, fresh materials, there was a boiled porridge of facts. It is not Val's intention to white-wash or to condemn, but merely to strike a balance which she believed essential.

The Russians at that time entered Afghanistan for reasons which seemed suspicious to all. Naked aggression was sufficient, and in need of punishment. But what about America in the Vietnam War and the Dominique Republic?

Both wars were unnecessary and hideous. To the defenseless people in an Afghan valley or a Vietnamese forest, or even in Beirut, the origin of the bombs which rained on them were of as little concern as the moral rectitude of the men releasing them. Death in war is a crime whatever the moral posture of its perpetuators.

It is a regrettable fact of life that the CIA and the KGB seem to be necessary and ordinary people like Val had even been touched by them, too.

Once she stood in a crowd of people, speaking with two African fellows. Val was speaking as an interpreter. The conversation lasted for one hour and a half in the Bryansk street. After it was finished, two guys in civil suits came up to her and said:

"Would you like to follow us, please?"

"Yes, sirs." she answered.

They went into the KGB office.

"Would you, please, write down on paper everything you spoke about to the foreigners", they ordered.
She did it.

Next time when she was working with some guys from Eastern Germany at one of the plants, she also was ordered to report daily on the workers from the German Democratic Republic during a three-months' period of their cooperative work.

It really was unpleasant. All of these people were not enemies but were still suspects.

There remained in those times the problems of the shortage of food products, the many goods of necessity for home - there existed the long-waiting lines for them every day. If someone does not show up, she or he will be excluded from the line automatically.

153

Every now and then the shopping trips started to big cities Moscow and Leningrad which were supplied with everything easier than provincial towns and villages. On arrival on the local trains one could see basically women overloaded with meat, sausage, cheese bags of around twenty five kilograms being pulled along the platforms to the expecting taxis. They were helped by nobody, having no husbands at all or just unreliable in their household.

Having worked at two or three additional places, Val managed to live as good as if not better than other people. She was able to buy nice clothes and even travel abroad. Twice she had been to Germany, twice to Italy, once to Suomi.

What a beautiful country is Italy!

Among the Italian landscapes that generate the most amazing Sassy forms, in effect, a city endowed with the "attraction of the incredible". In order to get a panoramic view, Val made her way to a natural vantage point overlooking a deep gorge. On the opposite side of this ravine, in front of the group of Russian tourists, was the city of Matera, in southern Italy, just above the heel of Italy's "boot". In the brilliant summer light, they saw houses clinging to the rock; they seemed to have grown one on top of the other. As the narrow roads between them wended their way down to the bottom of the gorge, they formed a tangled knot somewhat resembling the steps of an immense amphitheatre. In the many holes in the rock face they saw were, or had been dwellings. In short, they were the Sassy - cave houses wrought out of rock!

Many of the dwellings were below street level. Why? Because the entrance and some of the cave houses themselves were dug on a slight slope to exploit the sun's rays. In winter, when the sun reaches its lowest point on the horizon, its rays could enter the house, illuminating and warming it; in summer the sun's rays got no farther than the entrance, and the inside stayed cool and humid. On the back wall of the cave they were visiting, they saw a sculptured niche with several "shelves". It was a sun-dial, designed to indicate the sun's movement throughout the year. When they came back, the tourists had a strange sensation. The coolness of the cave had all too soon made them forget the summer heat outside!

In the early spring 1985 Valentina had faced many ordeals of her life, including the sudden deaths of her both parents. Death was always unexpected and sudden. On that date, 31-st of March, Val visited her parents' flat; Dad laid in his own bed, breathing coming and going at unfamiliar intervals. Now and then his eyes fluttered open, seeing no one. Her mother was there next to him, laying in her own bed, helpless and disabled as well, her sister, brother and a visiting doctor who said, "Don't touch him any more, he is dying".

A sheet strung like a shower curtain, separated them from this man, who was their close loved one and now he was terminal ill. Emma turned to Val with tears in her eyes, "I've never seen anyone die!"

Their Dad was not always easy with his family members except his wife Maria. He used to smoke very much, but when he quit smoking after the doctors gave him a warning he became more irritating at home.

Val stayed by Dad's bed for many hours. At last she decided to go home to her daughter as she needed taking care of. The daughter was already sleeping. Val wanted to do something and could not. She tried to concentrate her attention on a TV-program that was a game show, but could not comprehend any word. She turned it off. She tried to wash up dishes and broke some plates into pieces. She took a book off the shelf it fell down on the floor. Everything was falling out of her hands in the very direct sense of the word.

"What's happening to me? What's wrong with me?" Valentina thought to herself.

Somebody knocked on the door. It was a neighbour woman who said:

"Be strong, dear. There was a call from your home. Your Daddy has died a minute ago. 'Valentina', it was the last word he ever said ", the kind lady informed her.

"Thanks a lot, sweetie. What time is it?" Val asked.

"It's about midnight."

Val dashed to the entrance hall. A sudden thought like lightning flashed into her mind, "That was the reason for my odd behaviour in my apartment. Daddy's dying spirit flew to me to say

155

the last farewell". All night through Val and her brother walked to and fro, meeting each other in the middle of the street where their Dad had lived.

More visitors came. They cried with tears in the hall. Sometime during the watch a stranger in a fur coat went into the room.

Mommy tried to rise to greet him arranging her face, asking Val to offer a place for him.

On the third day Nick had to be buried finally in the spring soft ground. Relatives, his old friend Kuzin and grandchildren fidgeted politely in their fashions.

In the evening all of them prayed in the church in secret directly to Jesus and St. Nicholas, "Let the ground be soft for our beloved Daddy Nickolay Alexeevich".

Val wore a black solemn shawl for forty days in the moan of her favourite father.

Nine months later, in the cold winter on the 13-th of December, her Mommy died, whose date of death Val had predicted with the utmost precise accuracy. Leaving her with Emma and Larissa, she herself hurried to work, warning, "Today, my dears, I beg you to stay with our Mommy for all day because I saw a vision that our Mommy is dying tonight".

They obeyed and did not leave her even for a second alone. Nearly at six o'clock p.m. Mom observed the people being present in the room, her last word was, "Where is Gennady?" He was at that time very far from her. And she died, a simple Russian soul Maria.

The alives continued to live and resist unbearable things they suffered. Val's working life consisted of three years' at one plant, eight years' at another, and fourteen years' at the third one. Roughly twenty five years of technical translating the documentation of any kind.

Val always worked next to average engineers, sharing with them their common fortune to be such poorly treated, without appropriate respect from the senior bosses. Thanks to the famous policy of the Communist Party of the Soviet Union Russian villages started to be empty, the peasants wanted to go to the big cities where more products and supplies were available which meant one could live in an easier way.

Briefly speaking, the village citizens were transformed into city slickers. But everybody wanted to eat; therefore anyone had to collect the agricultural harvest, this is why average engineers and workers as Val had to pick up the crops.

It got started from March or April and lasted up to the late fall when the frosts came down onto the ground. Having forgotten about their direct service duties, they dug up the vegetable roots, separating them from the rotten ones, to be prepared for planting them in May. In vegetable warehouses there stood such a poisonous smell that at times it was impossible to bear, many people fainted from the smell. These handy operations prolonged for long weeks. Next job - to plant potatoes, then hay-making, guys to mow the grass with the help of handy-seethes; the women to turn the grass over for drying with the following women grabbing it and putting it into stacks.

Field work resulted in picking the crops, including grain, corn, beets, cabbage, carrots.

Six to seven months every year had been lost for those laborers as engineers but they fulfilled the urgent tasks of Party and Government, saving the annual harvest 1965 till1990.

Among the people with authority surrounding Val there was one Michael Petrovich Grekov, vice-chief of the designers' department where Val worked during the last dozen of years.

He was a Communist Party active member, not a bad boss of the Technological Department where he used to select mostly pretty women to fill a job, according to their appearances rather than business qualities. Women loved him although he possessed the character of a Gigolo, having a handsome face, always ready to smile, wearing a worn dirty colour suit, always ready to please the females.

Telling the very scabrous, indecent anecdotes about lovers, hookers and people of such kind, he acquired popularity among the men as well, being their immediate boss.

Unfortunately, Val's boss was Grekov, such an ugly personality to her thinking. Grekov knew exactly all about every woman whether she was married or not, divorced or was going to divorce, to stick to her and pester her till she agreed to accommodate him. The independent nature of Val simply irritated him, to say more frankly, he hated her and in any possible way he wanted to put her down.

His depraved mind could not admit how it could happen: Val was single and had no lovers, even did not want any.
Grekov could not grasp that a beautiful woman might be a lady of great moral principles. "How could it be, indeed ?" he misunderstood her and misbehaved.

Once early in the summer morning when all were hurrying for work, he sat alone at the desk where there lay a register for everybody's signature when one's arrival and at what time to work. Grekov used to come to this place earlier, watching and checking in the people.

Val entered approaching the register slowly. She was dressed in white pants and a wide creme blouse of "kimono" style, she leaned over the table and signed.

While writing, this bloody Grekov reached her pants' zip, unfastening it. Val was shocked: she did not expect such "games" from her elderly boss.

" It is necessary to be done something to stop such a disgustful playboy", flashed in her mind. Val slapped his impertinent face and quickly retired.

"What will happen to me?" she thought impulsively. "He is a vicious person. Will he seek revenge? Will he report on me to the Communist Party Plant Committee, falsificating the facts. I must tell the truth myself without expecting him to take action". Val told everything to her co-workers first, secondly, to the Communist Secretary. The latter advised her to wait.

Grekov never complained. From that moment on, he never approached her. All the women working on the same floor congratulated Val on the great victory over the improper, cheeky personality on that day. Many women dreamt about that, but Val managed to succeed.

That was a typical example of sexual assault and sexual harassment committed to Val by one in authority.

There is no definition for sexual harassment in Russian law.

The Supreme Court of Canada, for instance, has stated that the work-place sexual harassment can be "broadly defined as unwelcome conduct of a sexual nature that was detrimentally to affect the work environment or leads to adverse job-related consequences for the victims of the harassment".

All the following kinds of Grekov's behaviour were considered to create a hostile work environment:

a) making graphic or degrading comments about Val's dress, appearance, or anatomy;

b) displaying sexually suggestive objects or pictures in the work-place;

c) telling dirty jokes or making indecent gestures;

d) using such familiar terms as "honey" , "dear" , or "baby";

e) asking questions about Val's sex life;

f) offering descriptions of his own sexual conduct experiences;

g) giving leering looks, whistles, or catcalls;

h) making unwelcome physical contact, such as patting, punching, touching and so on.

Sexual harassment was a much bigger problem in Val's work-place than many employers realized.

Val's employers were the state plant's authorities, one of them was Grekov, he had the same behaviour as the rest. So who are the judges?

Val did not fear reprisals and ridicule but who could really protect her ?

The Russian Court had no laws for sexual harassment, she considered, the plant bosses worrying about the aim: to fulfill the state plan at any price; the people's future and fortunes were not interesting to them.

Val was just one small screw of that great state mechanism. After fourteen years' stalking by Grekov, her patience blew up. She protected herself in her own way, the only way she could.

She learned to resist all life hardships alone without hoping of help from anyone. These to be the sources of Russian female character who could survive anywhere and everywhere, under any conditions.

Val's daughter entered the Leningrad State University, the journalism faculty, and Val rushed to move to the big city, changing her Bryansk three-bedroom apartment for a smaller one in Leningrad.

Val loved Leningrad, many times she had been there before, she knew its history well, its founder Peter the First was not a new name for her, it was a matter of fresh attitudes and fresh values.

She dreamt of new meetings with the "Copper Horseman", a monument to Peter the First, Russian Emperor and the Great Reformer (the author of the project was the French artist Falcone with his helper Kollo, the artist from France, in August, 7, 1782). Val was dreaming about her visit to the famous St.Peter and Paul's fortress beach. That was also one of the sights of Leningrad - the first building of the city of Peter the First. The St.Peter and Paul's fortress was designed by the Italian architect Dominicko Trezini in 1703 and then built up by Bartholomeo Rastrelli.

Val loved this city because of the three revolutions that had taken place there, the reason why the city had been named after Lenin. A pretty historical place!

Val was pleased to see, outside, the roofs of the nearby buildings. A moon, nearly full, rode high in the autumn sky.

It was remarkable what had been achieved in the city, there was no question. In the early twenties, after the ruins of the civil war, how uncertain the course of the revolution had seemed. The leadership had had even to tolerate, with the new economic policy, a measure of capitalism for a time. What Lenin had begun, Stalin then had to impose his will. And the transformation had been astounding; the entire countryside turned into state farms and collectives; the independent peasants of the Ukraine were deported en masse to Siberia. The first stupendous Five Year Plan for industry was completed. Russia was now, truly, a world industrial power. Yet, at what cost? How many had perished? Nobody was concerned.

Russia had risen like a great bear: that was it. There was nothing, it seemed, the mighty bear could not accomplish with its huge strength, if properly directed. Everyone knew about Stalin's passion for Peter the Great.

Val, too, had seen how were treated men as nothing more than creatures whose purpose was to serve the state. But even Peter the

160

Great never dreamed of legislation like Stalin's. To turn ordinary children into enemies of their own parents - everything in Val revolted against that. The new Children's Law was very clear, though. Any child who discovered in either counterrevolutionary tendencies of their own parents should report on him or her.

Val grinned at the time. She happened to be present, at a meeting of repressed people to be imprisoned for many-many years by Stalin.

Their unsophisticated stories were told with great frankness:

Story No.1:

"It had been foolish of me, of course", started telling a man with a round face, balding head and fair hair, "to have made the remarks I had, even in private. The previous year the regime had actually declared that a number of scientific disciplines were to be abolished: pedology, genetics, sociology, psychoanalysis. The reason: Stalin's great constitution had just been published which declared Russia to be a perfect, democratic state. How then could there be sciences which spoke of poor children, inherited differences, social problems, or troubled people?

Once at home, with some friends, I said, "You realize, don't you, that this constitution is a flagrant lie?"

That was all I said, but it was enough.

A knock on the door.

My wife in the kitchen, stared with frightened, uncomprehending eyes. "NKVD. What have we done?" My little daughter awakened and began crying. My son, looking pale as a ghost, behind them.

I was suspected as a collaborator with Trotsky. And so, at the age of thirty four, I was surprised to be sent to a GULAG.

I was home from the war. In all but name, it was over, the Great Patriotic War.

I had fought well, nearly lost my life several times; but along with every other soldier at the front, I had been sustained by two pieces of knowledge: I was fighting for the fatherland and Comrade Stalin was commanding everything. It was well known, by now, that there was almost nothing the great leader could not do. The war, thank God, was done with. It was time to stay at home and build a new, bright future. I tried to find a job by my profession - a teacher. I was refused. Then I took a job as a boiler-man just to feed my family.

Now I am rehabilitated. But I have no health, no forces; I am too old at the moment to celebrate the victory. Life has passed by."

Man after man rose up and told their stories No.2, No.3, No.4 etc. They looked similar and differed in ends. No one had a happy ending. There was no such thing in Soviet reality. On the corridor walls there hang the endless lists of names of the repressive people; they were in their hundreds of thousands.

For Val it was like a thunderstorm in the clear heavens. In Bryansk, a small Russian town, nobody spoke about that, nobody even guessed.

Here, in Leningrad, there was quite a different life; people were more educated, life was moving and very exciting. The lights of the big city were attracting, proper like lights attracting moths at night time.

Several things were striking about the Leningradien people. The first was that, at the end of the eighties, they were politicized as it was in 1917.

The second was that, unlike most Russian peasants who wore felt and baste shoes, these people wore stout leather boots, which proclaimed their wealth and position. The third was that each wore a huge hat: one man's shaped like a bulbous dome, another's high and rounded, with a large brim, a woman's Moskvash cap, children's funny puffy knitted balls - so that as they walked along the Nevsky Prospect-Avenue, they resembled nothing so much as a sea of multi-coloured paints streaming in opposite directions. Val came to one of the reading halls of the public scientific library named after Saltykov-Shchedrin and took the newly published book by Alexander Solzhenitsyn, "Archipelag GULAG". She had been reading it for a month, every free Sunday or Saturday until the library closed at days' end. Val knew from the Soviet history lessons that massive repressions had been committed earlier, in the Tsar time.

The great Russian writer Alexander Radishchev, the first of the Russian intelligents, wrote, "My soul was wounded by the suffering of humanity," in his book 'An Ode to Liberty' inspired by the American Revolution. This sentiment caused his arrest in 1790 by the great liberal, Catherine the Second. He was condemned to death. The lesson was clear.

Do not criticize the regime. Do not ask questions. Questions are dangerous, the questioner more so.

It was a lesson each generation had to learn anew, yet with the passing years a tradition grew - tradition of violence and of repression.

Why had it happened to be in Russia?

In many ways and for many reasons Russia had been a laggard to European civilization. In part, perhaps, because of geography. In part, as Russians themselves insisted, because of the heritage of two hundred fifty years of Mongol oppression. More specifically because of the schism between the Eastern and Western churches. Moscow's Orthodox church held itself to be true Christian. But the great schism meant that Russia experienced neither Renaissance nor Reformation. Neither Church nor Court was swept by the intellectual hurricanes that blew through western Europe. Russia knew neither Da Vinci nor Luther, neither Rousseau nor Cromwell. Peter the Great and his illustrious successor, Catherine the Great, were "enlightened" autocrats but they permitted no diminution of imperial power. Their strong hands reinforced autocracy at a moment when it was disappearing in Western Europe.

In art Western Europe always influenced Russia, and Russia did the same on it. Leningrad was a great example of interconnections of works of great Italian, French, Russian architects. It was a superb example of a joint creative venture.

Think of Soviet Russia as the best democratic country in the world is how the Propaganda explained it, how could it happen that here hundreds of thousands of people had been persecuted?

Val's conscience worked with full strength. Why was the truth hidden from the simple people?

Why are so many Russian people nowadays emigrating? There appeared an odd term "brain leakage" from the native motherland. Why Solzhenitsyn wrote his book abroad but not in the Soviet

163

Union? Why did Andrey Sakharov suffer in isolation? Because of his human rights attitude? Those and many such questions came and constantly returned to Val's mind. All her heart turned to the question of new fighting democrats.

"What do you think of the new democratic Party?" Val was asked by her neighbour women.

"I believe they are honest people", answered Val.

It was really a spectacular time in Russia!

On TV screens, there were shown the meetings of the Supreme Soviet of the Soviet Union, of the Central Committee of the Communist Party of the Soviet Union OPENLY, following Gorbachev's glasnost policy.

Mark Zakharov, a prominent Moscow theatre "Contemporary" producer, had been burning his Communist Party Membership card publicly on a TV show, declaring about his leaving this Party who had compromised itself by repressions, by the Afghanistan War, by Tbilisi events. Edward Shevardnadze refused to be a member of the Central Committee of the Communist Party of the Soviet Union because of the bloody oppression of simple Georgian people in Tbilisi.

Boris Yeltsin excluded himself from the Communist Party and returned his membership card to the General Secretary Comrade Gorbachev in an open way.

It was unnecessary to go to the theatres at those times. All the country transformed itself into a big theatre with the main stage in Moscow. No one could be distracted as his or her whole attention was directed at the TV set.

Val also filled in the application form to resign from the Communist Party 20 years-membership because she was deceived by her Higher Superior leaders who were putting down the regular people in many violent ways.

At that time the mayor of Leningrad Anatoly Sobchak, a democrat by his political views supported Yeltsin. There were two referendums then, one to support Yeltsin, number two, to rename Leningrad after its original name Saint Petersburg. The majority of the population supported Yeltsin and wanted the old name for their favourite city. At long last this is why there appeared the original name of St.Petersburg in the nineties. It is one of the Russian aftermath results under millennium.

However the political battle continued. Nobody could have foreseen the cataclysm of August 1991 - the military backdown from the coup, the fall of Gorbachev, the splitting of Ukraine from Russia, the breakdown of the whole Soviet system.

What heavy days they had been. Dangerous ones, too.

Val appeared to be in the hospital with acute attacks of severe pain because of a gallbladder disease.

She felt the crimpy pain, usually in the right upper part of the abdomen, especially associated with digestion, excess burping, and feeling bloated. The physicians helped her and in a while she sat by the hospital TV set next to the other patients and watched something strange going on. A news commentator read some decree about the military position in Moscow and called everyone to join the coup. The Army obeyed the President. Immediately after Moscow news on the St.Petersburg TV screen appeared the city mayor A. Sobchak who held a passionate speech in defence of new Russian Democracy:

"Those who are supporting the new Russian democrats, I call upon you to fight. We must get together right now at seven p.m. at the Mayor's House".

Fresh news was reported every hour, in Moscow there were fights; in St.Petersburg all was quiet and calm. Not a single shot, no provocations, thanks to the behaviour of the city authorities who supported Yeltsin.

This was true Russian declaration to the whole world of the final change and commitment of the previous Soviet Union to democracy.

In Ukraine, mainly in Kiev and Donetsk, where Val's brother Gen lived, there was political unrest.

Gen called her by telephone and asked her about shelter as he wanted to get out of the city to somewhere where the political views of the politicians were not in turmoil.

"Can you take me in because I can't live here any more, no payments, no food, only troubles on the streets, I've got to get out of that permanently", Gen told.

Val replied, "Brother, come to me immediately".

Like most Russians, Val's brother drove her little car at break-neck speed, feeling free to use almost any part of the road as the mood took him. Once or twice, rather unexpectedly, the road surface of even this highway would abruptly disintegrate, and one would be traveling, still at the same speed, over a surface of caked mud or chips for half a mile or so until the smooth surface resumed again.

The weather was excellent. The sky was a clear pale blue, cloud-less, and with only a faint, dusty haze along the eastern horizon. The birch trees lay on each side of the road, their silver trunks and brilliant emerald leaves producing a sparkling effect.

The sister and brother were absent for three hours from Val's St.Petersburg's flat. Three hours, however, were enough to rob her apartment while they were walking.

Val's mood sank to zero. It was the second time that there was a home invasion; the first one, was her car, it was parked just before her flat's windows, the summer tires and rims had been stolen in the night.

Now, again, her apartment was robbed. She called the police who, as usual, put their trivial questions, "Introduce yourself, and look around, what has been stolen out of your flat?"

Val was astonished with the mess and disorder in her rooms. Burglars forcedly broke and entered the private home in the day time, importantly, when all the neighbours were in their dwellings.

In a moment there were taken the fingerprints of unexpected thieves who were guilty of the offense of trespassing.

The list of things taken away included fur coats, shoes, leather coats, expensive jewelry and two tape-recorders. The whole cost of the losses in roubles was about twenty five millions (five thousand American dollars).

"Are you upset?" asked one of the neighbours.

"No, I am not", answered Val, "I got angry because on our floor among the nine apartments it's been the third time of breaking in and entering: it means in our house the gang is acting. The next cat-burglary can be your dwelling, dear neighbour."

"You are right, sweetie. What should we do? It's dangerous to live here now", she added.

The women were right, it became dangerous and terrifying to dwell in their house because some time later, they heard, on the eighth floor there had been committed a murder, again in the day time when every pensioner was at home and nobody noticed anything.

The police had not done anything to discover these crimes.

Even though Russia has no formal victim's bill of rights, the following are some of the rights due to a victim:

a) the right to be treated with respect and courtesy;

b) the right to get back stolen property within three months of the offense;

c) the right to be informed of the progress of the investigation;

d) the right to attend the trial;

e) the right to receive compensation for crime injury from the territorial or government authorities;

f) the right to be provided with quick and appropriate medical attention, if needed.

None of these rights were given to the victims, like Val, who suffered from the crime and did not receive anything back. If the official bodies were unable to act, then one would rather unite themselves into public vigilant groups, groups of offending victims, out to obtain revenge.

There is a new face of Russia: organized crime, statistics of which was well developed in the book of two journalists, Dixelius from Sweden and Andrey Konstantinov from Russia, under the eloquent title 'The Criminal World of St. Petersburg', published in 1997. In every day life appeared a new word "racket". Organized crime poses a serious threat to the Russian government's efforts to stabilize society and promote orderly economic progress. That threat is compounded by nationalist and communist hardliners who try to persuade the public that democracy is fostering crime. The crime rate in Russia has gone up 152 per cent since 1991, when the central government of the Soviet Union collapsed.

Anybody who can afford to provide for his own security does so, and private security agencies are flourishing. One Canadian oil company hires a private firm to protect valuable equipment unloaded at docks in St.Petersburg. Then, to thwart hijackers, the company has armed guards riding shotgun all the way to the oil fields of western Siberia.

As for the benefit of new Russia one should mention that at least today, goods are available in Russian shops, including foreign boutiques such as Christian Dior and the Soap Berry Shop, a Canadian-owned business featuring personal-care products, if you have the money. And the frustrations of every-day shopping will ease as more and more as state establishments become co-operative or privatized, or at least introduce checkout counters.

Meanwhile, the most meaningful change in Russia is represented by something not seen: a new openness of ordinary people who are becoming less scared from government, if you are paying a visit to Russia nowadays, you will see the differences.There is no longer such thing as "official" opinion, as in the simple parroting of the party line that was so often heard under the Communist dictatorship. People express personal opinions with complete freedom.

"Mommy, I intend to quit you as soon as possible", said Val's daughter to her.

"Why?"

"Dear, dear Mommy, I want to try to live on my own ", was her reply.

"Well, it's high time for you. You're an adult and I have no right to disturb you", Val answered.

So Val found herself alone.

She had been expecting that moment for all her life and, now it had arrived. The gallbladder surgery was behind her, what are the keys to good health? She meditated. Good genes and avoiding risk factors such as smoking, drinking and high cholesterol foods are important. But they don't tell the whole story.

"Make love, not war" is one of the advices, in which the loving, supportive husbands play not the last role.

"Listen to your body" is the second recommendation, because your body constantly "talks" to you through aches, pains and that vague feeling the doctors call intuition. Pay attention at it.

"Love what you do" is the third piece of advice. Val really loved her teaching-interpreting work and enjoyed it as she could. Despite the life surrounding stressful conditions, she was quite happy with her job.

"Consider your soul," is very important advice, too.

Growing evidence links a belief in God, to better physical health, in Val's case, a communist atheist by views, the religion is found to believe in herself, in the best traits of character of a human being.

Plainly, robust health - a key to looking and feeling years younger - requires more than above mentioned a set of rigid rules. It also involves achieving an exuberant, hopeful, fun-loving state of mind.

Val has found out if somebody loves life, life will love him or her back.

For twenty years she was alone, raising her daughter, now her sweet child had graduated from the University, finding work and desiring to get her own life experience, Val felt herself alone again. She had a very good friend from Canada, John Pattison by name, whom she missed very much.

In December 1997, there appeared a chance to come to New York, and she took that chance hoping for meeting with John.

From the seat of a moving airplane, the sky over New York seemed empty, serene, an ocean of blue. Two weeks before Christmas Val landed at JFK airport, took a taxi and came to her friend who stayed in a hostel, which was not a usual type.

Have you ever read a book called "The Petersburg Slums" by Vsevolod Krestovsky, a popular Russian writer of the previous times? There was a precise description of the hostel of such kind. One captain managed to rent seven-rooms' apartment to live in; three ones for his family, and the four more to give for rent, to poor, miserable people, hiring the corners, simply speaking, as sleeping places.

So, in one room it happened to be ten or eleven persons at a time, in Brooklyn hostel. Four beds for constant residents, six or seven - on the mattresses on the floor.

The New York hostel hostess had about thirty five to forty people for one night in a five-rooms' flat. The corners cost seven dollars per night.

No special commodities, except one bathroom - for forty, one toilet - for forty, one kitchen - for forty, no soap, no fresh linen, no fresh towels. Anything of value was constantly stolen. The hostess's daughter's business was to pick up the money from the inhabitants. Many were in search of a job. In New York there exist a lot of employment agencies, which also, in their turn, fetch a profit from employers and employees, both.

First, Val made acquaintance with the new city: the American Museum of Natural History on the 79th Street, The Metropolitan Museum of Arts on the Fifth Avenue, Manhattan, the Museum of the City New York on the 53-rd Street of Manhattan and many other sights worth seeing.

She remembered, with bitterness, her custom to travel in Russia; it made her angry to think that she could not come or go as she wanted. She enjoyed the experience, it drove her to the streets. All her free days she walked through the Broadway, she walked to the Aright House or to the Fargo Store, and stood looking at the building for a long time.

She passed by the Penn Station and entered the Subway, went by the World Trade Center, Route Number Nine up to South Ferry.

She took the Staten Island Ferry; she rode to the island, standing alone at the rail of an empty deck. Val watched the city moving away from her. In the vast emptiness of sky and ocean, the city was only small, jagged solid. It seemed condensed, pressed tight together, not a place of streets and separate buildings, but a single sculptured form. A form of irregular steps that rose and dropped without ordered continuity, long ascensions and sudden drops, like the graph of some stubborn struggle. But it went on mounting toward a few points, toward the triumphant masts of skyscrapers rose out of the struggle.

The boat went past the Statue of Liberty - a figure in a green light, with an arm raised like the skyscrapers behind it.
She stood at the rail, while the city diminished, and she felt the motion of growing distance as a growing tightness within her, the pull of a living cord that could not be stretched too far. She stood in quiet excitement when the boat sailed back and she saw the city

growing again to meet her. She stretched her arms wide. The city expanded, to her elbows, to her wrists, beyond her fingertips. Then the skyscrapers rose over her head, and she was back.

She came ashore. She knew where she had to go, and wanted to get there fast, but felt she must get there herself, like this, on her own feet. So she walked half the length of Manhattan, through long crowded streets. It was four-thirty when she knocked at this door of one Park Avenue apartment.

"Do you need a house keeper, M'am?" asked Val to the hostess.

"Certainly. Are you from Jennifer's agency?" asked the latter.

"Yes, of course". Val introduced herself and since that moment on, she tried to do her best for this woman having a traveling-on-business-husband and two kids, three and seven.

Ponder this scenario: as a parent of children, named Connor and Kyle, this lady from Park Avenue thought she had been doing everything to help them develop their minds. She started reading to them as infants; she bought them educational toys; she took them to the Museums and to the library. Now the elder one is doing well in school, visiting sports schools at the same time. The junior attends the part-time Monte Sari's school.

But should the parents be taking credit? Difficult to answer in one way. In this complicated family Val was busy from six o'clock in the morning till ten in the evening, and always in short of time. More she had done, more had been demanded. Besides house-keeping, she became a nanny, then a cook and a nurse.

Because of the poor and irregular junk food diet the kids were both fascinated and troubled by their digestive systems.

In a Jewish family, for example, the children grew up in an environment with almost daily complaints directed at the "mar-gen". The "margen" was a genetic term in their house. Margen complaints encompassed everything from eating to defecating and all parts and functions in between.

Burping, gas and bowel movements were all important indicators of health and behavior.

If a child merely had to hint at the stomach, he was kept home from school and fussed over until his tummy magically self-corrected, a successful therapy that usually coincided with a missed exam or a test. Pleasant as it seemed the last mentioned, accompanied the useful.

"Connor", Val used to ask the little guy, "Did you do poop?"

"No, I did not", he answered honestly. Such inquiries lasted for more than a month.

His Mommy, a physitian by profession by the way, did not seem concerned about that. Her mind was busy in making more and more money, meantime her kids suffered.

The second problem of American kids at home: lice. Do not be surprised, in our time, at the beginning of the twenty first century, the lice, head or body lice, transmitted through shared brushes, combs and many other things, brought from schools. These little creatures live off your body by biting your skin and ingesting the blood.

Lice cause itching in two ways. First, the bite on the skin itches. Second, they leave "louse droppings" behind in the puncture wound, what has been delicately referred to by several patients as crab shit. Both head and body lice lay eggs, or nits, that attach themselves near the base of hairs.

For the whole week, Val did the sanitary treatment of the kids' heads, clothes, bedding. Regular washing at very high temperatures of all clothes, towels, and sheets used over the preceding week usually sufficed.

The last problem of the children but not least was stress. Two brothers, seven and three, were left at home with Val. The junior Connor, very active by nature, demanded attention to be paid to him: to play his favourite games of dinosaurs, to watch TV cartoons or Video, by all means together with him.

The older brother Kyle liked to play hockey and obviously his little buddy annoyed him a lot.

"Stop yelling!" shouted Kyle to him.

"I wanna play hockey, and you cannot take the helmet, stick and play with me", explained Kyle again.

Connor did not comprehend, started crying, complicating the home atmosphere more and more.

All of a sudden Kyle lost his temper, yelling back in such a high tone, that Val ran into their room in amazement, "What's up, guys?"

"Nothing special", answered the boy proudly and went to the bathroom where he stayed for a long time.

Then he cried from a tummy pain. Val jumped into the room; he was pale, complaining of the stomach.

They got through to his Daddy in no time by a mobile telephone.

"Dad, I feel badly now. Something is wrong with my belly", said he in a weak voice.

"Pass the receiver to Valentina", responded Dad. Val explained all her observations and meditations in this respect.

"Let him have a rest and lie in bed, no medications at all", concluded Daddy.

What has happened to this little boy?

To Val's pedagogical opinion, that was stress, a usual stress followed by the emotional nervous reaction to his brother's yelling.

It was a bad copy of the behaviour of his Mommy, who often yelled at them, having no patience and no time to persuade her favourite kids to cooperate, to get along.

She was a kind person who loved to talk about "me" and "I", after all, "I" - was the most interesting topic in the world, wasn't it. She was a very agile, slender person who always seemed in a rush because she frequently had taken on too much.

She could be described as hostile, impatient, tense, and restless (and those were just the most complimentary phrases).

She frequently interrupted Val to finish her sentence for her. She used to sit tensely at the edge of the chair and drum her fingers on the desk. She drove too fast and cursed at other drivers for being too slow (which they all were, of course).

She constantly jumped lines at the supermarkets to get into the fastest line, which, of course, immediately became the slowest line as soon as she entered it.

She ate quickly. She did not chew because it took too long. All the time she lost something and never found it, irritated at other people surrounding her. Her yelling was heard everywhere at home and in the streets. She shouted at her husband, her children, her Mommy. They shouted back at her.

173

Such abnormal, in Val's thinking, home atmosphere was considered by her very normal and clearly American type. Kids naturally inherited their Mommy's habit of shouting at everybody, and yelled at each other, boasting that they let "the steam out ", as their mother did.

This lady pretended to be a top society woman and never had been such.

Another experience as a caregiver Val acquired working for a ninety-two-year old Jewish woman, Pearl Greenfield by name, a tiny, skinny, tidy and very pleasant lady, in the vicinity of New York.

Pearl did not pretend to be an aristocratic society member, but she really was.

Pianist by profession, she was fond of classical music and drawing as well. In the middle of her small two-room apartment stood a gorgeous brown grand piano, on the walls hang her own pictures and a number of her family's photos.

What a treasure she was, this baby Pearl! She was fair, with very light brown hair, and though one could not exactly call her pretty there was simplicity in her rather round artist's face that was very attractive. She had a quietness about her, like a nun, that made her a pleasant, peaceful presence in any room she entered.

She was very devout.

Val and her would often walk in the rooms, heads nicely combed, so that from a distance one could not have said which was a lady and which was a caregiver.

Yet Val had also learned from her Russian grandmother a huge font of folk tales, and she recited these, Pearl's gentle face and blue eyes would seem to glow with pleasure and with a quiet amusement.

Besides her daily duties, it was this knowledge in which old Pearl rejoiced."Tell me, little Valentina, about modern Russia, how the regular people do live".

Val told her stories.

Sometimes Pearl asked, "Pass that book, little Val - those fairy tales by Pushkin. He has a story like the one you told".

"Your tales remind me when I was a girl", she would say to Val.

174

"Isn't it funny, we used to call our old grand mother Arina then. The tales you know come from another Arina - Pushkin's nanny, I suppose. That Arina, you know, was the real Russia, the enduring heartland. Always remember that".

Later there was a letter to Val from her old friend John from Canada,

The 2-nd of March, 97
Sparwood, BC.

"Darling Valentina, my Valentina,
I thought it is high time to write you as I truly convinced myself that I had lost you forever once and what a wonderful surprise to receive your card tonight, I cannot sleep for thinking about you, my very dear friend. And I hope soon to be able to care for you, me life-long partner and lover..."

And at the end:

"Then decide what you want to do and where to live, British Columbia, in my view, is the best province in Canada and, perhaps, any place in the U.S.A.
We have mountains of grandiose, many lakes, the Pacific Ocean etc. You won't get tired of anyone place as it is different wherever you go.
What a man need in this wonderful province is a true woman, honey Valentina.
So stop staring in the mirror, lazy, I love you for what you are, those tired eyes of yours will be at piece when you come to God's country.

Love you,
Yours only,
John".

Suddenly Val sat bolt upright in her sleeping place of Pearl's apartment, yanked awake by some dream or maybe a noise in the darkness outside. There was a dream about her old friend John. He came to her, big and masculine, with a face, open and frank, stretching his strong hands toward her. Her beloved man!

Val rose up, looking out of the window. The full moon has climbed over the steep roofs and is pouring its reflected glory down into the road, filling it with the colour of rubbed silver. Far away the lake was hardly visible. On the water, each ripple flickers like a white flame.

For all the beauty, though, there was something slightly menacing about moonlight.

Val got very thoughtful and deep about John, and herself, that old sleeping lady, the world itself.

How odd it was! This John, a far-away man, neither a relative nor a stranger, since a certain moment was becoming more closer to her. What was that? Love or magic of a full moon?

John felt the same. Every now and then, he called to Val, telephone conversations lasted for hours. Many things were in common between them: lifestyles, hobbies, tastes, views.

After their talks Val could not sleep at all, adding to her care giving night duties some mystery and adventure.

Behind the window she used to notice others pulled from sleep by the unexpected brightness of the moon.

Beneath the gauze-coloured light, the people's skin looked pasty, their eyes hollow and dark. "It could be a scene from a bad horror movie", she thought. No one spoke. They just moved, like zombies, mesmerized by the mystery of the moment.

Ever since humans first turned their faces towards its pale light, we have had a love-hate relationship with the moon.It symbolizes love, sex, birth, renewal and creation.

But we've also linked it with death, demons, werewolves, vampires and insanity.

"What are you thinking about, Val?" asked her awaken Pearl.

"Is it noticeable from outside?" Val asked in her turn.

"Oh, yes, darling".

"About a man who could be my destiny", Val replied and told her frankly everything about John.

"I don't believe he's honest", commented old Pearl doubtfully.

"Yes, I do", minded Val.

This time of early spring twilight she payed attention to small changes happening in mother-nature.

The pale sun, inclining, touches the tops of the swamp maples. She leaned her elbows on an occuring light as though spring required an act of faith. As the afternoon colours turned deeper orange, she rocked, waiting for a call from John who was decoding

176

her card reading, she was sure, the shadows in her mind. But at that moment there was just the fading day. No spring. Not yet. In the evening John called as usual and insisted on her coming to him.

"Sweetie, I have a hobby rabbit farm and cannot leave them without feeding. Rather you come to see me".

Again Val was inspired for the sleepless night of observing the moon. She loved the way the full moon transformed the night, making the familiar landscape serene and mysterious. Val made up her mind to come to Spokane, close to John's place.

Despite the fact she had seen him only a very long time ago, despite her hesitations, doubts, fears, she decided to go by Grey-Hound bus to see better America from the Atlantic coast to the Pacific.

Starting in New York when a station on the radio played jazz, the kind that gave a beat to the zipping dotted lines, she kept time with the blurred bridge streets, truck stop signs, and faraway towns' jittering light.

Val was heading to John, passing by Cleveland and Chicago, Minneapolis, Dickinson and Billings, Coeur d'Alene. From the Atlantic to the Pacific Ocean, crossing the country from the East to the West, past twelve American States. Val's body was like a reflex, part of the mysterious workings of an automobile. The windows are rolled up. The wind carried smells of fog and dust and fried food. Music oiled the pavement and the Grey-Hound bus held the turn as the driver down-shifted off the highway onto a small dark road.

Jazz, night, another humming journey to a man, her destiny. Unbidden, moments from her near past presented themselves like a show of shuffled slides, out of sequence, discrete.

One old transparency came into focus like a distant headlight in the rear view mirror: it's the middle of an ordinary day in old Pearl's flat, someboby evil whispered her, "John is a bad man, I feel". The same was repeated many times. She looked around.

The strangers were everywhere, someone tried to talk to her, when they had a rest between the towns.

"Look!" said one woman, addressing to Val and pointing out to the sky.

They saw a segment of a rainbow. A rain completed with the glowing afternoon in one of those speeding microclimates on Chicago roads in which something unusual was bound to happen. And it did.

The end of the rainbow had landed smack on top of a small white frame house at the back of the field.

"Guess the desire as fast as possible and keep it in mind. Do not tell that to anyone", uttered this woman in Val's ear. Val's thoughts were about John. "Let him be a very good man to me. God bless him and me, together", she thought to herself.

Val wanted to embrace a friendly woman. Before she could move, the rest of the rainbow appeared, its other end planted in the opposite corner of the field.

She gazed at the celestial stripes in their luminous entirety for two, maybe three minutes.

Then the whole rainbow disappeared in a gust of grey cloud and the rain diminished to drizzle, to mist.

On the last March Friday they met in Spokane. She walked at a measured pace, her eyes focused at his eyes, whose Val distinguished from the crowd at the instant when John stood on the balls of his feet, tense and ready in the cold white daylight, on the last step of the escalator of the Grey-Hound Bus Station.

He was magnificent in bright blue short-sleeved shirt tucked into the waistband of bright light-blue crisp pants, over the shoulders the blue-herring-bone tweed jacket, tan hands passing mechanically through brown hair.

Their eyes met. Val and John never parted from this moment on. The wonderful moments of Val's journey changed for the ones of Beautiful British Columbia in Canada.

At long last her loneliness was over, he was with her. Love joined two caring hearts of John and Valentina for ever.

One day, on their way to Lunbreck Waterfalls they met a couple.

"Could you possibly take a photo of us, M'am?" asked Val a woman politely.

"With great pleasure", answered the latter and helped them with pictures.

"By the way, where are you from?" asked the curious strange woman.

"I am from Russia", was the reply.

"Oh, we are also Russians", continued the lady. "My name is Mary Stoochnoff. My husband's name is Bill Stoochnoff".

Like this in an unusual way they befriended with a good Canadian pair of Russian Doukhobortsi origin.

Neither Val nor John ever heard of the Doukhobortsi. Who are they? What were and are the Doukhobortsi doing? In 1765, Archbishop of the Russian Orthodox Church derisively referred to a group of Russian peasants as "Doukhobortsi" or "Spirit Wrestlers", accusing them of wrestling against the Holy Spirit because of their rejection of certain aspects of Orthodoxy.

The Doukhobortsi accepted the name claiming they wrestled not against, but with and for the Holy Spirit in their efforts to live according to the law of God and the teachings of Jesus Christ.

By the 1890s, despite the harassment by state and church authorities of the day, the Doukhobortsi had developed a very moral and ethical way of life. Inspired by their high ideals and by dynamic leadership within their midst, they lived by the creed "from each according to their ability and to each according to their need". The consumption of alcohol, tobacco and meat was discontinued out of their respect for the sanctity of life and their belief that these substances harmed the human body, regarded by the Doukhobortsi as the true Temple of God.

For Val it was a discovery. She was a Russian woman by origin as were her new friends the Stoochnoff family.

Their moral rule "from each according to their ability and to each according to their need" was known for centuries among the Doukhobortsi, and as far as she assumed that principle was stolen by the communists for their Propaganda directed to the population.

That main principle was broken in the Soviet-Russian communist society in the line of the distribution of the food products, clothes, the goods of the first need, what was mentioned above.

Val asked Mary thoughtfully,

"When did your parents come to Canada?"

"In 1895".

"Where did they live in Russia before?"

"In the Caucasus. The village of Slovjanka was populated by Doukhobortsi".

How did the Russian people live then? I will explain.

The Imperial Russia of 1894 was as follows: from the Baltic city of St.Petersburg, built on a river marsh in far northern corner of the empire, the Tsar Nicholas the Second ruled Russia. So immense were the Tsar's dominations that, as night began to fall along their western borders, day already was breaking on their Pacific coast. Between these distant frontiers lay a continent, one sixth of the land surface of the globe. Through the depth of Russia's winters, millions of tall pine trees stood silent under heavy snows.

In the summer, clusters of white-trunked birch trees rustled their silvery leaves in the slanting rays of the afternoon sun. Rivers, wide and flat, flowed peacefully through the grassy plains of European Russia toward limitless southern horizon. Eastward, in Siberia, even mightier rivers rolled north to the Arctic, sweeping through forests where no human had ever been, and across desolate marshes of frozen tundra.

Here and there, thinly scattered across the broad land, lived not only Slavs but Balts, Jews, Germans, Georgians, Armenians, Uzbeks and Tartars. Some were clustered in provincial cities and towns, dominated by onion-shaped church domes rising above the white-walled houses. Many more lived in isolated villages of unpainted log huts. Next to doorways, a few sunflowers might grow. Geese and pigs wandered freely through the muddy streets.

In the country, the Russian people lived their lives under a blanket of silence. Most died in the villages where they were born. Three fourths of them were peasants, freed from the land a generation before by the Tsar-Liberator Alexander the Second's emancipation of the serfs. But freedom did not produce food when famine came and the black earth cracked for lack of rain, and the grain withered and crumbled to dust still on the stalks, then the peasants tore the thatch from their roofs to feed their livestock and sent their sons trudging into town to look for work.

The simple people lived very poorly, starved; opposite, the rich people who lived enjoying life supplied with the funds from the country estates to finance their pleasures.

It was the time, when the capital of Russia St.Petersburg still was faithful to Tsar Peter's wishes who had built it in 1703 on water and nineteen islands chained together by arching bridges, laced by winding canals. To the northeast lay the wide expanse of lake Ladoga, to the west the Gulf of Finland, between them rolled the broad flood of the river Neva.

St.Petersburg was the center of all that was advanced, all that was smart and much that was cynical in Russian life. Its great opera and ballet companies, its symphonies and chamber orchestras played the music of Glinka, Rimsky-Korsakov, Borodin, Mussorgsky and Tchaikovsky; its citizens read Pushkin, Gogol, Dostoevsky,Turgenev and Leo Tolstoy.

It was with special care that Fate had selected Nicholas the Second to be Tsarevich and, later, Tsar.

He was educated by tutors. There were language tutors, history tutors, geography tutors and a whiskered dancing tutor who wore white gloves and insisted that a huge pot of fresh flowers always be placed on his accompanist's piano. Of all the tutors, however, the most important was Constantine Petrovich Pobedonostsev. A brilliant philosopher of reaction, Pobedonostsev had been called "the High Priest of Social Stagnation" and "the dominant and most baleful influence of the last reign".

"A wizened, balding man with coldly ascetic eyes staring out through steel-rimmed glasses", he first came to prominence when as a journalist at Moscow University he wrote a celebrated three-volume text on Russian law.

He became a tutor to the children of Tsar Alexander the Second, and, as a young man, Alexander the Third was his faithful, believing pupil.

When Alexander mounted the throne, Pobedonostsev already held the office of Procurator of the Holy Synod, or lay head of the Russian Orthodox Church. In addition, he assumed the tutorship of the new Tsarevich Nicholas. Pobedonostsev's brilliant mind was steeped in nationalism and bigotry. He took a misanthropic narrow view of man in general. Slavs in particular he described as sluggish and lazy, requiring strong leadership, while Russia, he said, was " an icy desert and an abode of the "Bad Man" .

Believing that, national unity was essential to the survival of this sprawling, multi-racial empire, he insisted on the absolute authority of Russia's two great unifying institutions: the autocracy and the Orthodox Church.

From his special position - Minister of Religion, Pobedonostsev attacked all religious strains in Russia who were unwilling to be assimilated into Orthodoxy. Those who most strenuously resisted, he hated most. He was violently anti-Semitic and declared that the Jewish problem in Russia would be solved, only when one third of Russia's Jews had emigrated, one third had been converted to Orthodoxy and one third had disappeared.

It was the pupil of Pobedonostsev speaking to Alexander the Third when he wrote in the margin of a report depicting the plight of Russian Jewry in 1890,

"We must not forget that it was the Jews who crucified our Lord and spilled his precious blood".

Pobedonostsev's virulent prejudice was not restricted to Jews. He also attacked the Catholic Poles, Doukhobortsi (Fighters Against Spirit), Moslems scattered across the broad reaches of the empire. It was Pobedonostsev who wrote the document excommunicating the great Russian writer Leo Tolstoy in 1901.

Tolstoy had left the Church, and the excommunication was a formal acknowledgement of this fact. Still, Pobedonostsev may have taken a personal satisfaction in expelling the great novelist. Since 1877, when Tolstoy completed "Anna Karenina", it had been rumored that the character of Alexis Karenin, the coldly pompous bureaucrat whom Anna cuckolds and then divorces, was modeled on an episode in the family life of Constantine Pobedonostsev.

The Russia described to Nicholas by Pobedonostsev had nothing to do with the tasteless giant, stirring outside the tsar palace windows. Instead, it was an ancient, stagnant, coercive land made up of the classical triumvirate of Tsar, Church and People. It was God, the tutor explained, who had chosen the Tsar. There was no place in God's design for representatives of the people to share in ruling the nation.

For the thirteen years of his father's reign, Nicholas saw Russia ruled according to the theories of Pobedonostsev.

The tragedy of Nicholas the Second, essentially, was that he appeared in the wrong place in history. Equipped by education to rule in the nineteenth century, equipped by temperament to reign in England, for example, he lived and reigned in Russia in the twentieth century. There, the world he understood was breaking up around him.

Events were moving too swiftly, ideas were changing too radically. In the gigantic storm which swept over Russia, he and all his loved were carried away. To the end, he did his best and for his wife and family that was a very great deal.

For Russia, it was not enough.

The Tsar Nicholas the Second committed wrong things with his own people like the Doukhobortsi.

"What had happened to your parents in 1895?" Val asked Bill surprisingly.

"Peter V. Verigin, our Doukhobortsi' leader, advised us no longer to participate in the taking of life. At their meeting they decided not to be conscribed into military service, put down their weapons and refuse to attend a drill.

In support of their brothers, on the night of June 29, several thousand Doukhobortsi gathered all of the weapons in their possession and destroyed them by fire. With this action, they demonstrated their unconditional adherence to the commandment. "Thou shalt not kill" and their absolute rejection of violence and the use of force in their lives", explained Bill.

"What was coming up with them, then?" put Val her questions in astonishment.

"Then, something terrible had happened. The response of the authorities was swift and brutal. The Doukhobortsi suffered torture, imprisonment and exile - many lost their lives in 1899, after intervention of Leo Tolstoy and his colleagues, the English Society of Friends (Quakers) and others seven thousand five hundred people were allowed to immigrate to Canada", told Bill bitterly.

"What is happening nowadays?" thought Val.

We are trying to grasp the terrifying fortune of the Tsar Nicholas the Second from the communists, but he, himself, tortured the Doukhobortsi people.

The man who, sensing only imperfectly the dimensions of the storm which beats against him, still tries with courage to do his duty is a particularly recognizable twentieth-century figure. Perhaps for this reason we today are better equipped to understand the ordeal and the qualities of Nicholas the Second. In an earlier era when the world seemed ordered and disorder was the result primarily of human weakness or folly, then wars or revolutions could be blamed on a single leader. Since then, two world wars, the Great American Depression and fifty two years of the Nuclear Age have taught us, among other things, tolerance.

We have come to accept the fact that there are forces beyond the control of any single man, be he tsar or president. We have also adjusted our measure of human achievement. Facing together things which we only dimly see, uncertain which course to follow, we place a higher value on intentions and effort. We may lose - more often than not - but we must try: this is the essence of a rational twentieth-century morality. This was one of the lessons of the Russian aftermath at the dawn of the historical era.

The Russian Tsar Nicholas the Second broke the biblical law, "An unjust man is an abomination to the just: and he that is upright in the way is abomination to the wicked". And, "It is not good to accept the person of the wicked, to overthrow the righteous in judgment".

The Tsar was unjust to the Doukhobortsi and God punished him and his family as it became visible from the point of view of modern days.

Val and John's friends were of remarkable appearances.

Bill very seldom smiled: he could not see the point. Though he was already seventy-five, something in his square face suggested that on this matter, as upon most, his opinion had long ago been formed. With his grey hair, his not huge nose, and his hazel, watchful eyes, he was as formidable as his wife. His mouth was usually pursed into a thin line of silent defiance, and his firm, determined walk somehow suggested that, wherever he was going, it was because he didn't much care for the place he was coming from.

"Cheer up, Bill", said his wife. "Welcome all of you to the table", said Mary enthusiastically. She, warm-hearted and practical, had great gifts. She liked to supervise everybody in the kitchen; she would proudly make dainty pastries with her own hands, sitting opposite her husband, her face flushed with excitement, to watch his reaction. How delightful she seemed, how charmed, this simple Russian soul Mary. While eating the Russian borscht, kletski with the stewed goulash, and Russian traditional tea, between meals they talked a lot. They got interested in modern Russia, Val's life in Canada.

"How is your life in Canada, as a whole?" Val asked in her turn.

"In 1899, the first seven thousand and a half, Russian Doukhobortsi arrived in Canada to form a community in what is now the province of Saskatchewan. With the most primitive of tools, a lack of work horses, and barely enough food to keep body and soul together, they began their struggle for survival. They settled in 50 villages, setting up flourmills, blacksmith shops, a brick factory and other village industries, and began selling grain", told Bill.

"And was the Canadian government loyal to the Doukhobortsi after the exodus from tsarist Russia where they had been subject to persecution and exile especially because of their pacifist beliefs?" asked Val and John simultaneously. "No, it was not. In 1906 the Canadian government interpreted the Dominion Land Act in such a way that the land granted the Doukhobortsi would have to be registered and lived on individually, as ordinary homesteads rather than as a communal property. Furthermore, in order to register the land in this manner, each individual would be required to swear an oath of allegiance.

Following their religious beliefs the Doukhobortsi refused to take the oath.

The Canadian Government took over most of the land and sold it to newcomers, and the Doukhobortsi were again forced to move somewhere else. In May of 1908 land was bought in British Columbia, to the Kootenai, in the southern interior of BC, between Grand Forks and Nelson and up into the Slocan Valley", told Bill.

"Do the differences in Doukhobortsi exist, or the unique belief among them?" asked Val.

"Doukhobortsi divide themselves into three ideological groupings: the Orthodox or Union of Spiritual Communities of Christ, the Independents, who are the most assimilated of the three groups, and the Svobodniki or Sons of Freedom, the least assimilated and most radical group", explained Mary.

"Who was your leadership?"

"Peter Vasiljevich Verigin, by all accounts an extraordinary man. Look, Valentina, how he wrote in 1913: "Although of Russian birth we dwell in our community and consider ourselves the citizens of the entire globe and therefore we cannot regard our residence in Canada as fixed for all ages. Today we happen to be here, after sometime we may find ourselves in another country altogether", said Bill.

"In Canada the Doukhobortsi established a communal lifestyle which undoubtedly inspired the following observation in the Encyclopedia Britannica (1960 edition), describing the Doukhobortsi as: 'industrious and abstemious in their lives and, when living up to the standard of their faith, they present one of the nearest approaches to the realization of the Christian ideal which has ever been attained'", told Mary.

"Both of you involved in your faith with the help of your mothers and fathers. And what about other people's opinions in this respect?" asked and asked Val, greedy for knowledge.

Another man, a carpenter, said:

"Doukhobortsi are like any other people, physically. This, some time ago, was compared to the flowers. Some white, black, red, blue and others. It's understood that's how they are beautiful. We don't say, white is the most beautiful - flower or a person, black is the most beautiful - flower or a person. Each one slightly differs. That's what makes it beautiful. That's the way I see it".

"'People like flowers and flowers like people', what a wonderful image of a simple worker to be expressed in a few words. Simple and clear as Mother Nature, symbol of which for me", thought Val

186

to herself, " was Mary with her great passion for everything fine". Look around her house!

Everywhere there is planted a great many flowers of different sorts and kinds: sunflowers and goldenrod, asters, long-stalked plants to look like stars, what seem like their petals are finer and more numerous than those of daisies, named for the sun - the original name was "day's-eye", the eye of day, of course, being the sun.

In reality, the bloom of the aster is a flower head, each one of the "petals" is itself a flower.

Mary's love for asters was something especial. "In the aster", she told, "the "rays" of the star spread out from a central "disk" (reminiscent of a daisy's center) which is typically yellow. But the disk may turn to purple or to dark red as it gets pollinated. Not all asters have "ray" flowers that art lavender either- there are various shades of blue and purple and white".

"Mary, you are really fond of flowers, aren't you? You've got an artist way of composing the buckets?!" exclaimed Val excitingly.

"Oh, certainly. I love flowers growing since my childhood. My Mommy and grandma taught me that ", Mary spoke the last words sadly.

Her memory again and again returned to the previous, far long ago days, unforgettable.

Her grandma's story looked like "The Story of the Doukhobor Vasja Pozdnjakov", written by A. Chertkov in Russian and published in July 3, 1901 in Christchurch-Hants, England, about tortures and beatings of the Doukhobortsi by the fierce, violent Cossack troops. Here is his second story 'About the massacre and raping of the Doukhobortsi 14 women by Cossacks': "Again at Tanya P.'s house there was committed a raping crime. Her husband was not at home. Her cousin stayed there. He was locked in the stable. The Cossacks attacked several people. She was left hardly alive. Tanya got ill for about a month after that", etc.

A remarkable letter to those Doukhobortsi who have migrated to Canada by Leo Tolstoy came to mind whenever one met them:

"Dear Brothers and Sisters,
You suffered and were exiled, and are still suffering want, because

you wished, not in words but in deeds, to lead a Christian life.

You refused to do any violence to your neighbours, to take oaths, to serve as police or soldiers, and you even burnt your own weapons lest you should be tempted to use them in self-defense, and in spite of all persecutions you remained true to the Christian teaching...

Farewell

Your loving brother

Leo Tolstoy,

February 27 (n.s.) 1900."

What about today's life for them?

For how long Doukhobortsi hold regular prayer services, spiritual meetings and cultural festivals which feature their simple form of worship, rich tradition of *a cappella* singing and warm hospitality. They administer their own playschools, youth groups, publications, Russian language classes, community and cultural centers and heritage sites. And, changing times not withstanding, Doukhobortsi remain committed to the non-violent struggle for peace, freedom and justice, working together with like-minded people everywhere for a world without war - where love is the guiding principle of human relations.

On every Petrov's Day annually, it was on the last Sunday of June, more than fifty Doukhobortsi got together in the Lunbreck Meeting Hall, children and grandchildren of the exiled Russians, born in Canada, never seen their Holy Mother Russia.

Ever since they were little children, they had thought in terms of love for God, singing their psalms.

From as long as they could remember, musical *a cappella* notes had suggested colours to them.

As soon as their relations showed them the different keys on the piano, each had possessed, for them, its own distinct character and mood. At first these discoveries belonged to a musical world that they associated with the instruments they played. But then, when the little Doukhobortsi were growing older, something else took place.

"Can you sing?" asked Val a young Doukhobor in the Hall.

"Yes, of course. But why?" asked he in his turn.

"I wonder if the new generation is inheriting the singing traditions of their fathers and mothers", answered Val.

"All our Popovs' family is singing. The best of us is our grandma. She told me", went on the young man, "how her grandma, my great grandma, had been in the little church beside their home one evening listening to vespers. The church had a fine choir, and the haunting melodies of the chanting were still with her as she left. It was sunset when she stepped into the street and the sky above was gold and red. For several minutes she had stood gazing towards the glorious colours in the west.

And then, trying to express what she saw, she had chosen a chord. It was in the key of C minor. After a moment, she had added another and another one", told the young Popov.

"She did compose music, didn't she?" asked Val.

"Sure. She had imposed her first chords on that sunset. Yet as she looked, it was as though the sky were answering her, saying: 'Yes, that is my sound'. And in her mind the chords and the sunset became one".

"How wonderful it was", thought Val to herself, wondering whether it was the start of creation itself.

"How did your Great Granny feel while beginning to compose music and songs, did she tell you?" Val asked and got interested more and more.

"Yes. It was odd, she felt suffused with a strange sensation of warmth inside her stomach. When a moment later some children ran out into the yard, she was afraid, she might lose her thought, she found that with an effort of will she could hold the chords in her mind so that they did not slip away. And she experienced a small pang of fear, which she did not understand, as though the sunset said to her: "If you step forward now, little girl, you will lose yourself and belong only to music and God". And being uncertain what this meant, she had decided to preserve this blessed state of being in her mind, as, sometimes, she would preserve a dream that she might return to it later", he finished telling the story.

In the Hall, nothing reminded anyone of the trivial Church: no decorations, no icons, no candles, no altar, and no priests; the Doukhobortsi people were divided into male and female groups;

189

they looked like ordinary Canadians. Except the secretary Michael who wore a Cossack-fashion shirt and two or three women in beautiful Russian shawls.

The difference got visible when the choir started singing in many-many voice parts - listening to them seemed divine that the wonderful harmonies Val heard came from outside herself; they were given to her as though she could not say with certainty by whom or by what.

And before long, the musical otherworld began to invade the everyday world, like a light encroaching upon shadow, so that even such mundane things as a car were passing in the street, or a dog barking, now seemed to Val to contain their own music, which she would joyfully discover.

Her whole mind became crowded with musical phantoms: the people she saw: John, Bill and Mary, each with a voice - John a tenor, Mary - a soprano, like characters in some wonderful opera that was as yet only partially revealed to her.

Val never heard such beautiful singing of Russian songs, as following:

> *"It was in the Caucasus mountains,*
> *That a great event took place;*
> *Our forefathers burnt their weapons,*
> *Guided by our leader -Peter.*
> *For us, youth, so free and eager,*
> *These basic outlooks we must hold,*
> *Peace and toil's serene, bold banner,*
> *With love and forgiveness in every field."*

Or another one, 'Give Me Your Hand':

> *"How happy would be this old world we are sharing,*
> *If just one another we'd all understand,*
> *A neighbour would come to his neighbour declaring:*
> *'All people are brothers. Please, give me your hand'".*

After two-hours singing Val was asked to tell something about modern days in Russia; sufferings continued to be, tears rolled against her cheeks so she became overwhelmed with impressions about grief of her Russian brothers and sisters.

A combination of internal and external pressures eventually brought about a discontinuation of the communal lifestyle and has left the Doukhobortsi in a period of transition - whereby they strive to live in harmony with existing laws and customs, while retaining their fundamental spiritual values and beliefs, and cultural heritage. Not only with cultural traditions is interesting Canada but also with the natural history, particularly, in British Columbia. It received its name because of the beautiful Columbia River first. The Columbia River is flowing for nearly two thousand kilometers to empty into the Pacific Ocean off the Coast of Oregon in the United States of America, it is one of the major features of this irregularly shaped British Columbia province.

Other characteristics include three main mountain ranges, a variety of lakes and somewhat lesser rivers, ice fields, and many lash valleys, the Elk Valley where John lives.

On her way back to his Valley, Val admired the beauty of the rocky mountains and the chain of emerald blue lake surfaces, white pines and the western red cedar, blue Douglas firs, the western larch, hemlock and birches.

In the North of British Columbia it is known as the Chilcotin and the Cariboo regions where cattle ranching and wilderness still coexist on the enormous Fraser River plateau.

Wherever one could have a look, tall and small peaks of mountains ring the entire area, many of them topped by glaciers of blue ice, others keeping their caps of snow the year around,

Anyone who visits the province could enjoy everything around them. The birds of numerous species like the ruffled grouse, blue grouse, humming birds, whose females are single mothers. Males have nothing to do with nest building, incubation, or the raising of the young; robins, crows, sparrows are pretty good co-habitants of the human population.

Deer, elk, moose are tame here, and very often accompany you along the automobile roads.

What a wonder is this country, Beautiful British Columbia, where the fresh air and high altitude overpowers you; this is truly God's Garden of Eden!

191

It was John who invited his friends to visit Head-Smashed-in-Buffalo Jump on the Indian Paw-Wow-days.

About 150 years ago, according to legend, a young Indian brave wanted to witness the plunging of countless buffalo as his tribe drove them to their deaths over the sandstone cliffs. Standing under the shelter of a ledge like a man behind a waterfall, he watched the great beasts fall past him. The hunt was unusually good that day, as the bodies mounted; he became trapped between the animals and the cliffs. When his people came to do the butchering, they found him with his skull crushed by the weight of the buffalo carcasses. Thus they named the place "Head-Smashed-in". It was one of the oldest, largest and best preserved bison jump sites in North America, located 18 kilometers northwest of Fort Macleod, Alberta on Secondary Highway Number 785. It is a permanent Museum, well-designed and full of interesting features. Going to the Tipi village, you can pass by the country the Indians call "The Backbone". At barring time one must watch for foraging bears and fat elk as well as keeping an eye on the weather in case of sudden snow storms and taking into consideration the morning fog in the valleys.

You can see bighorn sheep and mountain goats grazing in precipitous pastures, appearing and disappearing like shadows in the rocks.

The road threads a pass packed and scabbed by loggers. Until the arrival of white European pioneers, Indians had lived throughout the far reaches of the Kootenai for thousands of years and then scattered everywhere. "Kootenai" means "water".

You went by lots of picturesque lakes full of fascinating blue water and came at long last to the Tipi to celebrate the Indians' biggest and most colorful event of the year.

This weekend they organized an extravaganza feature - three days of Native dance competitions, a traditional tipi village in a natural outdoor setting. Starting at one o'clock in the afternoon, the friends comfortably sat under the shelter of tree branches, breathing in the aroma of pine in the noon heat and the drumming and dancing shows, learning Native rhythms and admiring their arrowheads and unusual costumes.

One girl, their neighbour, apparently attracted everyone's attention to her appearance, born as an Indian, since her childhood she inherited the Native habits of wearing their holiday clothes.

"Girl, what's your name?" some asked.

"Oglala".

"How old are you, Oglala?"

"Six".

"Do you go to school?"

"No".

"Do you like to dance?"

"Yeah".

"Let's go to dance together with your Mom and Dad". So the women gave their hands to the little and big Indians and joined their fascinating and mystical dancing. Native people demonstrated their rhythmic tastes, displayed their artistic skills during the festival dance competition.

"John, you're going to visit the Interpretive Centre, aren't you?", proposed Mary.

"With great pleasure", answered John and the two friendly couples hurried up to the Memorial, in recognition of its significance, UNESCO declared Head-Smashed-In Buffalo Jump a World Heritage Site in 1981.

That was a new museum, a decoration of which three big buffalo stood proudly on a cliff, including the distinctive various animals such as coyote, foxes, rabbits, ground squirrels, and birds like eagles, hawks, falcons and so forth.

Their lifestyle was shown in details: how they air-dried fish like salmon, salted fish, air-dried the meat into jerky, they made biscuits of meal and Saskatoon berries which were also air-dried under the sun. They used to take with hunting parties and the village when it moved to a new location the staple diet of corn.

They were not savages; they lived close to the earth being very intelligent people.

Superb buckskin clothing and footwear, moccasins, mukluk boots for winter time were made up by them, as well as their own weapons like bow and arrow, lance, clubs and knives, tomahawks axes, later they obtained rifles from the white enemies.

In peacetime the primary task of the Indians was buffalo hunting, as shown in the paintings by George Caitlin, a Philadelphia artist who spent six years among the Western tribes.

The buffalo was more than just meat; it supplied virtually everything an Indian needed to stay alive, from tools and utensils (twenty-three items), clothing (thirteen items), ceremonial objects such as sun-dance altars, rattles, horse masks, winding sheets for dead, to tilt and furnishings, recreational equipment and riding and transportation gear (twenty six items), weapons.

Because this was of importance - and in tribute to its strength - the buffalo was worshipped as a sacred animal, its spirit praised before every hunt. The Indian movie, shown here at the theatre, was finished by the gun-shot of the Whites, symbolizing the great grief and suffering from the invasion of the White Men.

Again, grief and sufferings on the lifeway of the ordinary Indian people, like the Doukhobortsi or Jewish people.

All of them are as links of the one and the same chain which is called "life".

Is not it high time, really, at the beginning of the second millennium, to stop their sufferings and have the governments recognize the Pact which was signed with the Indians? And if they promised to pay the Indians for the land, then it's time to settle the debt.

It cannot be going on for ever and ever without settling this score.

As far as Doukhobortsi go they were given the land in Saskatchewan and the Government wanted each male to sign for the land and as it was against their religion to own the individual land, the Government did not understand them and took the land off them.

The Government ought to have altered their regulations allowing them to have one man accepting the land for all in the name of the Doukhobortsi.

Is it not a simple solution for all the problems at one time?

That's the same with the Jewish people. The Government just did not fully understand them. It's a pity, isn't it? Pities as the bureaucrats do not want to deal with something they do not understand. As Val understood for herself, life is to be continued in a thoughtfully organized society, with generous, good-hearted man like her old friend John who is not tired of daily repeating the sacred words, "I love you, dearest! " and reciting the verses:

> *"0 wondrous moment! There before me,*
> *A radiant, fleeting dream, you stood,*
> *A vision fancy fashioned for me,*
> *A glimpse of perfect womanhood".*

PART FOUR

GENNADY

"Oh, Brother Gennady, it's your Birthday,
If it's only ever once a year,
I think you should be told,
As brothers go you're special,
You're worth your weight in gold.

I know you love the flattery,
It never ever falls,
Now wipe the stupid grin off,
And get down off the scales!

HAPPY BIRTHDAY, the 18-th of January, 1942.
Sincerely yours
sis Val

18/01/1997"

Val was close to her only brother although the age difference between them was two years. Two years was enough, however, in their childhood to have a great respect for each other, Gen towards his older sister Val.

In Leo Tolstoy's story "Filippock", it is very well described how the little guy, Filippock by name, accompanied his elder brother to the village school daily but was not admitted to attend classes because of his young age. How unhappy he was, a poor tiny soul! Next day came and Filippock again was going to dash for the school. This time, on his own.

The dogs were barking, he was scared of them very much, then he found a stick, and tried to protect himself against the angry animals, so he went on and on till he came to the school.

Again he was not allowed to enter the school in order not to disturb the pupils.

Since then Gennady's nickname became Filippock, who greatly resembled Leo Tolstoy's character by his attraction to school, after which he used to meet his sis Val.

"What are you doing here, Gen?" Val asked him amazingly.

"Nothing. I'm waiting for you", he replied.

"Why?"

"To help you with your schoolbag", answered the little gentleman.

"If so, let's carry it together", Val said, generously allowing him to touch its handle.

Nobody was at home, the parents being at work, the eldest sister Emma - at school.

"Let's play a little", Val proposed to Gen. He agreed. "You'll be my horse, and I'll be your horseman", Val explained, yoking him with some ropes which happened to be lying randomly around. "If you are a horse, you need some oats to be fed. I'll go outside and try to get it for you, sweet Gen", she said and left the room.

Val spent many hours outdoors, playing with her neighbour girls, forgetting all about her home-"horse" errand.

Their Mommy came back from work late in the evening, saw Gen standing in the corner quietly, and tied to the chair, meekly expecting his horseman Val.

"What are you doing here, Gen?" Mom asked.

"I'm expecting the corn", he said.

"What?!"

"The oats."

"What for?"

"To eat."

"Why have you been tied up?" questioned his Mother.

"I am a horse and have to stand calmly in a stable", he told her.

"It's clear to me now ", murmured Mom.

"How long have you been standing in the corner?" asked she.

"I don't know. First, I met Val at school, second, I carried her schoolbag, third, we started to play", explained little Gen.

"Where's Val?" the angry Mother asked.

"I am not sure. Perhaps, in the yard", Gen answered. Mom

looked out of the window and called her daughter,

"Come home immediately!" she ordered.

As Val appeared in the room, she grasped in a second that Mommy was angry, as she was waiting for her with a wet towel in her left hand.

"What's up?" asked Val innocently.

"Nothing, except your brother", cried Mommy, chasing Val in the hopeless attempts to catch her and punish her with the towel.

"You left him for a long time, he is still expecting you but you have forgotten everything, playing in the yard", grumbled the Mother. "Now I'll show you how one must behave in such a case", shouted the young woman, running around the table which was round.

So the chasing supposed to be around the circle. The alert Val jumped under the table and escaped through the door. Disappointed Mom remained motionless with the towel in her hand; the water was dripping onto her feet from the wet towel.

Gen's behaviour and successes were perfect when he entered the school at long last.

Having possessed a pretty good memory, he soon learned to read, write, tell and retell stories. Thank goodness! His two sisters were the first audience, and how grateful listeners they were!

"Do you want to do something interesting for your sisters?" asked Gen to himself.

"Yes, sure. Good. That's the spirit! Then listen, please."

Joke Number One.

Question: Why does an elephant want to be alone?

Answer: Because two's a crowd.

Joke Number Two.

Question: Why did the elephant stand sideways on his head?

Answer: He wanted to keep a low profile.

Joke Number Three.

Question: What did the elephant do when he came to the water hole?

Answer: He sliced his drive into the woods.

Joke Number Four.
Question: Why does an elephant rub vanishing cream on his body?
Answer: It helps the elephant hide.

Joke Number Five.
Question: Which king did the elephants fear the most?
Answer: Richard the Mouse-Hearted.

Joke Number Six.
Question: Why did the elephant eat lOO-watt bulbs?
Answer: It wanted a light lunch.

Elephant jokes were very big in the Gen's reading field. What did elephants ever do to deserve that? Nobody tells hyena jokes, but hyenas laugh at elephant jokes and everything else.

Joke Number Seven.
Question: My grandfather was the kind of man who went to a barber-shop every day.
What was he, an actor?
Answer: No, a barber.

Joke Number Eight.
Question: What's your favourite kind of dog?
Answer: A hot one.

Joke Number Nine.
Nothing I know of
Would please me better
Than to see a giraffe
In a turtleneck sweater.
Joke Number Ten.
Gen: I should never have shown anybody but you the watch I got for my birthday.
Sisters: Very nice.
Gen: There's no present like the time.

And then Gen told his next story:

"Years ago our grandfather gave me his clock - now it is called "a grandson's clock" - but the only trouble is, it runs backward. Instead of going tick-tock, it goes tock-tick. And have you ever seen a balalaika clock? It's shaped just like a balalaika, and instead of going tick-tock, it goes laika-bala. I even had a stammering balalaika clock once that went bala-lala-laika-ka. Otherwise it was a perfectly normal balalaika clock. It had an hour hand - that was the first hand, and a minute hand - that was the second hand, and a second hand - but that made the second hand the third hand!

I've never understood that. Somehow it puts me in mind of a man in a circus sideshow who ate razor blades and broken glass. Once he ate a clock, but he didn't like it. It was time-consuming. Which reminds me - did you hear about the railway station clock that struck eleven? It fell off the roof and hit a football (soccer) team! You remember, sisters, it consists of eleven footballers. At eleven hit eleven".

Little Gen was really fond of sports; he tried football, basketball, volleyball, ping-pong, chess.

What is chess: art, science, or sport?

Uncannily, chess contains elements of all three - and yet chess remains a game, the best game ever invented, Gen gathered.

Chess is a game loved by his father and friends. Chess imposes a set of rules and has finite limits, but just as you start to think that you're finally solving its mysteries, chess thwarts you. Sometimes, therefore, the game is frustrating but far more often chess proves both surprising and delightful. The deeper you dig into chess, the more of its secrets you reveal - but the game has never been tapped out.

The point is that not only chess is an excellent educational tool, chess is fun, too. Persuading kids to play a game of chess is far easier than enticing them to do math exercises, believed senior Filin! The great thing is that the kids are actually learning how to think while playing. They can't help it!

Parents all across the world are waking up to the fact that chess is an inexpensive and effective option for developing skills, such as the ability to sit still and concentrate, that are directly transferable back into the classroom.

Chess was for little Gen an endless source of pleasure. The degree of fun derived from a game of chess was rarely a function of one's absolute playing strength, but rather of the relative strengths of Gen and his permanent partner, Daddy. If two players were horribly mismatched, neither was likely to have much fun. The best situation occurred if two players were evenly or closely matched. Some days one won in such matches, and some days one could lose - but the issue was always in doubt often right down to the end of the game!

Sometimes when the chess atmosphere became more and more intensive, Gen's mother would interfere, "You, old fool," addressed she to her husband, "can you see how your son is suffering because of the losses. Look at him! He's about in tears, you stupid ass and pompous-all-fool!" Maria cursed Nick. "Step down and let your little son win! You understand that, don't you?"

At long last justice celebrated its victory. The young man won his first chess game and the old one pretended to be joyful about this fact. Even he stretched his hand to his son to congratulate him on his victory. Val witnessed all and enjoyed it more than everyone.

In one moment she organized the theoretical chess quiz game, the answers of which she knew beforehand. Her brother was the centre of her interest, not Daddy. She put repeatedly her sophisticated questions to Gennady and Dad.

"Who was the first chess world champion?"

Gen answered first, it was as in a modern Jeopardy game. The role of Alex Trebek performed Val. "Emmanuel Lasker from Germany," was the answer.

"How long?"

"From 1894 until 1921."

"And what about Jose Raul Capablanca?" "He also was world champion from 1921 to 1927", Gen answered again.

"What can you say about the Russian chess school? Who was the beginner?"

"Alexander Alekhin was single-minded in his pursuit of the world championship and his drive eventually overcame

202

Capablanca's skill. From 1921 through 1927 he competed in 15 major tournaments and won 8 of them", told Gennady.

"Who were the other Russian prominent chess players ?"

"Mikhail Botvinnik, Mikhail Tal, Boris Spassky, Tigran Petrosyan, Vasily Smyslov, Mikhail Chigorin, Paul Keres, Viktor Korchnoj", counted Gen, bending his fingers in turn, trying to remember all he knew. Gen was the winner of the quiz and got great satisfaction doing it. Val leaped up, kissed him and gave him a big hug.

Gen grew up, doing very well at school. Once his mother was invited to school to explain on local radio how she raised her child's IQ and her experiences.

She told the other parents verbally her address over the inter-com,her report had been prepared by the teachers beforehand.

"There seems to be a timetable for programming the young people's brains - of a lot of opportunities", as one scientist put it. If you miss an opportunity in childhood, you can lose the time. But developing the children's brains continues throughout their whole lives.

In my case, there is a little community of three children. They teach each other, learning from each other, as well. We, working parents, can influence on them exclusively by our own example of lifestyle. That's all. Thanks for your attention", and added, "I'm a regular woman. There is nothing really special or unique in the way I raise my children. They grow up naturally as everybody else in our society".

Eight school years had been completed by Gen with a top-mark-certificate. In all subjects and his behaviour noted as perfect.

In the mid-fiftieth, when he was a teenager Gen started changing little by little:

> *"Heavenly Daze!*
> *When someone tries to tempt you,*
> *Into doing something wrong.*
> *Temptation put behind you!*
> *Be noble! good! and strong !*
> *Recall this old-time rule;*
> *Remember how it goes:*

Evil whispers yes,
Goodness only noes!"

(S. Corbett)

One day his mother crossed through the mall and met Gennady's teacher who asked her: "Hello, Mrs. Filina, tell me what's the matter with your son. He's not been attending school for two months or so?" "Oh, really?! Every morning he takes his schoolbag and heads to the classes and comes back from school also on time. Where does he usually go?", she asked in astonishment.

At home she asked Gen passionately:

"My honey love, you're getting older and beginning to pull my leg, aren't you7"

"Mom, no, I'm not", he answered.

"Then how do you explain your two-months-absence from school? Your school master informed me this morning," she kept on questioning him.

"Oh, well", grumbled Gen, apparently not hoping for this direct question 'en face',

"You see, Mommy, I did not notice the time had been passing. My friends and I, we, guys, first went to the woods, you know, second, we played and talked, then wandered around marshes, ponds, and wet places".

"Oh, really?!" his mother was amazed.

Gen and his pals needed the tonic of the wilderness, to see cattails in the marshes to bring the female mature flowers for making an attractive home decoration; to hear the booming of the snipe; to smell the whispering sedge where only some wilder and single fowl builds her nest. The guys did not break the birds' nests. They admired them, they loved and saved everything.

The young nature explorers watched a squirrel leaping from tree to tree, listened to the symphony of sand hill cranes and yellowlegs. Bryansk area teamed with life - from insects and green frogs to the furred and feathered. Gen was of especial curiosity about wild plants, in which habitat it grew and in what range, it was so rich in these areas.

"Look!" exclaimed Gen, cutting out one of them, "this is veronica".

"Show me, show me!" cried the gang of boys.

It flourishes along streams and in wet ditches, scattered throughout the forest region.

"Oh, I know the legend about Veronica!" shouted one of the fellows.

"Tell us, tell us, please", everybody cried in chorus.

"According to the legend, the last chapter of the Holy Bible "the genus" was named after Saint Veronica, who wiped Christ's face when He was on his route to be crucified. On her handkerchief there was left a "true image" (Vera iconica) of Christ's face".

"Oh, it's marvelous. Who told you that?" they all got interested in the answer.

"My grandma in the village. Look. The Veronica looks like "forget-me-nots", but they are entirely different from them", continued Gen's friend.

"Blue flowers, whether they are forget-me-nots, veronica, or something else, are a traditional gift of good luck and remembrance for departing guests.

The greeting "God speed" or "speedwell" that accompanied the present basically means "God be with you".

"Speedwell is one of the nicknames for veronica", concluded the clever boy.

"Look out! When picking any water-loving greens like veronica, cattails, mare's tail, or buckbean, always be certain to avoid polluted areas!"

"By the way, cattail has a great number of other names: cat-o'-nine-tails, Cossack asparagus, rushes, flags, broadleaf cattail, or bulrush like in North England. Do you know the puzzle?" asked Gen to his comrades.

"What? What kind of puzzle?" cried out the children.

"Why did the bulrush?" asked he. "Who knows they answered".

"Because it saw the cowslip". Everybody laughed. The game started, the good old puzzle-game.

"Why did the garden fence?" asked one.

The other answered in a second, "Because it saw through the

window box".

"What is it? That is of one and the same colour in summer and in winter, throughout all the seasons of the year?"

"A fir-tree."

"Who knows the limericks?" asked Gen .

"What's this, the limerick, Gen?" asked the boys.

"Limerick is a nonsense poem with the rhyme scheme like that aabba, stresses on the first, second and fifth lines (five anapestic lines, as my Dad said), popularized by Edward Lear" , explained Gen .

"Give us an example, Buddy".

"Here it is:

> *There was a young lady named Harris,*
> *Whom nothing could ever embarrass,*
> *Till the bath salts one day,*
> *In the tub where she lay,*
> *Turned out to be plaster of Paris " ,*

recited Gen the rhyme.

"Oh it's simple enough", said a guy, "I'll try:

> *'It happened in Brazil'*
> *A grass snake from Rio, Maximilian,*
> *Was adored by a girl snake named Lillian,*
> *But the snake-in-the-grass*
> *Snatch away from the lass!*
> *What a rotten reptilian Brazilian!".*

Then tried another one:

> *" 'The Fidgety Type'*
> *I used to think planes were all right,*
> *But I hated my bargain-fare-flight*
> *To Moscow and Leningrad,*
> *Orel and Stalingrad*
> *I only stayed there overnight!".*

Everybody wanted to try the limerick-game:

"A fish that was caught up in the Banks the White
Said, 'If I could once have the only right;
I'd want a vacation
Then reincarnation.
And come back as some kind of fish aright'".

The next one:

"There was an old man of Capri,
He played a violin on his knee,
The people laughed,
And thought him daft,
And so did you and me" .

The following one was:

"Who is it?
The Thing that appears is mysterious,
I sometimes believe I'm delirious,
I don't know how near It is,
When suddenly here It is!
The situation's quite serious."

And the last and shortest one:

"School play.
Had to stay.
Bored.
Snored.
I was away. "

"Now I understood the reason of your absence at school, my love Gen. You enjoyed your games instead of school classes", insisted Mother.

207

"Excuse me, Mommy", said Gen," I forgot the time passing entertaining the limerick. Here is one for you:

> *"It was my Mommy being alone,*
> *Who insisted on my coming home,*
> *She troubled my mind*
> *Since I never could find*
> *A suitable rhyme for returning,*
> *Because my heart was truly yearning".*

Mother's heart melted after her son's dedication rhymes, she forgave her charming and very beloved son.

Gen grew up and his jokes were growing together with him, becoming more and more obnoxious even grotesque:

> *"Teacher's Pet*
> *Only someone who's an absolute sap'll*
> *Give an old crow like our teacher an apple!"*

A rhyme to a girl:

> *"You look like an orangutan ,*
> *And you smell like a goat;*
> *If you were my Valentine*
> *I'd cut my throat!"*

Or this one:

"Don't let your parents tell you, 'Kids were nicer in the old days!' Naturally, it was not true. The kids at all times remain kids with their advantages and disadvantages."

When Gen was a toddler, he loved his friend Igor who had got a big wheels' cycle. Igor kindly shared his bike allowing Gen to ride on it. Gennady spun it in circles and tried to fly off cardboard jumps. At night, he'd bounce into bed with his parents, Maria and Nick, wake them up, and squeak, "It's me ! It's the bed-jumper. And the foot-smuggler."

Then he'd rub his cold toes up and down their legs.

Gen loved to talk. By the time he was six, if he could not corner someone to listen, he would walk up and hit him or her. It wasn't an angry hit. He just wanted a person to know he was there. And he wanted you to listen - right now!

He'd follow you around, tugging at your sleeve, as he spilled over with imaginary stories of war and spy adventures and Russian national heroes like Chapaev, Budenny, Gastello, Matrossov.

His blue eyes sparkled under uneven bangs. His friend Igor was under Gen's great spell. Excited Igor would tell you that he had magical powers and then throw his arms around his waist, or pull your head down and give you a hug.

As the friends grew from toddlers into active little, and then big boys, they played together basketball, football. But they never really cared very much if their team won or lost. They played for fun and to be with their friends.

Gen often asked to his Dad, "How come people are so mean to each other ?" Gen thought that people should be kind and helpful to everyone, no matter who they were, and give everybody a chance. In spite of weird looks, he yelled "Hi!" to all the strangers in the shopping malls.

He cracked original jokes, such as: "What's round and red and you can wear it?". Before you could come up with a clever answer, he'd shout, "A pimple!"

And then he'd bound off laughing.

It was two friends who drew posters, verses and songs about nature. They worried about pollution. When they saw a documentary about an endangered species of penguins, they cried, they looked like twins. They asked questions about dolphins, too.
Would they be around when they were old men? Was there a clock ticking away somewhere? Was there only a little time left for the Earth if people didn't change? Gen told to his Dad, "Kids will be the ones to teach the adults to take care of the Earth".

The two friends decided, "We can help people change. People are the pollution solution. We'll be defenders of the planet. To keep the world healthy and beautiful".

One day they told to their teacher, "We want to start our own club. We want to call it, "Kids for Saving Earth".

They talked with their school friends and started making plans. Igor often behaved in an absent-minded way, his glasses slipping down his nose, as he startled into space if the teacher or anyone else scolded him for not listening, he would reply in his slightly nasal voice, "It's just that what is going on in my own mind is so much more interesting".

But while Igor worried about the Earth's future, there was another clock ticking away inside his lungs.

In the fall of 1958, Gen's friend began to show strange symptoms. He'd wander out of his bedroom at night, and walk around the rooms with a disoriented look on his face.

He developed headaches and began to vomit.

Igor's parents grew concerned. They decided that Igor needed to see a doctor. After an X-ray at the hospital, they received the shocking news: Igor was diagnosed as having a lung tumor.

The doctor put him in the hospital that night for tests, and two days later performed a delicate lung operation. In spite of many hours of surgery, the doctor was able to remove only 75 percent of the huge mass in Igor's lungs.

The family remained positive. They fully believed that Igor would recover. His father used to say, "He always kept his sense of humour - through everything".

Igor never doubted that things would turn out okay. After all, he was the kid with magic powers!

Igor returned to school full time. He had grown thinner and thinner. But even with deep hollows in his cheeks, he kept grinning. Gen supported him as he could. They never lost their faculties. They both were alert and maintained their sense of humour. "What is it? Black and white, And read all over? - A newspaper."

Their week long vacation expanded into three weeks at Christmas as they continued on to Moscow.

While they went by train, they sang:

"Let be always the sunshine!
Let be always the heavens!
Let be always my Mommy!
Let be always Gen and me!"

210

Each day was more wonderful than the last simply because it was so great being together. Igor added his usual dose of home-made humour: "What's red, yellow, and green and makes you want to scream?" He threw out his arms. "A traffic light!"

When the friends returned home, they grabbed the ball and headed for the backyard.

"Igor could really smack that ball", Gen remembered.

"By March, Igor could still hit, but he stopped running around", Gen said. "He grew tired. His legs wobbled beneath him", Igor's Dad paused, cleared his throat and then continued , "Soon he didn't go out at all".

"This was a special kid", said the school principal, "In those last few months, you knew, he was hurting. He'd miss a few days of school, then you'd see him in the hall, and he'd have this big smile. He'd say, "Hey, Mr. Principal, how ya' doin'?"

On the First of May, Igor sat with his family around. The table filled with apple pies and cranberries. His friend was next to him. They shared with one another all the things they were grateful for. When it was his turn to speak, Igor said, "I'm grateful for my family and all my wonderful friends".

Four days later, the kid with magic powers slipped away. His father was with him at the end. He doesn't like to talk about it. He wasn't certain exactly which moment Igor died. He just sort of slipped away, like a puff of smoke.

The funeral was attended by many of Igor's friends, teachers, and adults. As his parents pulled themselves together following the funeral, Gen set about fulfilling the promise to Igor to be a faithful friend to the Mother Earth…

. . .

So Gennady soon was a student of the Bryansk Forest-Technological Institute, the faculty of the Mechanical Engineering in 1960.

Together with the scientific technical knowledge, Gen used to spend a lot of spare and vacation time in the forest wild grassy meadows and sunny forest openings.

One poet William Wordsworth somehow exclaimed:

"How does the meadow flower its bloom unfold?
Because the lovely little flower is free,
Down to its root, and, in that, freedom, bold".

When Gen observed that white forest flowers seemed to have the most enchanting fragrance, it appeared that the less snowy white blossoms have developed exquisite "floral perfume" to attract pollinators .

It is intriguing to watch the vital partnership between flowers and insects, bees and flies, as well as mosquitoes.

Meadow flowers such as wild roses, violets, and monkshood are also common in forest openings.

"A rose is arose is a rose".

Whether wild or domestic, roses were one of the easiest flowers to identify. "The best flower in the world is the wild rose", Gen considered, recommending to his Mom a tasty jam or a vitamin-crammed tea or a Christmas tree garland or a beauty bath. Roses could fill all these needs, and countless more. Besides being the "flower of flowers" and the symbol for beauty and love, the rose (from the Greek 'rhodon' meaning 'red') signifies silence. The expression "Sub Rosa" originated in Rome, where roses were suspended above a table or engraved on the ceiling to indicate the confidentiality of all conversations.

For a natural Russian Christmas decoration, string rose hips and wrap the garlands around your tree. After the holiday, the dry hips were used for tea, or the garlands were placed outside as a treat for the feathered friends.

Gen loved the birds that were fond of rose hips and helped distribute the seeds. Wild roses were ideal ornamentals, being both attractive and versatile.

Following a Desna river upstream to its source was Gen's delight.

"Water comes from a faucet", was his childish city wisdom.

"Water comes from a well and flows farther into Dnepr river near Kiev", was its country counterpart. But actually witnessing water that flew from an opening in the forest offered a special connection to, and appreciation of the pure water Mother Earth gave the people so freely.

"The wild is calling, calling ...let us go" and Gen had followed streams to their sources, quenching his thirst with icy water from a mountain spring, meeting with a hare, or a fox, watching the water and dipping his hand for insects were just a few of the joys he had experienced. Gen had been a philosopher and a scientist in his own way, and like those of his time and country his interests had extended into all things. He had questions to ask and answers to seek.

He learned to do as he could. Gennady had a restless mind.

Now the girls had aroused something in him that he could not explain. As far as he recollected female students' faces and figures, made his young blood boil for him and he started having headaches. Girls seemed to live in quite a different way and they appeared to be so charming, intriguing and attractive. They were strange ones, the girls and him, but the result was less for them than for him.

The girls he had known belonged to their own families, and the parents demanded that each family member conform to a certain standard. Now here and there Gen, a good-looking, intelligent youth, was coming among them with disturbing new ideas, and new proposals.

"Nataly, would you like to go with me for a walk?" asked Gen, peeping at a young girl passionately.

"What walk have you thought out, Gen?" asked the pretty girl in her turn.

"If you don't mind, it would be a ride in the boat along our beautiful Desna river", he explained, "Do you agree, Nat?"

"Sure", Nataly answered.

"I'll show the beauties of our nature and tell you lots of stories about them", Gen promised.

They met on the bank of the river near the Black Bridge. Nataly was dressed in a blue skirt and a white blouse, she had been dropping a pebble into the pool of her thinking, and who knew where the ripples would end?

"Let us hire a boat and swim from it, in the middle of the river the water's cleaner. Have you got a swimming costume, Nat? You should have tried sunbathing, too", said Gen and they hurried to the river boat station.

The bright sunny morning came suddenly to the river. The shadows under the trees appeared and became more visible and distinct, tentatively at first. Bullfrogs spoke loudly in the river, and some large thing splashed in the water.

"A fish", Gen said, "a big one".

The thought of their flimsy boat was not a pleasant one. He made a motion for silence and began dipping his paddle with great care. The boat glided through the dark, glistening water. There was a smell of rotting wood and vegetation from the shore.

Once, on a fallen tree lying in the water they passed only the length of a paddle from a huge snake. She was as startled as them, but Gen and Nat slid past in the dark water and she gave only a surprised shish.

It was very still but for the sounds from the forest and the soft rustle of water. In the distance and across the river they heard vague sounds of childish yells swimming in the river.

Then a large island came between them and the town. "Sweetie, you are crazy as a loon", said Nat turning to Gen. "Where are you going to land, here ?"

"Sure. Look! How nice it is around here!" exclaimed he in a pure amazement.

He turned the boat into the now strong current from their right and then he dug in, the paddling with all his strength. Now they, no longer drifting with a current, were breasting one, and a strong one at that. The island was rich with dandelion flowers and lovely wild country roses and there was beauty where the river ran.

They went on the shore.

The yellow colorful blowballs touched the green carpet with the new cheery banners of spring.

"How marvelous the dandelions are!" exclaimed Nat, rising up both of her hands. "As though all were big yellow fury bees landing for a second allowing us to admire them! I'd rather plait a wreath of them to put on our heads".

"Go ahead", responded Gen, "I'd like to check the boat to see if there is any leakage in it, or not ".

After some time had been passing, Nat made up two dandelion wreaths, one - for herself, the second one - for Gen.

Wearing them, they looked like two funny old-fashioned, Russian youths out for a walk, being ready to give hands to each other and to start leading in dancing circles, very smoothly and full of grace.

They did not take any musical instrument with them, but they heard the music of the hearts within them, so their eyes sparkled as one thousand lights of a grandiose firework.

"Nat, do you know that some call the dandelions 'the liver herb'?" began Gen.

"No, I don't. Tell me, please, Gen", continued Nat.

"This plant lowers cholesterol and high blood pressure, and gives support in emotional problems", said Gen.

"Oh, really? My grandma told me its stems is a folk remedy for warts", added Nat.

"During the Second World War my Dad told me, the latex like substance of the dandelion roots was cultivated by the Russians as a commercial source of rubber", told Gen.

"I heard that in America this flower was intentionally imported on the Mayflower", said Nat and after some time asked Gen thoughtfully:

"Do you know the legend about the dandelions?"

"No, not yet. After your tale, I suppose to be familiar with it", Gen looked at her meaningfully.

"Producing about 150 seeds each dandelion blowball, according to legend, if one seed remains after three puffs on a blowball, you have a faithful lover", told Nat and could not guess at the moment because nowhere there was seen any blowball, they must appear three weeks later, what a pity!

So it was the start of Gen's love-games with females.

One long June night his fellows and Gen went to a dance hall situated within their block of houses, but over the Black Bridge, which was famous for gang violence.

By midnight Gen used to come back from his walks, dropping

in his home to have a glass of milk with a slice of rye bread, and then heading for his summer sleeping place in the cow's barn outside their lodgings.

The clock beat twelve times: everybody at Gen's home slept, except for his sister Val.

She read the philosophical books, preparing for her exams. Expecting her brother obviously, however he was delaying why, she did not lnow.

At one a.m., at two or three nobody showed up. Val woke up her mother, complaining at Gen's absence.

"Go to bed. He is apparently sleeping and dreaming about some sweet girl," Mom said.

Val was scared to death, she was afraid of the darkness, and she was afraid for her brother's safety.

Overcoming her fear, she went out alone, crossed over the yard and checked the barn's door. There hung a big lock, showing that Gen was not here.

Val became worried more and more. Her heart felt that there was something wrong had happened to her brother. She no longer disturbed anyone in her family, but she could not sleep a wink. In an hour she approached the barn again, in an hour - again.

Gen did not appear, some while later Val was about to lose her temper, clenching her fists, asked herself: "Where is he, at long last? What is up, too?" When she came to the barn next time, she saw Gen lying in a pool of blood, unconscious and pale.
Val called the emergency ambulance, the doctors said: " One hour longer and he would be dead", doctors started the fight for Gen's life. Fortunately, he was saved this time.

What had happened that night?

Gen and his friends made a big mistake of walking down the boulevard with the girls from those gang members to pass time. The girls giggled and laughed, provoking Gen's pals to behave silly.

Another pretty girl from a rival gang hollered from across the street, she was accompanied by young gangsters.

Gen's friend could not accept the taunting and ran across to fight it out with his rival.

The fight was with knives, although Gen remained on his side of the street, some boy's knife hit him under the ribs.

Then everybody ran away in fear of the police. Nobody wanted to get arrested.

Gen rolled back his blue eyes, for some time he walked without purpose, then he fell to the ground and crawled behind the fence.

Val was in shock, some hours after she investigated this case with the aid of Gen's comrades.

Finally she got fed up with the violence. She went to the police. It had not been too hard for her to speak before a select group of fifty students. But when Val saw the adult men in police uniforms staring at her she almost swallowed her tongue.

On the hour of her speech, Val recalled, "I was afraid of being made fun of. All the gang members have still freedom. I was afraid of what might happen after the speech. What could I do? Should I run for the bus or ask a policeman to take me home? My mother couldn't get off work to listen to my speech. Neither my father. I had no one with me".

The more Val thought about it, the more her stomach flipped around. Her palms grew sweaty. Her cheeks felt hot. Should she back out? It wasn't too late, yet. Everyone would forgive her.

But she remembered her brother Gen lying in a hospital bed, dying. Then her mind forced her back to his friends' faces bleeding in the night.

She pushed her feet underneath her body. Somebody had to have gutts to call a halt to those gangs.

She stared at two young policemen. They smiled and seemed to say, "Go on. You can do it".

Val left her fear lying there in the corridor, like a shed skin. She spoke with a steady voice for five whole minutes. It was a sister's speech in protection of her brother.

"I am sick and tired every time I come out of my house, getting harassed, beat up, or killed. We really want things safe for all the people. The only thing you can get from a gang is a hole in your body or six feet under.

Take your choice. Either way, you end up dead..."

And then Val noticed the hundred eyes staring at her. It was so quiet that the whole audience seemed to be holding its breath. She looked straight ahead and went on talking, meaning every word.

"The gangsters' parents have so much hope for their children. What is happening? The best way to get out of this is to get a good education. It's the only passport out of this neighbourhood..."

Val finished. There was a pause, and the clapping began. It grew louder. The policemen stood up and cheered. She looked out at the white eyes, the white teeth, the bright smiles. And she swallowed a thickness in her throat.

She felt like she had just saved the whole world, not only her brother.

Before graduation from the Institute, getting his diploma of a mechanical engineer, Gen was going to visit his love in one small Ukrainian town; on his way there he stopped in Kiev to visit another acquaintance, Galina Michailovna Izilenko by name, a small, ordinary woman, the same age as him.

He did not reach his love that time, but soon returned home and declared, "I have to get married".

"To whom?" the family members asked with interest .

"To Galina from Kiev. I left my jacket with my passport as a deposit for my return to her", he added sadly.

Something unusual was in his voice. We don't marry nowadays just for security and protection, but for love, romance and emotional fulfillment. Nothing of that kind was foreseen.

"Do you love her?" asked Val.

"I have to", he answered. "We are expecting a baby to be born soon. The wedding is planned for some day in February."

Nobody understood the true reasons of his marriage. After the wedding celebration he was directed to a big Gorno-Altaisk furniture factory as a certified engineer.

Working as a chief engineer in the day-time and as a simple worker in the evening shifts he tried to earn as much money as possible to help his wife to buy a descent flat for living in Kiev. Since that moment on, Gen fell in love with woodwork: cabinetmaking, carpentering.

By mid-December a pretty baby-girl Larissa was born. The love of their daughter could not join two people like Galina and

Gennady whose personalities were quite different: twice he left his family, twice he got back.

Over the hours, during telephone conversations, Val had heard many of Galina's complains that her husband was no longer as attentive or interested in her, as he was early in the relationship. She wondered, what happened to the man she fell in love with?

Val's answer was that Gen was still there, and with a little effort and understanding on her part, she had the power to bring romance back into the marriage.

Romance? As a matter of fact, there was no romance in their relations at all, there was no love from the very start; practical Galina just grabbed a young perspective man for sex playing, without understanding his romantic nature.

The hysterical jealous scenes from Galina added to the full picture of their relationship which was on the verge of divorce.

Twice they got divorced, twice they married -it meant that both of them tried to achieve a lasting passion, intimacy and happiness.

Gen would do all sorts of things for Galina and Larissa at home: fixing up the toys, plumbing, electrical jobs, fulfilling all the technical home assistance.

He felt that sharing his income and the rest of his life were much bigger gifts than as simple little thing like emptying trash, as Galina insisted on.

He was surprised and deflated when it didn't win him more appreciation.

Galina turned the situation around. "I know how hard you work", she said, "and that you want to rest when you get home, I would really appreciate it, though, if you would just empty the trash for me".

Being goal oriented, men find it hard to shift directions. So in the beginning Gen grumbled. But the fact that he emptied the trash made Galina feel more special than the work that captured most of his attention. And as her husband saw how strongly she valued what he did for her, he emptied the trash because it made his wife so happy. The secret of getting more from a man is to appreciate what he is already giving and then ask for more in small increments. Having solved the trash problem, Galina knew that over time she could demand from him more and more. But nothing more had happened.

They parted for ever: there remained their pleasant, blue-eyed daughter in the beautiful city of Kiev, the jewel of Ukraine.

For his daughter this was a time of discovery. The summer drifted on far into autumn that year, into the time of Indian summer that the Russians call "Granny Summer".

Gen's daughter liked to visit her grandma in the village of Mironovka near Kiev, she walked all around the area, sometimes alone and sometimes with granny, a small, rather old woman, who showed her where to find herbs - Saint John's wart, belony, ribwort - where there were medicinal ferns.

They walked through a little pine wood to the south, above the river and there on the mossy ground grew bushes of bilberry and cranberry. Here and there, as they walked, she would point to a particular tree and say, "There's a squirrel nest up there. Look." She would point to the littler tracks made by the squirrel's claw on the trunk as it went up, again, and again, to fill the deep hollow in the trunk with nuts for a winter.

How lovely the woods seemed, how friendly. Above, in the brilliant blue sky, billowing white clouds passed from time to time, gleaming in the reflection of the late-morning sun.

This girl grew up under the great influence of her granny who was proud of that.

Before the First May's holidays,1986, nobody in the Soviet Union knew about the great disaster at Chernobyl Atomic Station's explosion, neither did Gen's daughter.

She, a young 18-years' old girl, accompanied her granny and mother and walked across the Kreshchatik square. Suddenly her head began to be dizzying, then vomiting and she fainted. Doctors could not diagnose the disease, later it became clear that it was the dangerous consequence of the nuclear catastrophe which was thoroughly hidden from simple people by Gorbachev's government until it was forced to reveal the truth.

Since that moment on, the young girl could not continue her education, could not work physically, could not love young guys and bear normal children. Obviously she got disabled, a young girl grew into an adult woman with a hard fortune like a silver birch tree. Its branches were bare, wintry; but the eastern morning sun was making its silvery bark, shiny. "You look as if you were made of snow and ice", she thought, "yet, inside you are still warm".

The Russian birch was a hardy tree. It would grow anywhere, in any conditions, supplanting trees that had been burned or cut down. "I will be like that, too", the girl vowed. "I shall survive".

Meantime Gen had to survive, too.

Coming back to Bryansk, he lived at his Mom's flat and worked as an engineer in one of the plants.

Once the enterprise's communist party representatives offered Gen to join their Party. After putting him hundreds of questions they decided to refuse him because of the immoral behaviour towards his family: two marriages and two divorces with one and the same woman. What an embarrassment. They did not understand him at all.

At that time Gen met another woman, who was not ugly, but wearing eye-glasses, an engineer by profession, divorced, with a baby-boy, she was seven years younger than him. Her name was Ljudmila.

"I met her", Gen explained, "and took pity of the bad situation she was involved in. Her native aunt got rid of her after quarrels, her baby was under her Mom's care in the Ukraine".

Gen was too honest to deny there was a problem, but it was a phase that would pass, he assured the young woman. "Remember, we are at the very first beginnings", he said. "We have no separate flat to live; have no money in savings; but we have good occupations and can start our cooperative life in my Mom's apartment. We'll work together, and in future all the problems will fall away", he added .

Ljudmila was puzzled. She had listened intently to all that Gennady had said. She had caught his vision of the better life to come, and it had touched her profoundly; she had never heard anyone speak like that before. Yet, when she considered her own life, and her memories of what had passed in the Ukraine, there was something she found she could not understand. And so now, she faced a little awkwardly and asked in a soft voice: "But when

221

will it be this future?"

Gennady stared at her. It was a question of such dazzling stupidity that, for a moment, he had not known what to say. Was she trying to be funny? No. As he gazed at her large, serious eyes and pale face, it was obvious that she was entirely sincere. What a striking-looking woman she was.

He smiled. "I'm afraid you misunderstood me. The future better life we will build up together. And it depends on us, only on us, when we'll manage to do it and how long" , he said kindly.

Did she believe him? Or not?

She had no idea. But one thing she did know. He was the most handsome-looking man she had ever seen in her life.

In 1987 Ljudmila bore Gen a new baby-boy, Danil by name. By that moment the scandals had burnt at Gen's Mom's house; the two women, young and old sick, could not get on any more with each other.

"You, dirty old witch, you stole my butter", cursed the younger one, "give me it back" .

No, I did not", Gen's mother protested.

"Yes, you did, you stupid woman. It was only yesterday I bought half a kilo of butter, and now nothing is left. You've eaten it. I don't intend to feed you, old sick ass". She offended the old woman openly, crying out with bad words. Conflict between his wife and his mother was getting more and more serious.

Gen with Ljudmila had moved to the Ukrainian small miners' town Enakievo of Donetsk region.

Changing his engineering degrees for a new profession as a worker, he had to work in an underground mine in very old-fashioned, dangerous conditions and with very old equipment.

His work was hard but gave him the opportunity to receive a new three rooms' flat and raise two sons calmly. The boys admired Gen badly, calling him "Daddy", traveling with him a lot across the Ukraine. They remembered the school winter vacation, which fell on January 3-10, the week was celebrated the same as in Russia in a very beautiful way.

It was a lovely and delicate New Year holiday calling to mind images of New Year trees decorated with lots of light garlands, ornamentations and many other sweet things.

In Kiev the ceremony of folk walking and Christmas celebrities were of particular beauty.

The two brothers were excited therefore when their father announced that morning that they would all go to Kiev's main New Year tree to watch.

The weather was fine, they recollected. There was only the faintest wind. The cloud cover was high and thin, so that the pale presence of the sun was sensed, if not seen. The streets were full and by the time they reached the Dnepr-river, a huge crowd was gathering. They crossed the street of Darnitsa and took up a position in front of the high walls of new buildings.

Right on the bank of the frozen river, inside a large area enclosed by rails, stood a big New Year fur tree with electric garlands, whirling around, like a Maypole.

The children approached the tree, surrounded it, playing, dancing and singing in the fresh frozen air; two boys and their Dad joined as soon as they could.

The three men's brotherhood had been strengthening with years, unfortunately Mommy Ljudmila grew more and more angry with her husband having promised her a better life and golden mountains and did not accomplish none. She was disappointed. The second Gen's marriage failed. Ljudmila and Gennady were split off, but there still remained a great men's friendship among three close people, Gen, Denis and Danil, everlasting men's strong love for ever, Gennady thought, and his work, which saved him in all hard times.

New social times were slowly coming; the changes were taking place in the very region the people lived.

In the Soviet Union there had been always several sources of wealth. The salt beds and the furs in the huge northern wilderness, the wonderful black earth of the warm Ukraine, and since the time of Ivan the Terrible there had gradually been added the minerals of the Ural Mountains, far to the east, and some very modest trade from the huge, barely colonized wastes of Siberia that lay beyond. Gen was involved in mining the great Ukrainian national coal resources which became poorer with years, the mining facilities had not been renewed since the last century.

The miners' work was really hard, being for a whole hours' shift underground, under extremely dangerous circumstances; their wages were still the same but grocery prices were growing fast and constantly.

It was when Michael Gorbachev came to power and declared new reforms, including glasnost.

Undoubtedly, Gorbachev was a fine Soviet fellow. However Gen also had friends among the trade-unionists who opposed the reforms and who objected to Gorbachev's high-handed ways. He mistrusted the Ukrainian and other politicians who were sent to the Enakievo mine.

He was jealous of their influence and considered them too communist -too far from the simple people -for his taste.

Gen preferred to stick to his old friends, who decided to declare the first All-Union strike throughout the country: "To us, Soviet miners, to simple workers, only one thing is of importance - how long we can live like slaves without normal conditions to live with our families. That is all that matters". And then here was used a word that was, and would long remain, close to the heart of every Russian:"We must live our lives with pride of honest men like free people".

The impression on the whole Soviet people was as if an explosion came through the clear skies; everything was translated by the television set openly, according to Gorbachev's glasnost.

Gen participated in this one and a half month's strike. Imagine, my dear reader. For this period of time, daily and at night shifts, after eight work hours had been passed, several thousand miners in dirty, greasy overalls, muddy boots, mining helmets with lamps changed each other for another group, standing and lying before the building of Local District Communist Party Committee. They went to this place daily as if they came to work by 8 o'clock in the morning, demanding the normal life standards and working rights.

Huge, organized crowds of working people for the first time in the Soviet period dared say the truth, they wished to be free.

"What is freedom, itself?" Gen thought to himself.

224

Lately he read one foreigner's book about that, who wrote: "Freedom of thought is possible anywhere; in prison, in labour camps, in moments of solitude or collection. No power on earth has yet managed to eradicate this right". "No, this author is not right", he thought.

"Even freedom of thought cannot be possible in prison or at places like that when the authorities are above, no possibility to write, to read or to communicate like in Soviet prisons. Poor little thing, this foreigner, he just does not know the truth about Soviet prisons, doesn't he?" meditated Gen. "Freedom of action is possible nowhere, unless we allow the ability of a rich person to buy an expensive object as a freedom, but this is denied by a poor person, and therefore cannot be considered as a right, but merely as a privilege", continued the foreign author. "How odd this writer is! He cannot understand the main thing about the freedom that it is undivided, the freedom of thought and freedom of action. Now the Soviet citizens can at long last acquire the possibility of expressing their thoughts free and that is why, to act according to their thoughts. The example is my comrades in the mine", gave Gen the second thoughts what is happening around him.

To his regret, he participated in the strike for just ten days, then he proceeded in his turn one month's holiday and left for his native town.

After his return the strike results were announced loudly: there was a big salary increase but the bad work conditions were still aggravating life in the Ukraine as well as in Russia; it became worse and worse for regular people.

For seventeen years' experience underground he got the right to be retired and live on a pension.

However, the pension was so small, but the prices for food, clothing and renting a flat went ahead so fast that his mine pension was not enough to live on.

He made up his mind to continue to work underground because there were no other work places on the ground in such a small town as it was Enakievo. The economical situation in the former subjects of the Soviet Union as it was called the Ukraine grew worse. The strikes did not help. Everywhere there were four-five months' delays of salary payments and pensions. It was obvious for everybody that it had been organized by the political opposition, communists, who lost their power in the country. The only objective for them was to sabotage, to harm wherever it was possible being contrary to the new oncoming democratic forces headed by Yeltsin. The simple people seemed to suffer most of all.

It happened to be like a very famous Ukrainian saying: "The landlords are fighting but the serfs' mohawk hair is vibrating with electricity".

Gen told everything to his sister Val, complaining at the unbearable living standards in the Ukraine.

She invited him to Saint Petersburg to stay at her apartment unless he finds a new job and can feed himself.

He liked this idea of moving to a big city, the lights of which were always tempting and attracting at the same time.

How wonderful it was to go there. As soon as he prepared, it was midsummer.

There is no stranger or more magical time in the city of Saint Petersburg than midsummer. It is the season known as White Nights.

For around the summer solstice, in those northern cities, the endless days do not give way to darkness. Instead the daylight lingers, far into the evening and beyond until, at last, for the space of half an hour or so in the early hours, it is transformed into a pale, glimmering twilight. The atmosphere is charged, the world unreal. Buildings seem like grey shadows; the water wears a milky sheen, and on the distant northern horizon, the twilight greyness is punctuated by the flashes of the aurora borealis.

Season of White Nights: electric season. Surely it must have been some dangerous magnetism in the atmosphere that led Gennady to commit such acts of complete insanity.

No other explanation is possible. For by that summer, the world for Gen had entirely changed. He met his first love, Vera by name.

How delightful it was just as if they were meeting for the first time twenty nine years ago.

Vera would pile up her rich hair, put on a light yellow ball gown with billowing sleeves and her dainty, flat-heeled dancing slippers with their white ribbons; the men would put on uniforms and take turns dancing with her. And he danced with Vera most of the evening, but the star of the party was Gen himself. He borrowed a balalaika and led the musicians in haunting Ukrainian melodies. Then he danced crouching almost on the ground while he kicked out his legs, and next leaping high into the air while the musicians kept up a frenzied beat.

Once, drawing himself up and arching his back, and jamming a tall sheepskin hat upon his head, he gave a brilliant version of a stately Georgian dance - moving across the floor with precise little steps, turning his body from side to side as he went, so that he seemed almost to be floating.

"He's good", Vera remarked.

Now Gen's heart was dancing, there was another reason for his excitement, he met his young old love.

Gen and Vera sat side by side on the bench, his arm around her shoulder, and her head from time to time resting upon his chest as they talked softly together for long hours.

She was not happy. Neither was he.

She was lonely, without a husband, no children. Only hard-sick parents. No close friends.

His position was easier, having two faithful sons for his benefit. The more they spoke, the more he understood how changed they were since their brilliant youth, how different and incompatible they were.

After several months' dating they parted; he had recited a poem with the dedication to Vera:

> *"I shall remember till my ending,*
> *How I first saw my love, my light;*
> *Just as the darkness was descending;*
> *A fleeting angel in the night.*
> *Your spirit calmed me, waking: sleeping,*
> *I saw your face across the night.*
> *Divinity and inspiration,*
> *And life, and tears, and love".*

PART FIVE

LARISSA

"What are the little girls made of?
-Of honey and spice and all things nice,
That's what little girls are made of."

Little Larissa came to be born a pretty, funny baby-girl. Her Mommy used to cuddle up with Lara and talk not in their childish primitive language but in the adults' serious way because she knew for sure she had to make it seem natural for toddlers. The aim was to create an ongoing listening climate where the tone would remain the same always.

Lara's Mommy was aware that her growing baby was curious to explore nature, to investigate the world.

The first and the most important link to this world was the Mother. Oh, how many grateful words were told about mothers, how many nice songs were sung for the Mothers and with the Mothers.

"Red River Valley", "The Band Played on", "I'll Take You Home Again, Kathleen".

Lara's Mommy used to sing to her child, her voice floated, a deep soprano, sometimes without words, her voice itself being an instrument.

Sometimes her clear voice sailed way above, a wild, perfect harmony with a child who did not understand anything yet, but listened to her with two tiny-tiny ears! Mom stopped as though she had screamed.

Shocked at herself, she looked at her beloved child to see if what she had done was okay.

Yes, the kid said with her eyes, as Lara tried to imitate her Mom's song "Sleep, my baby" with the sounds "ba-ba".

Mom looked back with eyes full of wonder, as she must have looked at her on the first day of her life.

Lara's first words were funny, indeed. Nobody could understand what they meant. Did the "ba-ba " sounds resemble a Russian word "babushka" for Grandma or a shorter "ba-ba" for an English sheep or lamb? Or were those words comic words repeated after Mom's words "baby" , singing in English to her?

Mom did not know. Neither tiny Lara.

Although Lara's grandmother knew it for sure - the reason was because of her influence on girl, her talks. In a quiet but musical tone, old Maria began to speak.

She told Lara about the sacred springs and the spirits that inhabited them. She told Lara about the magic ferns and flowers in the forest, near which there was her village. She told her about the souls of lovelorn girls - the rusalki -who lived in the river, she recounted the story of the firebird, Ilya of Murom, and several others.

Old Grandma often visited Val's house, she loved her grandchild Lara. How lovely, Val used to think about Maria, and how stately was the traditional dress of the Russian woman of 1970. She wore an embroidered blouse with billowing sleeves, instead of the usual simple skirt and shirt as it could be worn in the last century.

Over that blouse, and reaching to the knees, was a long sleeveless gown - the famous sarafan - coloured red and embroidered, as it was the style in the town, with geometric birds of oriental design. And crowning this splendid ensemble was the head kerchief embroidered with gold and silver threads and river pearls. Old Maria and young Val look like the same, the only difference was their clothing and their behaviors, the manners of telling their stories.

Old Maria told about an old Russian and Ukrainian legendary traditions of a curious feast, this was the day of John the Bather - half Christian, half ancient, pagan Slav - and it was hard to say where one began and the other ended. Upon this day, the folks made little dolls of Yarillo, the old fertility God and his female counterpart, whom they called Kupalla; and having paraded them around the river, in a ceremony that was half baptism and half a ritual sacrifice, and which in either case signaled an ancient rebirth.

It was celebrated on the first of June, a Saturday night when the girls guessed about future husbands throwing the flowery wreaths into the river: wherever a wreath was caught, at that place her husband or beloved man must live, it was called the Yanka Kupalla feast that is how it was called in the Ukraine.

Under the warm sun all of them walked back to the house, where a charming meal was laid out: meat pies, cold shchi - the summer version of cabbage soup, trout, turkey and pan-cakes.
There were cherry, apple and raspberry pies, accompanied by mountains of sour cream. To drink there was kvas, wine, and half a dozen different flavored vodkas.

The mellow atmosphere was made softer yet when a little later the women, all in their wonderful dresses, arrived in front of the house and, standing in a circle, sang those most lovely of all Russian and Ukrainian folk melodies, the ancient Kupalla songs.

It was perfect, Lara's mother thought. Everything was just right, like in a fairy-tale.

In real life everything was quite a different situation. The shortage of financial support forced Lara's mother to go to work when the baby was three months old.

From that moment on, Lara was raised up by a working Mommy who shared her busy time between her daughter and her husband, who did not support her, either morally, or physically, especially after work.

Little Lara confused the day-time with nights: at nights she demanded playing with her, and in the day she slept like a log. Mommy was working a full-time job and had no real time for having a rest.

Thank goodness! Such confusion did not last very long.

Lara started walking when she was one year and a month old, avoiding crawling as each baby of her age did.

In a simple way, once Lara rose up and toddled up towards the opposite wall, held up by Mommy's hand. Since that exciting moment, the grandpa's role had been increased; he taught Lara to hold a pencil, to draw lines, to talk to her in his specific way. Lara's first independent "picture" was called "A girl is doing 'pi-pi' , fulfilled in a very modern way.

The artist's age was one year and six months.

Later there appeared the coloured pencils which were sharpened by her first teacher Nick pretty accurately. First steps, first drawings, first books - they were the most memorable and changeable.

Lara's Dad liked to walk with her to the riverside. This type of no confrontational setting kept a parent as well as a kid at ease.

Though they were rarely aware of it, most fathers did it.

They had no time for educational games because of their constant business and an extraordinary love for work, but such a time together with the child could involve almost any activity.

Walking and trips in the boat along the beautiful Desna-river gave a great satisfaction to both, father and daughter.

They told Val how they saw a flock of ducks, thousands of them, they rose as one from a field. In a moment they were in their midst. The air was full of ducks - in front, below, above, behind - wings flashing in the light. The thrill was indescribable. They seemed to accept Dad into their number, and he winged along, just another bird in the squadron. For a second Dad forgot about his little companion, Lara did not frighten. No wonder.

They were birds of a feather.

"Are you again wet after this walk?" asked Lara's Mommy, gazing at them.

"No, we aren't", answered Dad.

"Where have you been, both of you? Look at the mirror! You are covered in mud and feathers! What have you done?" she asked him .

"Nothing. We'd been at the river and watched the ducks flying in the sky", explained he.

"Oh, it's clear, then. Take your shoes off and go to the bathroom immediately", ordered Mom.

By this time one can relate to the first Lara's musical experiences on the piano, which was the only decoration in the livingroom.

As a teacher, Val realized that music, aside from being one of the highest manifestations of human intelligence, is the most scientific of the arts, relying for its best effects on mathematical knowledge of pitch and duration, the weights and measures of strings, the bore of a pipe. In fact, Pythagoras, the first theoretician of music, considered it a mathematical discipline along with arithmetic, geometry and astronomy.

It's increasingly apparent to-day that the ancients were onto something; music instruction can improve a child's spatial reasoning, which is essential to success in math, the sciences and engineering.

Val's friend Nadezda Kabanova, a music teacher, tested toddler Lara and gave her the first music lessons. After eight months of piano and singing lessons, she found that Lara's spatial reasoning had improved by 35 percent.

One scientific research pointed that children who had received no instruction showed negligible improvement.

And in another research, Nadezda told, it indicated that musical training permanently wired a young mind for enhanced performance in the future.

So, strange as it may seem, music really is an appropriate course of study for a child destined to grind out "life skills" or career directives.

Mercifully for the child, music does offer more. It gives enjoyment, for starters, and it provides perhaps the best chance a student will have of developing grace and beauty in school.

It can help her or him explore and cultivate their emotions, and suggests a form of self-expression. It is an interesting way to learn the value of practice, discipline and (with a band or chorus) collaboration.

"And what about Larissa, her musical hearing?" asked Mommy to the musical teacher.

"She does not possess a superb capability, but for general developing it is enough", Nadezda answered.

"Music also permits us, in a small but important way, to look to the long-term objectives of our education system. And one of those objectives must merely be to impart and preserve the riches of our cultural inheritance", added the young teacher.

"Thank you very much, dear", said the girl's mother. "You're absolutely right. Because music is one of the nicest things in the world".

The second important thing, Val reckoned, was reading. Lara's first books were to be about her favourite toys, cartoon characters, nature inhabitants, such as:

> *"My Teddy-Bear was dropped on floor,*
> *With torn off left and right paw,*
> *I'm not going him to throw:*
> *He's my sweet pie, I know! "*

Or:

> *"There is a swinging Bully-toy,*
> *My honey, sighing Mickey-boy,*
> *The board is coming to the end,*
> *I might unluckily to land".*

The song of the beloved tortoise, Tortilla by name, from the same name cartoon:

> *"I am lying in the sun,*
> *And me looking at the sun,*
> *Still I look as in book.*
> *And I'm giving her a cast,*
> *Alligator's swimming fast,*
> *I went on lying in the sun,*
> *And observing Mother-Sun!"*

First reading steps were done by Lara with the help of Val, teaching her gradually, step by step, the letters of the Russian alphabet during playing and drawing, and reciting the poems. "Lara, can you say what it is", her Mom asked showing a big capital letter "A".

"It's a roof", she answered.

"Let's draw it", and on a sheet of paper there appeared pretty funny signs.

Every month there were organized little shows with Larissa's vernisages; actually those were parents' parties with drinks and much talks, among which Lara's first portrayals were widely debated and highly estimated. However Larissa herself did not like to be the centre of everybody's attention, to her character, she'd prefer to watch everybody and everything in a hidden way. Such a little detective at home, with her own anticipation.

Val tried to educate her child as much as possible, opening in Lara as many "windows of opportunity" as feasible.

She began teaching her three-year' old Lara a foreign language to understand and talk in English.

"What's your name ?" Val asked in English.

"My name's Larissa", replied the kid.

"What's your last name?"

"My last name's Kostina".

"What's your Mom's name, then Dad's name, grandma's and grandpa's names ? " and so on and so forth. So far, so good.

They stumbled at the numbers when they started counting. "One, two, three". The new Val's pupil could not distinguish between a Russian sound "s" and an English one "th".

Since there was no "th" sound in the Russian language , the Russian infant generally failed to retain the connections for that sound.

As a result , Larissa could not succeed, when exposed to the difference between "s" and "th" before age three would have trouble discriminating between the two sounds as an adult.

Lara began speaking Russian with an English accent, pronouncing the Russian words with typical English hissing.

As soon as Lara's Dad heard her pronunciation he demanded a stop to his daughter's English lessons immediately, the reasons were as follows, "I don't know for sure, if any foreign language is needed in her future, but it seems to me that she will speak in Russian, in her own language, in an incorrect way and it's a shame!"

Val had second thoughts.

"In learning a new language if you miss a window of opportunity, will your baby be forever handicapped?" and answered to herself, "No, because opportunities to strengthen the think progress abound throughout childhood. We start our life with more neutrons than we need. This means that children can learn faster than adults because throughout their developing years children's brains have an abundance of connections.

Consider, for example, the process of learning to speak a foreign language. While a kindergartner picks up an unfamiliar tongue more ease than a nine-year-old does, the nine-year-old learns it more readily than does a high-school student. I failed with my Sunny-daughter at the young age, I wish to try it later when she's nine!"

Meantime Lara's grandma got seriously sick, and she could no longer be a favourite baby-sitter for the little girl. Lara aged 5 started to visit a day care, acquiring the social experience of communication with children of the same age.

It was so important for a child to be involved in a great number of interesting games, friendships and social activities.

At home, in the atmosphere of everyone's love and mutual understanding a child is growing up a little bit soft, generally speaking, unprepared for the real world!

In the day care a toddler gets the first experience of living in a community. Her or his behaviour changes basically.

"My Sunny," used to say Granny to her beloved granddaughter or grandson, "what would you like for breakfast, dinner or go for a walk?"

"I'd prefer candies to soup ", answered the spoilt baby.

In the kindergarten all children are equal and none of the staff is going to make a difference among them. No Grannies, no Mommies close to them, no baby-sitters. The children tried to be independent and communicative.

"Be my true friend", offered Lara to a little guy in the day care.

" OK, it's you who gave me your new wind-up acrobat-monkey to play with, didn't you?" asked the lad.

"Oh, yes. By the way, what's your name?" questioned Lara.

"Andrey. Let's make friends. You're a kind girl", continued the fellow with satisfaction, winding up with the key the unusual toy.

"And your name?" asked the wise guy.

"Lara".

"I'll be defending you against all the hooligans. I'm a strong boy. Look at my muscles, Lara," and Andrey showed to his new girl-friend his bared arm muscles proudly. He behaved like an adult and apparently copied his own father.

Almost every child has tried, at one time or another, to play one parent off against the other.

Kids, however, are even more likely to play this game if they see their parents discussing their problems aloud; they are inclined to copy their parents' behaviour.

Frankly speaking, if parents weren't often practising good manners at home, how could they expect their children to do the correct things.

One day Lara and her friend Andrey brought home two kittens and a pregnant cat.

Lara's mother would watch incredulously as they went upstairs. It didn't matter whether the creature was a dog, a cat or a ferret. Their approach was always the same: love them, pat them and feed them, take care after them.

"What's that?" asked Val in astonishment, gazing at the three animals.

"The cat family. They are screeching in pain. We are sorry for them", explained the children.

"But they are ill. What can we do with them?" asked the young woman.

"I don't know", answered Lara.

"Neither do I", echoed Andrey.

The cat, a tabby kind, had delivered already one kitten, but another was stuck in the birth canal.

That was the reason of her screaming, about which Val was informed in the veteran hospital where she hurried with the children.

The tabby cat had to have an emergency cesarean section and every one of the three people breathed a sign of relief. Two little grey balls of wet fur were still alive.

Carefully the kittens were plucked from the womb and handled to Val. They cried and cried. When the tabby cat rushed to the kittens' box and started licking their fuzzy bodies, Lara's mother grew more and more agitated.

The Vet could read her thoughts: "What should I do with three kittens and a cat in my tiny apartment?"

Some minutes later he declared: "The cat is seriously ill with skin decease. It must be killed. The kittens seem to be also infected with this desease. We cannot give them back to you until they are free of infection", the old Vet concluded.

The children were very unhappy, they wanted everything better but it turned out for worse. Val bought them a Teddy kitten for both, two cones of ice-cream and calmed them down, "Don't worry, children. Life is not as simple as it seems to be. That's not as great a loss as it seems to be. The most important thing in the world is that you are healthy".

In fact, they were not healthy: they had become infected with the skin desease from this damned homeless cat; it took one month to heal the children, luckily. Moreover, many kids were infected because of those children.

Val knew absolutely that she had to be a model in behaviour in front of her daughter's eyes. But how difficult it was sometimes! Being a parent means being mature enough to help a child adapt to disappointment, as it was in Lara and Andrey's case with the kittens.

Disappointments were expected by the children at every step. As Lara had not been chosen for a concert or- sports team, she appeared troubled.

"What's wrong?" her mother asked.

"I wanted to play a main part of Baba-Yaga in the fairy-tale performance. But I was given another small part, which I don't like", said Lara in tears.

Lara's mother was neither angry nor livid. She didn't fly into a rage, cursing and calling her daughter's teachers all sorts of names. No way. Val tried to calm down her daughter convincing her to take part in the future performance in any role she was proposed.

"My Sunny-daughter, you will act Baba-Yaga character next time. It's not the last performance in your life", said Lara's mother.

Parents who can't accept when their child isn't number one send message that when you're frustrated, you blame the source of frustration instead of looking for a way to cope.

A better message is to teach children that while they cannot always control the outcome of every situation, they can control their response.

Children must learn to behave more gallantly than they feel. Being gallant is more than simply saying 'please' and 'thank you'. It's about not boasting or calling someone names behind his back, about winning fairly and losing graciously, treating everyone with respect. Val tried to do her best when one spring day she asked Lara's day care teacher:

"Could you possibly ask my daughter to tell the gist of the opera we visited last night?"

"Why?" the teacher asked in her turn.

"I want my daughter to learn how to talk logically and correctly and how to retell stories to anyone else", explained Val.

"Oh, superb. I'll do it for you", promised she.

These were the first lessons for Larissa, aged six, how to talk to anyone, anytime, anywhere.

A little sweetie girl Lara never wanted to be a talker. But to her mother, the ability to talk well was one of the great pleasures in life and could bring with it some of life's greatest rewards.

Nobody can say it's always easy.

The vast majority of people would rather jump out of an airplane without a parachute than speak to someone unknown.

Of course, all the training in the world won't persuade a child to behave and talk perfectly if her parents become aggressive, demanding and rude at the slightest provocation. That's why one could say the best way for parents to improve a child's manners and enrich her word power was to improve their own first.

Parents need to be especially vigilant not to say something casually that they may be alarmed to hear later in the mouths of their children.

A wife who tells her husband to shut up and a father who calls a neighbour a jerk are likely to hear their children speak the same way to them.

Children copy their parents all the time.

Once Lara's father dashed for his editorial staff work as usual he was late. And every one of his comrades was worrying why he still wasn't at work: they used to gather for discussing the weekly plans every Monday morning.

239

One of them called to Lara's father's home and asked, "Hi! Who are you?"

"Hi, I'm Larissa Kostina ", the girl answered. "Where is your father?"

"He's gone to work."

"Where's your mother?"

"She's in the toilet".

"What is she doing there?"

"She's very busy. She's doing pee."

"Oh, really?" and the caller hung up.

As soon as Lara's Dad had arrived at work, thirty journalists were waiting for him, he would be asked in no time: "By the way, Comrade Kostin, what is your wife doing at the moment?"

In a serious mood lined, Kostin answered: "1 doubt if I can reply in a correct way".

"Don't doubt. We know it for sure, your daughter told us that she is doing pee in the toilet", and everybody laughed in a loud voice. That was how the reporters entertained.

Another funny story had happened to Lara when she was visiting her grandma's place and staying there for a night.

Old Granny and the youngster decided to sleep together in one and the same bed.

They finished with washing, cleaning the teeth, changing clothes for night gowns and at long last they lay in bed and talking. Granny began:" Once upon a time there lived little Red Riding Hood…"

The wonderful fairy tale was over; Larissa was about to sleep and suddenly started searching for something under the blanket touching the place under her Granny's bum. "What's up, honey Larissa?" Granny asked the little girl agilely. "What are you looking for?"

"A tail, Granny, your tail", answered the cute child.

"A what?"

"Your tail."

"Why? Who told you that I must have a tail?" asked the surprising old woman.

"Mommy. It was my Mom who told me the stories about the

origin of a man", explained Lara eagerly.

"And what the hell was that origin?" Granny continued to question her granddaughter.

"My Mom told me that I was originated from her, she was originated from you... The first man on the earth was originated from a monkey. But monkeys have tails, I saw them in the Zoo", explained the little girl patiently.

"What? What did you say?!" poor little Grandma could not help laughing.

"Do you realize, Granny, that the last generation is me, the generation before last is my Mommy, and the first generation is you? And you must have a tail, mustn't you?" explained Larissa.

"Stop talking like that. It's nonsense. Sleep tight. I am tired of your silly talks", said her Granny in an angry voice.

Actually she smiled and smiled; Larissa was full of a sense of self-coscience for her age.

Now Lara was embarrassed, why her Granny started to laugh, she told her very serious things and very sincerely. Frankly speaking, Val was also about to laugh when she heard this story from Maria's mouth. As a matter of fact, she was impressed with Fridrich Engel's work "The Origin of a Family and the Private Property" where the author considered a monkey was the first reason of existing in the world and later on there appeared mankind. Lara's father, a journalist by profession, also influenced on her in his own way.

He taught her by his own example how to communicate to the people.

The first rule: you don't have to be quotable;

The second rule: you must love and respect your converser;

The third rule: remember to take turns while you are conversing;

The fourth rule: broaden your horizon in order to talk in many subjects as possible;

The fifth rule: keep it light; do not stay too long;

The sixth rule: be genuine, willing to reveal what your converser's background is, what his likes and dislikes are.

At the same time he underlined that it was not necessary to

open your soul to everybody up to the end. Something must be left as a secret.

His professional secrets were watched by his daughter when he took her to the interviews with. Little Lara heard and observed how her Daddy talked to the very successful illusionist Emil Kio, he was absolutely charming as an interviewed guest.

Emil Kio was doing his tricks again and again, Dad was up-front about the circus, joked about them, and was completely at ease with himself that he put him at ease, too.

As for Lara, she was offered a marvelous horse ride sitting right on its back around the circus arena for ten circles. What a pleasure she had, one could not describe it in any words!

Whether her Dad was talking to one person or a million, the rules were the same. It's all about making a connection. Show empathy, enthusiasm and willingness to listen, and you can't help becoming a master of talk.

Lara could witness it herself when again she was taken into the reporter's car where her father was running a coverage about the sports festival in town on one of the first days of May.

It's now talk-shows come into our homes easily and naturally, and they're not afraid to reveal their tastes or tell stories on themselves.

Without making themselves the focus of their talk, they are themselves. If they - or a guest - tells sad or a joyful story, they are not afraid to show their feelings.

It's now but then, in seventies in a Communist Soviet Union Lara saw the sprinter running with the relay-race baton, her Daddy talking something into his microphone. The spring weather smiled at her, as did the passers-by and fans watching a little girl's back, which a reporter used as a desk for penning some notes.

What can a parent do at home to bolster a child's intellectual qualities?

Young children do not need direct instruction. What's necessary is to create a stimulating environment in which they find learning exciting.

Val experimented with the learning playing on the carpet floor,

242

looking her daughter in the eye.

That tracks brain connections that's strengthened with each exposure, and helped Lara sort the world into what's familiar, what isn't, what's different, what's the same - crucial skills in learning.

At the pre-schooling age Lara visited a dance school, which was situated on Petrov hill, the highest point of the town in a former Church of the sixteenth century. The place itself was very picturesque, indeed, and the interior was changed in the original way, decorated with long wall mirrors and wood. The most distinguishing thing in the whole ensemble was a parquet hard wood floor that was attracting many young people and their parents who were fond of dancing.

The teacher of all dancing skills was beautiful Alla Petrovna. She was really a striking woman. With her tall, powerful body, her head thrown proudly back, and her brown eyes gazing, apparently, down upon the world, she seemed more like a member of one of the princely families than a dancing teacher. When men looked at Mrs.Alla, however -as they always did -it was the fine points of colour on her cheeks, the creamy flesh of her wonderful, sloping shoulders, her splendid, rather small breasts that they noticed, while becoming instantly conscious of the powerful, controlled sensuousness that her elegance did not trouble to conceal. If she'd let me, a strong man thought, I could make that body glow; while others, less certain of themselves, could only muse: NOW, that, my God, would take a proper man. A few, more poetic, thought they saw in those proud eyes a hint of sadness; but then, watching her on the dancing floor, it was hard to know whether this might not be just an element of her art. One thing in any case was certain: Mrs. Alla Petrovna was in full bloom of her maturity, as a Goddess of dancing.

Everybody admired her and her style of dance teaching. After a great number of rehearsals Lara's pals and her gave a big dance concert on the central circus stage with great success.

Lara built intellect and learnt about the world by reaching out to new experiences - by exploring.

The little girl experienced high levels of adult involvement and encouragement.

"Good! Excellent! Bravo!" used to exclaim Lara's mother when her little one first learnt to drink from a cup.

"There's a dear!" Mom praised her with such words when her little Sunny one first walked, first danced.

Val knew that cheering her child's accomplishments not only delighted her treasure but also reinforced connections in the midbrain, the seat of emotions. Lara was seven years old and was approaching for the first time her first class at school, the first grade, the start.

For her Mom, that was the task of the greatest importance. She realized that actual IQ scores might not change dramatically as her child grew older, but academic achievement could. These were the years in which the child's brain was finely tuned and environmental influences continued to count. Val's attention could not necessarily create an Einstein, but it remained a vital ingredient in the child's intelligence.

Most of the Russian mothers whose children were going to attend the primary school tried to obtain a leave from their work to help their children in their first grade students' step, because the school programs were very oversaturated with the knowledge of skills, physical and mental exercises.

Larissa had finished the first grade as a straight A-student. How did a high-achiever like Lara do it? Brain wasn't the only answer.

What people tend to think of as intelligence was probably overrated. More important were interrelated factors that included motivation, family and school support, and sheer effort.

In fact, Lara's mother knew it for sure by her own experience that those students, who scored high on traditional measures of intelligence such as IQ tests, became bored in school and didn't put in the effort. They could wind up developing bad habits and fail to live up to their potential. That is why Val organized at home such a play school atmosphere where her daughter played the role of a teacher.

Her friend Helen was a student who used many last names to represent 30 more imaginary classmates. At home there hung a small blackboard with chalk to write with.

There was a special class register with all needed notes and, of course, result marks. The teacher Larissa Vikentjevna Kostina told her pupil about the rules of plain Russian, arithmetic, geography, history, natural sciences.

She gave Helen tasks, estimated "the pupils" very strictly, in general, she copied her real school teachers' conduct. When she had no students, she used sometimes her dolls, giving them the names of her real classmates.

Lara played her home school lessons long after she had grown up, because her Mommy realized it helped her daughter tremendously.

The decision about divorce was taken together by mother and daughter.

"Larissa, I am going to live separately from your father", Val told to Lara.

"Why?" asked the daughter.

"Your father doesn't respect me, misbehaves, you know, and doesn't want to stop drinking alcohol", Val explained.

"You'd better give him a chance, Mommy. And wait," advised Lara.

"My dear, sweetie daughter, I gave him lots of chances, I sacrificed my life for him, but he doesn't value it, he just doesn't respect me any longer", Val said.

"Then", said the wise girl, "let us divorce", as if Lara were Kostin's wife but not his daughter.

So Larissa got alone as well as her Mommy did. They felt like two single adult women in one family, one - little, another - big, but with the similar thoughts and the similar fortune.

From this period of time, Larissa lived as if she were a grown-up: Mom always consulted with her as if they were the same age and very good friends. After the divorce they moved to another street. Larissa changed her school volunteerly.

She was doing well at her new school like at her previous one.

Once Larissa's mother met her daughter's first school teacher who taught her before.

"Thanks a lot for your noble and extremely hard work related to the first graders", Val spoke gratefully and continued: "Larissa finished your class with excellent top marks, the same has been done at her new class with a new teacher".

"Oh, no, no", answered the surprised teacher, "That's not what I deserve, that's the result of your great work with your daughter".

"Oh, really? I've not noticed my efforts. I consider them as natural as life has to be", Val was embarrassed.

"I thank you immensely anyway for your great appreciation of my work. It was more pleasant to hear it from the professional highly educated person like you". They exchanged courtesies for some while. It was for the first time when Larissa's mother faced her real educational results.

It meant for her that she had to go on, it was the right direction. Val noticed that the high-achieving student Larissa actually did fewer hours of homework than her lower-scoring classmates.

She got them by mastering some basic techniques, among them the most important was learning how to read.

Larissa in her reading highlighted the main concepts to help remember them. As she read, she also paused at various points in the text and restated aloud concepts she had just covered. "I try to put it in my own words", Larissa said. "That way it's easier to understand".

And, of course, the academic reading should not be like reading a mystery novel.

Larissa first looked at how a textbook was organized by checking its table of contents and headings. Val encouraged her to write the chapter headings down on paper so she had an outline of the chapter before she began to read. The secret of Larissa's reading well was to be an active reader - one who continually asks questions that lead to a full understanding of the author's message. Val's concern was home reading together with her daughter aloud, taking turns. Books were collected in the bookcase. On each side of the bookcase was a picture - not the classical scenes her grandfather would have favoured, but bright, informal studies, one of a country landscape at sunset, the other of a wrinkled peasant's face. These paintings by the new school, known as the Wanderers, gave Larissa huge pleasure.

"They are the first truly Russian painters since the makers of icons", Val would say. "These young fellows painted Russian life as it really was". Indeed, in their living room, the young woman and her daughter even had a little sketch by the best artist, the brilliant Ilya Repin, which showed a humble barge-hauler on the Volga River, straining on his harness as if he were trying to be free.

Further evidence of two the inhabitants' character lay on the square table, in the form of several thick periodicals. These were the so-called fat journals, in which one might find in serial form, the latest works of the greatest novelists of the day: Valentin Rasputin, Daniil Granin, Michael Bulgakov.

Among the books in the bookcase one could read the classical names of the great Russians: Tolstoy, Dostoevsky, Turgenev, Pushkin, Lermontov, Blok, Akhmatova, Tsvetayeva and many others.

Whenever Val saw young Larissa, she would recite the lines of Alexander Blok on Russia's years of stagnation:

"Let the ravens croak and fly
Over us who daily die.
God, Oh God, let better men
See Thy Kingdom come" .

And poor young Larissa would watch morosely.

Until her senior classes at the High School, she managed to finish two additional schools one after another, the musical in the piano class, and the drawing one, each during a four years' term with satisfactory results.

The first thing people noticed about Larissa was her mousy brown hair. She was allowed to wear it long and loose so that it fell in lustrous masses over her shoulders to her elbows.

In a black-white-red plaid dress, a red waist-coat, silk tights, black lacquer shoes and a big, wide-brimmed hat from under which her hair poured down, she looked enchanting. And then people would notice her eyes. They were deep blue-grey, and they knew everything.

It was amazing what Larissa knew. Yet how could it be otherwise? No sisters or brothers, only her mother who was an exceptional teacher and an example that Larissa copied and criticized constantly during all their joint life.

It was natural, therefore, that her mother should turn to this bright little girl to be her companion.

Larissa knew every painting in the local gallery. There were the outstanding people - wonderful natural evocations of the country by Repin, Surikov, Serov, Levitan. Levitan had done a huge landscape of one small Russian town like Bryansk - a haunting vision of it on the high bank, seen across the river under a deep blue sky full of retreating clouds.

But Larissa's greatest delight was to speak to Mommy's friends about European painters which were dazzling, and middle-aged who were scarcely familiar with such wonders they would be astonished as teen Larissa prattled: "This is a Monet; here's Cezanne, Renoir's nudes always seem to have the same two faces, don't you think?"

Or:

"This is by Gauguin. He ran away from his wife and children and went to live in Tahiti. But those are Picasso and Matisse".

Her mature opinion about the arts allowed her later, when she took her first job as an artist at one Bryansk enterprise at the age of seventeen, to judge her own abilities in drawing:

"I will never be as a great artist as Vrubel or Levitan were, but be an ordinary painter, mixing up the paints I do not want", and she changed her work for another one.

Before finishing her school year, Larissa's favourite Grannies died. It happened in spring on the 31st of March and in winter on the 13th of December,1985.

Two mysterious figures 31 and 13, reversed, were the same, and frightened Larissa since that moment on. She used to be scared of the "devil's dozen" enclosed in two nasty numbers "three and one" and tried to escape into her future life considering that they could bring unhappiness to the people. She avoided going upstairs on the thirteenth floor, to seat at the place under such a number.

It was just the time when Val delighted in taking this bright little person with her on short and long journeys to show her the world. As a tourist group guide Val went everywhere and knew everyone. Already she had been to Leningrad, Moscow, Kiev,

Minsk, Odessa, Simpheropol, Batumi, Sukhumi, Sochi and many other big and small Russian towns.

Nothing had changed in them as it may seem from the first sight. For in this land, every wooden house sooner or later was lost to fire or age. Every town had its old part and a new part added on.

How else should the old part look but a group of cabins on one side of the stream, and a little fort surrounded with brick walls on the other? There was a brick church with a little tower, inside the fort. In the Ukrainian or Russian manner it was arranged as a simple Greek cross with a cupola over the centre and smaller cupolas over its eastern and western ends and over the two transepts. In the tower was a single bell.

The new parts look like familiar as in every town. The four-to-five storied panel buildings built like boxes, made no difference in whichever town they had been erected; they had the same face.

The impressions became repeated and Larissa's traveling passion began decreasing except for the people. She liked watching them with anticipation of each episode that can have happened on the way. The first priority was Mom's deeds.

Larissa saw once how her Mother rescued a child at the bus stop. It was a splendid fall day when a group of tourists,which mostly consisted of women and their children, tried to get on the bus. Everyone dashed to the entrance doors to occupy the best seats. Mom was getting in, as usual, as the last in the line, watching if everything was in order. The bus driver closed the doors and started moving without having glanced at the side mirrors. The young chauffeur did not notice how one preschooler with his schoolbag behind was stuck between the two halves of the back bus door, his body had been pulled along the asphalt pavement, the schoolbag inside.

Val shouted, "Stop him! Stop him! " and rushed under the back wheels saving a boy. Val grabbed the kid with his unlucky crushed bag. At the same moment the crowd of people cried out, "A boy under the wheels! A boy! A boy!"

The bus driver had stopped, nobody had been injured. The boy was rescued. The entire crowd sighed with relief. Larissa wrote this story about her Mommy later in her school composition, and her teacher informed Val about that.

As Lara was growing up, Val realized that she had to change her behaviour tactics and came up with three rules for herself: the first - be a consultant, not a manager; the second - present a united front with your child; and the third - give your kid privacy. Val knew by heart those regulations, but how hard it was to imprint them when your child reaches fourteen years old, it is the most dangerous age in the human life. Teens recoiled when parents gave them advice. They did not need a manager, they needed a consultant, an ally.

"Think!" ordered Val to herself,"Think about what a business consultant does. Instead of jumping in and suggesting change, he carefully listens and helps you sort out your thoughts and options".

It was very important in this transition period of Lara's life that the parents do not make mistakes.

"Where are you going to-night, Larissa?" asked the mother.

"We're going to the discotheque", replied the daughter.

"With whom ?", Val got interested.

"With my school friends."

"When are you going to come back?"

"It depends."

"No, sweetie. I am expecting you back before midnight. Otherwise it will be pretty late, and it's dangerous in the streets", advised Val softly.

During Lara's early teenage years Val found that her personality and the way she behaved were changing dramatically. Part of this was due to an awareness of her own sexuality caused by the start of her monthly periods and physical changes in her body, and part was due to hormones, chemicals produced in her ovaries, which have an effect on her moods.

Larissa was growing taller and her proportions were altering. Her waist narrowed, her hips swelled and her thighs became fatter. Val did not explain anything to her daughter. Larissa had a school-friend Helen whose mother worked as a gynecologist; that woman collected girls together and it was she who explained everything which was happening to the girls' bodies, she told it in the correct

250

way.

Larissa often complained to her Mommy:

"I think I look terrible! Seriously! My clothes are wrong, my make-up is wrong, my hair's wrong. Nothing is right at the moment! I haven't laughed in four weeks and that's no joke, either!"

"No, no, Darling", Val said to calm her down. "Without doubts. You look very pretty, ask somebody else". But her girl-friends behaved in the same way in their families: "I feel a bit disappointed about my changes that are happening to my body. What if I couldn't enlarge my breasts and reduce the size of my bottom".

Another of Larissa's friends said, "I'm trying to accept the way I look, but most of the time I wish I looked like somebody else". Or:

"I'd like to be prettier and older".

The girls were not alone; nearly everyone felt exactly the same at this time. It was a horrible time for parents to survive; but they tried to come through.

"Sweetie, accept yourself for what you are", said Mom to her daughter.

"Why?" asked Larissa.

"Because if you expect too much of yourself you may never feel that you are an 'OK' person", advised Val. Parents realized that it may be painful to think that their own children may never be award-winning novelists, great advocates, powerful journalists, the greatest actresses who ever lived or the most beautiful models. Very few of them achieved that much, so they didn't go on striving for something which was probably beyond their capabilities.

"Set your sights a little lower, maybe settle for less, and like it", used to repeat Val to Larissa's friends. So her two friends Olga and Anna settled for less, at the age of 14, they decided to enter the Cooking Secondary School to be professional cooks.

Larissa missed Olga and Anna, coming up to Mommy and said in a very categorical voice:

"Mommy, I'd prefer to join the Cooking Secondary School as my friends Olga and Anna".

"What are you going to do there?" asked the astonished

Mother.

"1'1 be a tart decorator", answered the naughty Larissa.

"A what?! A tart decorator?!" Val was surprised.

"Yes, after finishing the drawing school I can now do decorative rose design, can't I?" continued the daughter.

"No, honey. It's excluded. You should go on with your education and then we'll see together what profession you are choosing. Am I right, dear? Think twice and later you'll give me the answer".

So Larissa went on with her studies at school but the serious problems of her future profession orientation were on the agenda of the present day.

The solution of this problem was getting "to disturb" a growing desire to know boys. All teenagers were awkward at the beginning and starting off a friendship was difficult for everyone.

"Remember", Mom used to say to Larissa, "you are with a boy both in the same boat and the other person, I mean a boy, is probably feeling just as shy and awkward as you are. Be careful! Do not offend boys. They are human beings as you are.

And second. Be yourself. Don't put on airs and graces and don't try to make out that you're someone you're not. Do and act exactly as you feel, not as you think you ought to. Remember that what a boy-friend wants from you is exactly what you'd enjoy in him.

Started friendships at school, it was the easiest way because it's part of the normal daily routine, and in mixed classes boys and girls were naturally thrown together" .

"Who is the best girl in the class, in your opinion?" asked the boy's Mother of Victor Gaponenko.

"Larissa Kostina", he answered.

"Why?"

"Because she is fair".

What girls and boys look for in each other was of great interest of parents, too.

When boys in the Larissa's class were asked, "What are the most important qualities that a girl must have for you to want to go out with her?" here were the ten most frequently mentioned qualities: 1. Good looking and a good body, not necessarily pretty ,"but if she has an awful personality I won't ask her out again".

2. Friendly and not conceited, "a girl who is willing to show that she likes me".

3. Intelligence.

4. A sense of humour.

5. Honest "doesn't play games or tease".

6. A good conversationalist, "she has to be able to talk to me".

7. Similar interests and values.

8. Sexually candid and frank, "I wouldn't like her to be a prude, but on the other hand I don't want her to have been with a lot of other boys".

9. Outgoing, not shy.

10. Mature "I'd like her to have a serious side too".

The girls answered about the important qualities that a boy must have for a girl to go out with him were:

1. Intelligence.

2. Good looking and good body but not necessarily handsome.

3. A good conversationalist, "easy to talk to".

4. Sincere and honest, "not just out for sex".

5. Confident but not conceited.

6. Sense of humour and fun to be with.

7. Clean cut, "well groomed, doesn't take drugs or drink alcohol to excess".

8. Romantic and affectionate.

9. Popular at school.

10. Gentle "doesn't feel that he has to prove that he's a man".

The parents were wondering why their children had chosen one person or another.

Why Larissa's classmate Victor Gaponenko called her best trait of character as "fair"? Why fair?

Val held herself in darkness until she once watched the following scene.

There was a usual after classes time meeting, something was discussed. Val dropped in, by occasion, she needed to tell something important to her daughter.

But Larissa was involved with the problem solution.

She said in a loud confident voice,"On the one hand, he's

right", and then counted the reasons "why…", "On the other hand, he's not right", and again there were named a great number of whys. Val watched her daughter in a secret way, from the far corner of a long school hall corridor, hidden by the pile of desks and cabinets. She watched Larissa as if from a stranger's site.

Many things can attract you about a person, his or her face, smile, appearance, the way he or she talks or moves, and you may feel attracted intellectually, emotionally or sexually.

Suddenly Val understood why this young boy called Larissa a fair girl. The object of his adoration had a profound effect on his life, full of unfair judgments and deeds in his own family and at school. A cheerful smile from the loved girl, very kind by nature, made him blush and fill blissfully happy, whereas an angry word or a frown or even a stern glance plunged him into despair. Larissa kept a safe distance from him as well as from other boys. That allowed her, however, to have her first experience of love without the possibility of being injured.

There existed an unwritten bill of Larissa's rights which read:
I have the right:
To be me,
To affection,
To love,
To support,
To ask for help,
To be depressed sometimes,
To be nervous,
To make mistakes,
To be listened to,
To say what I feel, want, need,
To be silly sometimes,
To show my feelings,
To time on my own,
To time with my friends,
To time with my family,
To make my own decisions,
To have my own values and opinions,
To respect or disrespect,

To ask questions,

To be angry,

To be concerned about those I love,

To time for school /work / sport / hobbies,

To say no.

The time had arrived for giving Val's child privacy. Teen Larissa needed to have a sense that her Mommy was not in total command of her life. Her room was especially important.

Val faced this issue with her teenager, who said one day:

"Mom, I need my own territory, and I see, you don't want me feeling like I have to leave the apartment to get in".

"Yes, certainly", agreed Val. "Now you can invite your friends into your own room but I can live in another one. It's very simple".

Since then on their house was full of teenagers: talking, eating and playing different games. But that was fine. Val was just glad they were there and they were safe.

It was a Pancake day when eight Larissa's friends got together at the table served with different kinds of pancakes stuffed with caviar, strawberry jam or just with sour-cream. Lara's mother moved with the noblest feelings, addressing to polite kids, said,

"Dear friends, let's try to eat pancakes with forks and knives as it is supposed to be by the etiquette in the top society families like British Queen Elizabeth the Second".

"Oh, it is tempting", commented one of the girls, trying to eat with the necessary cutlery.

"How difficult it is", replied the other one, committing all these manipulations so clumsy that Val smiled.

"No, no", insisted Val on, "the only condition to be followed is to eat in the right way. All the others are forbidden now," and she left their room for the kitchen. Behind her back she heard such a burst of laughter that in a second she jumped into their room.

They were sitting and eating so innocently in Val's presence that Lara's mother smiled back at them. As soon as Val had been retreating, they stopped eating normally, mocking and giggling at each other.

When Val appeared again, they became still and very polite. That was like a game, everyone felt a sense of humour.

Another part of the demand for privacy was a teenager's emotional and physical withdrawal: monosyllabic responses, pulling away from parents' hugs, refusing to go to places with them.

Some parents felt upset and rejected when teens retreat or push them away, but it's a normal part of adolescence.

Many parents don't realize that while the teenager is retreating, he doesn't want the parents follow too.

In her teen years Larissa had been acquiring the categorical notes in her voice, declared:

"I do not want, Mommy, to travel with you any more. It is not interesting. I'd better spend my free time with my friends".

"Oh, yes. We've seen a lot of sights. I would rather stay at home and do lots of my own things", retorted Val.

Parenting teenagers was process of negotiation and redefining the parent's relationship with the child - and communication was the key.

The rude words appeared at the time in Larissa's speech, while she was arguing with her mother.

Val was offended and the main punishment of her teen daughter was to stop any kind of communications with Lara. It could last for one - two days: such a silence, blockade in response to Larissa' s bad words.

Then the telephone rang, Val picked up the receiver, one of her acquaintances spoke to her.

"What's happened at your home ? Larissa ran into me, took a library book and I asked her about you how you are doing" .

"Oh, that's nice. And what did she answer how I was doing?" asked Val.

"She explained to me with tears in her eyes that my Mommy had not talked to me for two days" , told the woman.

"Did you ask her why her mother did not want to talk to her?" continued Val.

"No, I did not", confessed the former .

"It's in vain. Because she's using bad words, even while conversing with me. That was my reaction. She was punished like this. Now I see that she's suffering, that means she understood her bad behaviour and I'll take away my silence blockade", concluded Val.

It was one of the pedagogical approaches which she used to treat her daughter.

What teens really needed is a guide: a wise person to whom they have access when they needed help.

When a parent can fulfill this role, she or he often experiences a new kind of satisfaction.

Watching teenagers learn who they are and solve their own problems is among the most rewarding parts of parenthood.

The main problem of Larissa was to choose what to do in the future.

Stressful situation at home, did not allow Larissa to solve her problems at this time. After finishing school she worked first as a designer, then as a courier in one Bryansk' newspaper.

In Val's opinion, it was visible that Larissa's inclined to study literature, arts etc. Concerning Larissa's future profession, she proposed to her daughter to sign up for part-time journalism course and try herself for a journalist.

For Lara's mother and father, a natural order of things was to keep on education for University degrees.

It was Gorbachev's time, the glasnost period, when openly speaking out was allowed. A great deal of information was poured all of a sudden on the unprepared heads of Soviet citizens. In 1988-1989 it was extremely difficult to pass the entrance exams to the Universities. The children were taught by old-fashioned Marxism-Leninism programs in history, language and literature, but at the entrance exams they were asked about the modern new attitudes to the events happening in those days. No text-books, no special manuals and recommendations how and what to do. The flood of modern coverage and materials to be discussed was published in newspapers and issued on TV-shows.

In such conditions to formulate young brains was the main parents' concern, they filed and cut up the articles from periodicals.

For Larissa there started home classes to prepare for University entrance exams, including knowing the following questions as:

"What was the role of the Chief Commander George Zhukov in the World War the Second?"

(Nothing was informed about it earlier),

"What is your opinion about the collectivization years of Stalin period?" and so on.

What opinion can have an eighteen-year-old when everything was mixed up in her head?

Val acted then as a tutor in all subjects at a time, simultaneously helping her in public activities.

By the way one prominent local TV showman Alexander Googlja came up to Larissa's father in his editorial office and said:

"I have a proposal to your daughter".

"What?!" Lara' s father blushed to the ears, frightened to death because of her very young age for marriage, he considered, she was far too young, "What proposal?"

"I want your Larissa to be my assistant show-girl in a new TV-program", explained the young man.

"Oh, yes, certainly. It would be interesting to her", sighed the father with relief.

Larissa's first interview attracted much attention. It was really amazing to view how the sixty-year-old priest talked with dignity and great respect to the young journalist Larissa Kostina:

"Tell me, please, Father Sergey, how are your dealings now after a long period of banning the church in our country", asked the girl.

"As a matter of fact, Mother Larissa," he began explaining the situation around the church of the old pope.

So Larissa was renamed into Mother Larissa and for a long time after, this name had still stuck to her.

Thus the first Lara's steps were rather successful in the field of joutnalism.

Her birthday celebration at eighteen was marked with a great bouquet of roses, carnations, a type-writer as a gift from both parents, and verses:

> *"Let calmly life of years does flow,*
> *Let you be always need in people,*
> *Let a hundred friends want you to go*
> *To visit them and cheer up a little.*

Let be the passion for your friendship,
Is guided not only by fear,
But by the heart sincere and the candid,
For which you're famous everywhere".

One of the things that Larissa realized was that her Mom's main worry was about daily necessities. She noticed that she could not go on without things to make sure that she was well off.

Larissa was aware that her Mommy worried not to deprive her of clothes and outings and all kinds of things that better-off children got.

Larissa was compassionate by nature, never complained, was helpful as she could.

The grown up teen remembered that her Mommy found it very hard to refuse her requests for money or treats and probably felt full of guilt and didn't forget that if her Mom had to deprive her, she was feeling insecure and concerned lest she could lose her love. Everything was okay in Larissa's family. Two-years-experience of a full-time job made her sure that there was enough money to go around. Their family ran smoothly. They both, Mommy and Daughter, had to mend things and deal with money in a responsible way. They felt proud of doing these things rather than dismayed.

One of the most difficult things Larissa was not going to have to do was adjusting to a step-father. Even one thought about that got her angry. She saw, as examples of girl-friends' families, how the girls suffered. For her Mommy, it was unnatural and not understandable to see how new people as intruders who disturbed the family were stealing the only parent's love and attention. Children might feel not only emotionally threatened, but even pushed aside in their own home and their own space had been invaded by a stranger.

"I did not want him here, either", confessed one of Lara's close friends Tatiana to Val. "I wanted him to go. I kept thinking 'It's not my home, it's everybody else's but it's not mine. It doesn't seem right because I was not consulted and Mom started letting him stay the night and then the weekends. Then he started bringing his stuff in and he kicked our sofa out, our television and our table".

Larissa felt a great compassion for her friend and was glad that she did not feel such a bad experience herself.

It was very hard for the teenagers to cope with what seemed to be the loss of their mothers' affection, particularly if they were fearful that the new "so-called 'fathers' tried to play the role of their true Dads. Tatiana felt resentment and anger and resisted the new authority. Tatiana's mother, because of that, changed her partners many times, and every time unsuccessfully.

The worst fear of Larissa's mother was a possible incest as sexual relations between close relatives, or sexual abuse. The most common relationship of this type was between step-father and daughter.

Another Larissa's girl-friend Helen told her story, "Sexual abuse got started when I was as young as five or six. At this age I accepted largely what adults said and did as being right, so I went long with an adult who asked me to do. I thought that it was normal and natural and that other people did the same".

"What's happened then?" asked the worried woman.

" As I got older I realized that the relationship was wrong. It was unpleasant to me and I wanted to escape from it", sobbed the poor girl.

"Did you tell it to your Mom?" asked Larissa's mother.

"No, I didn't. I felt too afraid to tell anyone save you, aunt Valentina. I thought if I was involved with my stepfather, who is in control of things, it was impossible to find a way out. I thought that no one would believe what I said or that they blame me for what had happened".

"How awful! I'm frightened of the consequences. It's dishonest keeping something bad from your mother. I'll try to speak to your Mommy. I know her as a very good woman", promised Val and did it.

It was important from Helen's side to tell someone and to stop the sexual abuse. If not, the burden may affect her for the rest of her life. She might carry the feeling of shame, guilt and blame around the years. These feelings might prevent her from trusting anyone again, might make her worry of new relationships and cause difficulty in forming new friendships.

If she, however, could talk to someone and eventually get help from somebody, she would find that all her anxieties had gone and she could look towards the future with confidence.

Helen's mother got rid of her partner and their family got normalized for the better.

Larissa's mother never intruded into her daughter's privacy. She did not wish to tell her daughter too much concerning the facts of life.

Larissa entered the Leningrad State University, the faculty of journalism in 1989 and graduated from it in 1994. Her new job was connected with a TV network and was to give her great satisfaction, which up to now, continues to be her chosen profession.

"If nothing else I can leave my daughter, but if I have left her a love of languages, of literature, of people, a taste for Homer, for the poets, the people who have told our story - and by "our" I mean the story of mankind - then she will have a legacy enough", said Val to Larissa's friends at the graduation party.

On April, 24,1997 she bore a baby-son, Gleb by name.

"What are the little girls made of?

- Of honey and spice and all things nice," recollected Larissa.

"What are the little boys made of?

- Of bats and snails, and puppy dog tails!"

The second half of this saying whether it is the truth or not Larissa will discover in the years to come.

May the jorney of life though it is not easy be as guided by all that you have learned and experienced, may those be as guide posts on the road that you follow wherever it will take you.

All the best, Larissa.

Good luck!

PART SIX

JOHN

"Ferragosto"

Dedicated to John Pattison,
born in August, 15, 1930.

Once John appeared in the world,
Amidst the August he had swirled,
A year thirtieth had been this era,
The happy Pattisons had cleared.
It's tough to be so handsome,
The people would think he'd care,
But the jealous looks of a few some
Are hardly for him to bear.
It's rough to be so clever,
They wished him weren't so resourceful,
For the jealous fits of the lesser wits
Can make him feel remorseful.
It's awful to be so unhappy,
With lucky women should him enjoy,
But the jealous sights of the average guys,
Have known an occasion him to destroy.

It's a burden to be so delightful, generous and extra-kind, but
one can guess that God meant it in mind. Though I wish the things
could not change, nothing to be rearranged,
'Cause gorgeous that JOHN well to be !"
  With love
  Valentina Filina.

August, 15, 1997.

It was March 1997, 9.49 p.m. to be precise, Valentina had be embarking her long journey West by Grey Hound bus, as John had advised her to do so - she could see some regions of the United States of America and form her own opinion about this part of the globe.

John remembered the last time they had met, it had been in Berlin on the Kurfurster Dam, she was sitting at a table drinking a glass of red wine and nibbling various types of cheeses. He was drinking in her beauty. She looked so sad and lonely! John sent her two red roses, he saw her look around. Her eyes locked onto his, they could not break the connection, so John rose up and went to her. He spoke to her in German:

"Guten Abend , Miss. Darf ich sitzen hier, bitte? "

She answered, " Sure. Guten Abend, Herr".

John could tell she was not of German origin.

"Wie heissen Sie, Miss? And do you speak English?" asked John.

She replied, "Ich heisse Valentina Filina. I do speak English but I am Russian". John represented himself.

He was here on holiday, and Valentina told him that she was an interpreter and she was working for a trade Commission from Bryansk area, which was located midway between Moscow and Kiev, roughly 600 km, to any of those cities from Bryansk.

They talked and talked for, perhaps, three hours, they exchanged addresses and telephone numbers.

John told her he was born English but now was Canadian, he asked her out to visit the Zoo next morning. So they met again, walked and talked. She was divorced, but he wasn't. The reason she was unhappy, because the commission was to be returning to Bryansk the next day. Valentina was slim, tall and 37 years old; John was 47. They had lunch, then visited his room at hotel where they held each other and kissed all afternoon. Finally they made love in the evening, and Val started to cry, they promised to each other and swore to remain in touch by mail or phone if nothing else.

It was a parting they both hated. Valentina was so God damn beautiful, John was in love with her and he knew he would never forget her, now twenty years later Val was on her way to collect her lover, little old him.

She came to New York to take work and to make enquiries where John was now, was he still at the old telephone number, if so, where the hell was that in Canada; they finally made contact, John couldn't believe it.

He picked up the phone when it rang, he heard her say, "John", "That's you ?! Valentina!" he answered, "Where on earth are you now?"

"New York," she said.

"Why are you there? Where did you come from?" John asked.

"To get you at long last", she replied .

John wrote her number down and phoned her every day till it was time for her to catch the Grey Hound bus to Spokane, Washington State. She had two days-three nights' trip ahead and he arranged to pick her up personally in Spokane. John followed her journey on the road map, he assumed the bus would be traveling at 100 km per hour. He looked at the map till 4 a.m. on Wednesday, then he lay down to sleep, which didn't come easy.

As he was thinking back over the years to when he first met her.

She had returned to Russia from Berlin, it was 1977, the next time John heard from Val it was from Czechoslovakia 1979, she sent him a letter, and by the time he received it, she was back home in Bryansk.

The reason she wrote outside of Russia was due to the "Iron Curtain" policy of Brezhnev and the KGB. John never heard from Val for fourteen years.

His first wife had died that was Anna, his second wife Margaret he divorced, and his present wife Chris had run away due to alcohol. And debts of fourteen thousand dollars.

Now his dear friend Val wrote again to him from Finland, describing what had happened to date, again John could not return her letter as she was only three days and it was not allowed to write to her home address as all foreign letters were intercepted by the post and KGB (1993). The following year Val telephoned him from Italy, she had just arrived by tour bus having passed through many countries to get to Trieste.

John phoned her daily, and they renewed their love for each other, it was in 1994.

Again in 1996 she went to Hamburg, Germany, for ten days and also contacted him. Now she had her sights set over here (1997) and come hell or high water she was barreling across the USA like a sputnik.

The woman was entirely different to any woman he has ever met: Valentina gives herself 100% to her man, she is honest and truthful, and John was dying to see what time and life has done to his Val.

Wednesday came, John awoke at 8.00 a.m. and looked to see where she could be now on the map. He was terribly worried for her, Valentina was on her first trip across the USA.

Now a retired foreign language teacher, also an interpreter.

He was hoping she would not be afraid and return to New York without seeing him. They had a date for meeting, Friday, on the 21st of March, 1997, at 9.40 a.m. in Spokane at the Grey Hound Terminal.

That Wednesday John checked the map every hour until late in the evening, He also made his plans for the trip to Spokane as well as cleaning his apartment, here in Sparwood, British Columbia, Canada.

Thursday was no better. He was washing, dusting and polishing till midday. He packed his travel bag, checked the map again and tried to visualize what Val was doing at that moment. John was nervous but could not help it. She was his long lost love of twenty years. Finally coming home, away from any Russian influence, it finally got round to midday, he picked up his bag, locked his apartment and drove away heading for Spokane .

Many thoughts were going through his mind as he traveled. John remembered his childhood in England, when only a few months old he was circumcised, it hurt him so much that it was imprinted on his mind; he remembered standing in his cot at the hospital: he was holding the cot railing crying with pain, the whole room was full of babies crying in their cots, he was near door and on the far wall were three high windows were rounded at the top, they were narrow windows with small panes of glass. John saw his Mommy and Daddy looking in the right hand window near the bottom.

266

He told his mother about it years later but she wouldn't believe him, saying he was too young and couldn't possibly know what happened.

He had every childhood illness going plus some extras while a young child, a mastoid in his right middle ear drum which made him blind for three days until the mastoid burst out over, had it bust in over, he wouldn't be here today.

Then John caught St. Vitus dance where the nervous system made him twitch and jerk continually. Each time he twitched or jerked he got slapped. He finally after two years recovered, age six years old, the time was 1936.

At age of nine (1939) the phony war broke out and (1940) the air raids started, bombs falling, food was rationed, lights extinguished on the streets and houses.

Germany invaded Poland and Russia on Germany's side attacked Poland from the rear.

John read the newspaper daily, and it didn't seem long before Hitler attacked the Soviet Union. The Russians had been stabbed in the back by their ally, they were hundreds of kilometers into Russia before Stalin accepted the fact that his ally was now his enemy.

John was ten years old and devoted his whole energy to securing food of any description for his mother. He would come home from school, grab some home-made bread and jam, take his dog "Toby" and disappear into the woods and fields to look for berries or eggs, it didn't matter if the eggs were from pigeons, pheasants, partridges or pee-wits. He looked for rabbits or hares, ducks or duck eggs; he took everything he could find.

He checked all the ponds and lakes, even abandoned gardens he visited to see what he could collect.

They had a Castle at Branspeth belonging to Lord Boyne, he gave it to the County Regiment, the Durham Light Infantry as their Head Quarters, and they occupied the Castle but neglected the walled gardens by the Golf course. John claimed it for his mother, he visited it and found an old green house which had lots of broken glass pane windows; it was huge and had blue and green grapes in it.

When the grapes were ripe enough he picked them up.

There were apple, pear, plum and cherry trees. That fruit he picked by the sack full too and it found its way to Mom.

Red and black currant bushes, gooseberry, strawberry and raspberry bushes, canes and beds were picked. There was rhubarb, it must have been many years old, the stalks were red 2' inches thick and over six feet tall. John took it out, and his mother thought it would need lots of sugar but it was sweet. Returning home after harvesting the rhubarb he read the Durham Advertiser:

"The war in Russia was going badly for the Russians, Leningrad was under siege, Germany's 6th Army was at Stalingrad and Moscow was almost reached. The German Forces were only 15 km away but the city was ringed by heavy defenses and was thought to be impregnable. Fresh Army units moved up to the Front from the Sino - Soviet border".

John considered then: "Look out, you, Germans! The Russian boot is going to kick you in the ass." One day his Mom said to him, "Son, we are getting down with our coal. Can you look for some?" John had a home-made cart: he used baby chair wheels and strong boards, there were sand bags at home, too.

So he took off for the railway gradient going west towards Branspeth Castle. The fireman on the train locomotives had to stoke and fill the fire box to get a head of steam big enough to tackle the slope, spilling coal and cinders on the track. John intended picking up all the bits in his sand bags, when a train came he stepped to one side to allow the train to pass. The driver saw him and told his fireman to shovel some coal out of the locomotive's door. John thanked the driver by waving to him.

He was in the cubs when he reached 11 years, he transferred to the boy Scouts; the Scouts collected waste paper and card-board for the war effort. They received five pounds per ton into their troop account which the Scout Master used to buy tents and camping equipment. So they could go camping in the lake district, to get away from the air-raids for a while.

The following year when John was 12 years old, he joined the St. John's Ambulance Brigade, to learn all there was to learn about the First Aid as no one knew when it would be needed next.

He read in the newspaper that America had been attacked at Pearl Harbor in the Pacific Ocean and had lost most of its fleet. To a surprise Japanese Air Raid carried out by Carrier Aircraft, again, a foul stab in the back. So America was now fully involved in the Second World War.

While in the Boy Scouts they still found time to have fun; each summer they would go to the lake district or - to a farm on the West Coast at a village called "Greenodd", they would go by train over the "Pennines" which is a range of hills forming the backbone of England. It was an exciting trip; the little train would halt at every village to let passengers on and off. Finally they would arrive at Greenodd where the farmer, Mr. Kellop would be waiting with horse and cart to take their camping gear to the farm. He was a very friendly person whom they all liked. While Mr. Kellop took his horse and cart the long way round to his farm, they would line up and march over a railway bridge to the beach on the other side, then on to their campsite behind the farm house.

It was beautiful there on the inland estuary, small beaches with rocks dividing each beach. When the camping equipment arrived they were very busy erecting the bell tents and cookhouse shelter, storing food, laying out their sleeping bags and personal belongings, and, of course, preparing their first meal! Mr. Sands, their Scout Master, had lots of help preparing potatoes, carrots and other vegetables as well as cooking the meat, other scouts hauled water from the farm house.

When the tide was out, the bay would drain except for around the edge, there it was like a shallow sandy river, perhaps, three feet deep, they caught flat fish called "flooks" by walking slowly, feeling with their feet for the fish which would wriggle when they stood on them. All they had to do was bending down and grab them. Mr. Sands showed them how to gut and clean them, then how to cook them, too.

A scouts camping holiday was also a work camp, they all were shown how to cook, light a fire even on a wet day, how to improvise to cross a stream by building a bridge or using their staffs to vault over it, hiking around the bay, reading a compass or at night if it was clear, reading the stars. They were constantly studying and taking tests to earn their cloth badges which they sewed onto their sleeves. Mr. Sands also showed them where to look for mushrooms and, of course, Mr. Kellop instructed them how to milk his cows, to muck out his byres and feed his cows, chickens, ducks and geese, his horses and pigs.

John found that he took to scouting like a duck to water. "I recommend scouting for any boy as it prepares him to be a man", used to say John to other people.

The most interesting class was how to read sign, to be able to tell what animal had made the tracks and how long ago as well.

All the scouts read the newspapers and held talks on how the war was progressing. John's eyes were on battle of Britain Air reports, of enemy losses against their own; they were obviously winning and the North African War was finally going their way too.

In Russia the Germans had been pushed back to the borders but would counter attack soon, John felt very sorry for their ally. But supplies to Russia were getting through to Murmansk by ship, however, at a tremendous loss of ships due to U-boats and air attacks.

Mr. Kellop's eldest son Bob was always visiting their camp. He brought his fishing rods to them and showed them how to catch cod fish when the tide came in, he took part in all their activities and when they had to go home, Bob saw them off at the railway station at Greenodd, always promising to write, which he never did. They always saw him again the following year.

The Americans came to Britain with masses of aircraft and bombed the occupied countries of Europe as well as Germany in day light raids. They suffered terrible losses in men and equipment until they changed their tactics and flew night raids.

The war at sea in the Atlantic Ocean had been won against the "U-boats" due to better detection methods and through the German loss of an ENIGMA decoding machine, so England could now decode the German signals and intercept the Wolf Packs. They sustained heavy losses in U-boats, so supplies were reaching England in vast quantities. John assumed they would win the War in the end, which they did.

At first they had thousands of Italian prisoners of War working on the farms. Then they started to get more German P.O.W. until they were in their tens of thousands, many more were sent to Canada and the USA.

John's time at school came to an end in 1944, that year the school leaving age was extended for one year. His head master wanted John to stay at school for another year but he wanted to earn money as soon as possible.

So he refused and took an apprenticeship at a Tap-and-Die Factory as a machinist. There he worked two years and finally transferred at age of sixteen to the "C" Pit at Brandon Colliery till he was 21 years old, having served his time to be a fitter/turner, a double trade which enabled him to earn a good living.

Up till sixteen and a half years John did not bother girls at all, he liked them but did not understand why. One day he met his first love, 27 years old, ex-beauty Queen from Brandon. He was walking home from Durham city via the stepping stones over the river Browney.

It was a warm day, and before leaving the city, he went into a pub to buy a shandy, half beer and half lemonade. There he met Edith Blenkensop, she spoke to John and he enjoyed talking with her. She asked him where he was going; he told her that he was planning to go home on foot. Edith said she fancied walking, too. So they left the pub and crossed the river walking through the fields towards home, they talked about everything. She asked if he was courting anyone. He replied, no. Then she asked if he had ever made love. When he told her that he did not understand the question, she looked at him in amazement,

"You haven't made love to anyone? You are still a virgin?" she asked.

"I suppose so", he replied feeling shy and angry at the same time.

Edith steered him into a field, well away from the footpath and finally selected a grassy corner where they sat down.

She showed him how to kiss and putting his hands on her breasts, he could feel her hard nipples and he got aroused. She opened her blouse, showing him her pointed breasts and while he

271

caressed them she opened his trousers and took his hard penis in her hands and started to masturbate him. He was so excited and she pushed him onto his back and mounted him putting his penis into her vagina.

Well, it was so damn beautiful; she rode him like riding a horse till he came time after time. John finally rolled her over and mounted her, coming all the time. They were rolling down a grassy hill, still locked together, and making love all the time. He did not know exactly how many times she and he came, but they blew themselves silly till they could not do it any more.

Edith, he met daily for six months and all they did was making love. By now she was carrying their baby, and she always ended up crying before parting.

He did not realize it till she disappeared, he found out later that she got married to someone else and had left the district forever, he was love-sick for her, and searched for her for months, she broke his heart and he still cannot forget her.

John buried himself in sports, swimming, playing water polo, ice-skating, ice-hockey and speed-skating, cycling, rowing a skiff on weekends, attending dancing school with his sister Muriel untill they got thrown out for jiving, when they should have been doing ball room dancing. So he started attending ball room dancing in the evenings.

His Saturdays started early, he took his towel and swimming trunks with him, also his hockey-skates, caught the bus into the Durham city, on arrival at the Bus Terminal he would take a luggage locker and leave his skates there, then walked across the city to Brown's Boat House. He would hire a skiff and row two to three miles up river, turn around and return to the Boat House, hand in the skiff, take his swimming trunks and towel, walk along the river path to Bath's Bridge, cross over to the Swimming Baths and swim till noon.

Then he would get dry and walk back to the Bus Terminal, changing his towel and trunks for his hockey-skates, go to a 'fish and chip' diner and eat his lunch, and then again cross the city to the ice-rink where he would skate till 5.30 p.m. Returning to the Bus Depot, he deposited his skates in the locker, went into the

Gents' washroom to get washed and cleaned up. He would have tea and a sandwich somewhere till it was time to go to a dance (they opened at 7 p.m. till 11 p.m.). John used to enjoy dancing so much that sometimes he would miss the last bus home which left the bus station at 10.30 p.m. just for the sake of an extra half an hour dancing. He would have to return to the Bus Station for his skates and swimming gear before walking three miles home.

When he met a new girl-friend at the dance he would arrange to meet her the next day in Durham City. If she was a stranger to Durham he would spend time to show her the city visiting the Cathedral or the Castle. The City is a University and College town with many places of learning, scattered around and apart from the River Wear which snakes through the city in the shape of a large 'S' on the map.

It, the city, is built on seven hills and very-very old, dating back to the time of the Normans and earlier, as he believed the Cathedral was started in the Sixth Century.

When John was seventeen and a half years old he called into the King William pub on Silver Street in Durham City, he wanted a shandy as it was a hot day and he was thirsty. He went into the lounge to drink it as he was under age. There he met his friend Bill with whom they discussed their present apprenticeship jobs. John worked long overtime hours and had not seen Bill for some while; Bill who was six months older than John had just been to the recruiting office and joined the County Regiment.

When John reached the age of twenty one he followed his friend Bill into the Army, only he made a difference: he joined the Royal Electrical and Mechanical Engineers. He was sent to Branford for basic training for 12 weeks. After that he was posted to the R.E.M.E. school where he attended various courses for the next sixteen weeks.

He was sent to the overseas depot where he was at first assigned to be sent to Korea, but this got changed at the last minute, John was redirected to West Germany to British Army of the RHINE, this was in 1952.

His first posting was to Lunenburg, then Nienberg, and ending up in Willick near Krefeld. Five years had passed; he reenlisted for

273

a further seven years and was sent to Aden for two years in Yemen, while there he went to Mombassa in Kenya. His next posting was back to Germany, for a further five years, and then he was discharged in 1963.

John returned to England where he entered civilian life as a machinist, working for a German company which manufactured underground mining machinery. He bought a house, kept it for three years, but then moved to Newton-Aycliffe nearer his job. But he was not happy with his life because John remembered Germany for its picturesque scenery, industrial development and the friendly and down to Earth people who lived there. His mother, Ethel by name, was pretty dominant and loved her son very much and wanted him to settle down close to her, but he had itchy feet and wished to see more the world and explore the unknown lands.

In 1969 he applied for work at Lynn near Boston, Massachusetts, the USA, for the General Electric Co. they were making the Huey Helicopters. John happened to work here only one week before the workers went out on strike. John did not wait, he moved to Missouri to Carter Carburetor and then to St. Louis worked in the Tool Room for one year. The American continent impressed him, it was a new way of life, the food was different, the people were different and very friendly to work and live with. Even the black people were still not free, he thought, as they were classified as second class citizens although the civil war was long over but nothing had been changed. He found them to be a very sympathetic and simple people.

"Hi, John. How are you?" asked one coloured female.

"Hi, Dolores. Fine, thanks. And you? How are you?" replied John.

"Oh, not bad. Could you, perhaps, come over and take your coffee-break with us?" she offered.

"Sure." John said and went with her to sit with her friends.

"Are you from England?" they enquired.

"Why?" John asked.

"Because we have heard that coloured people are treated differently in England. Is this true?" they asked.

"We don't care what colour your skin is in England. We accept you for what you are. After all you are human beings like everybody else," answered John.

His relationship with these people remained very close and extremely friendly.

This beautiful country was rich not only of good people but also of intriguing scenery like the Merrimac caves, where visitors could go underground to see the stalagmites and stalactites and coloured rocks. He drove through the Ozark Mountains and visited the home of David Crocket, a hunter, a trapper and a guide in this region many years ago; saw the large paddle boats tied up on the Missouri river, the stainless steel Archway representing the gateway to the West and many more sights.

Due to the number of various reptiles in Missouri John's wife refused to emigrate. He made his mind up to return to England in 1970. John's heart called him, however, to Germany, where he worked for three years and emigrated from Hamburg to British Columbia, Canada, in February of 1974.

In 1977 John with his German wife Margret took a holiday to visit her son in Bremen. Margret stayed with her son, but John drove to Hannover, then onto Helmstadt where he passed through the East Zone to Berlin where he met an old friend Hans.

Hans was pleased to see him whom he had not seen for four years. So Hans made him welcome. They drove around the following day visiting the Berlin wall and climbing up the platforms to look over to the East. It looked depressing, grey buildings, no people to see, just decay everywhere and soldiers armed and walking along the opposite side of the wall, 100 meters back, as close to the wall were land mines.

They went out to the cafes and ordered coffee and German cakes; they discussed the situation in Berlin. Hans remembered the Berlin blockade.

"Everything was flown in by the Americans, British and French Air Forces. Even coal and planes were landing every minute of the day and night. It lasted six months", Hans covered as if it were at the moment.

John looked across the tables and saw a beautiful woman sitting toying with her glass and cheese. She looked terribly sad and lonely. A young lady came to the tables selling flowers. John bought two red roses from her and asked her to take them to that sad lady across the room. Something stirred inside him, the great Scottish poet Robert Burns's verses came to his mind all of a sudden:

> "Oh, my love like a red, red rose,
> That sweetly smelt in June,
> Oh, my love like a melody,
> That sweetly played in tune".

John watched that beauty took the flowers, smelt them, their glances met, he smiled and she smiled back. So John went to her, begged her pardon and started the conversation in German. From her answers he knew that she was not German. But who she was, he wondered. When he sat down, they continued their conversation in English. He discovered she was Russian and there on business trip and the day after tomorrow she had to return home. John asked her to excuse him for a moment and went back to Hans and told him he would be busy for the rest of the day. "I'll see you when I get home", John said to the friend. Hans grinned, "Be careful not to get lost".

The Russian lady still sat at her table, so John went back to her and sat close as he did not know if someone was watching or listening to her talk.

The more John learnt, the closer he felt to Valentina. She was charming! Even her name "VALENTINA" sounded to him like a beautiful piece of music.

He repeated and repeated this name as an oath not to forget.It was obvious to him, he was falling in love with Val, but they had to part, unluckily.

Everything was interesting in their talks to both of them: to her, life in Canada, in England, in Germany, how good the German market seemed, and how odd supposed to be an old enemy had it far better than the winner and why it should be so; to him, how pitiful the Russian life was, she complained, how hard it was to buy goods and make ends meet. John begged her like an oath to always keep in touch, that the future could have the key to her happiness. He explained he was not at the moment free but perhaps in the future they could get together.

Valentina was crying bitterly. John tried to comfort her, and in the end she dried her tears, it's the thought of going home, she said, the unhappy day, she's not looking forward to it.

Val returned to Russia, John - to Canada, both worked very hard.

In 1992 John's British wife Christine, 24 years younger than him, left him leaving him terrible debt to the tune of fourteen thousand dollars through alcohol; she was an alcoholic and a mother of four children, including two of John's. John supported his children as much as he could. John's separation now was like a torture and he crucified it as Jesus in his life. Because of Christine's unstable behaviour in her family, she had a conflict with her children who finished with the police and social service taking charge. So John's kids happened to be under the permanent government custody. John finally divorced her. What was he now? A single man, much suffered, and badly unhappy! Thank goodness, all was over.

Like a star of a new hope Valentina appeared in his horizon, his far Russian beloved friend. Their meeting was like a dream come true. Look at the sky! The weather helped and supported their reunion, John had prayed to God daily to keep the roads free of snow and He, their Lord, must have heard because up to the date of their marriage the winter weather looked like spring. Spring is always considered the personification of newly born life, the blossom of everything alive, the building up of a new happy loving family of John and Valentina.

God bless them forever!

Forever, however, had lasted just one year and three months. John passed away on the third of August of 1998 because of the lung cancer.

Loving John's soul was streaming far away to the horizon and beyond.

Eternal memory.

ISBN 141200036-X